Records of Colonial Gloucester County Virginia

A collection of abstracts from original documents concerning the lands and people of Colonial Gloucester County

Compiled by

POLLY CARY MASON

Volume I.

Mrs. George C. Mason
Post Office Box 720
Newport News, Virginia
1946

Please direct all correspondence and orders to:

www.southernhistoricalpress.com
or
SOUTHERN HISTORICAL PRESS, Inc.
PO BOX 1267
375 West Broad Street
Greenville, SC 29601
southernhistoricalpress@gmail.com

ISBN: 978-0-89308-403-5

Printed in the United States of America

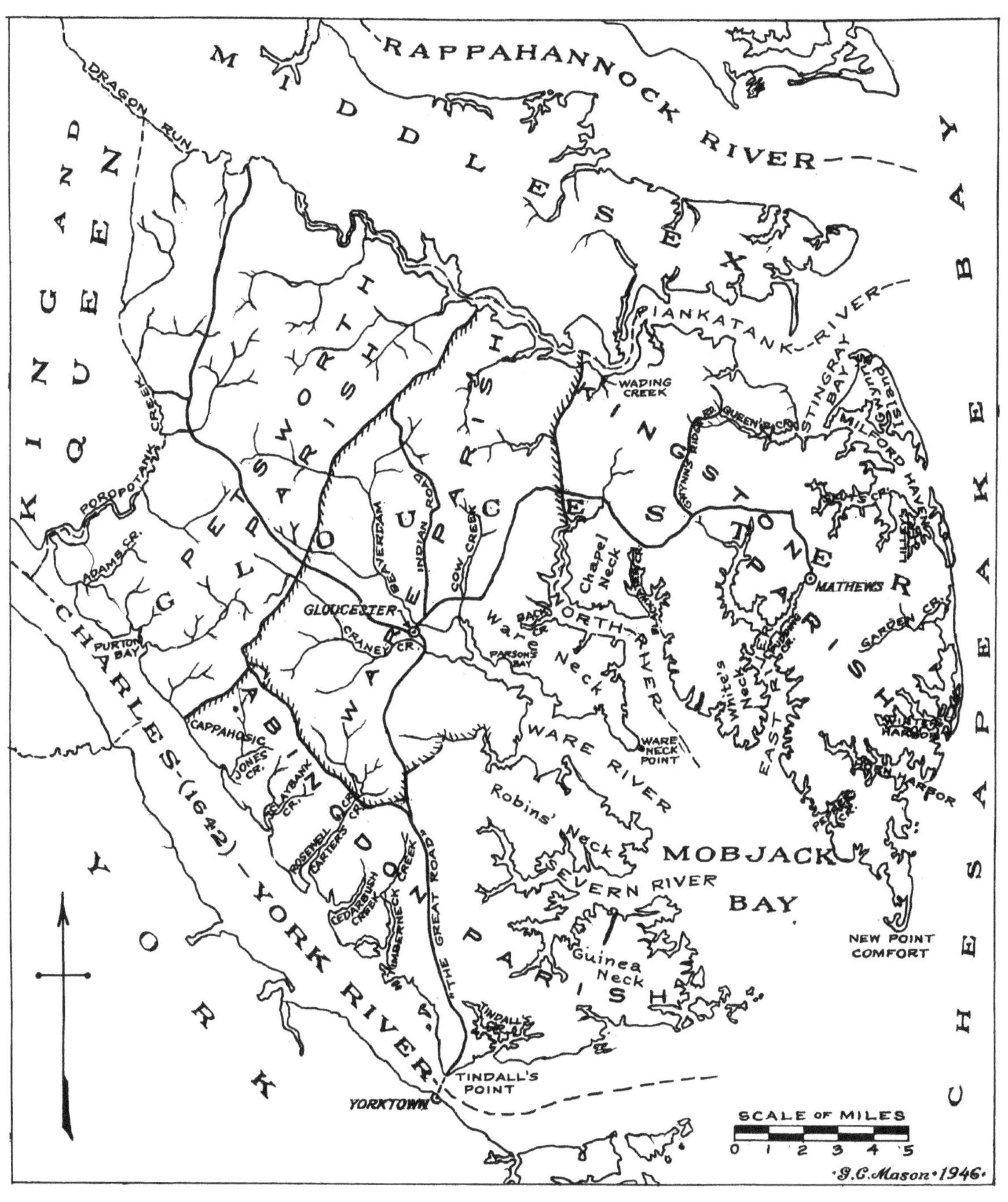

MAP OF COLONIAL GLOUCESTER COUNTY: showing parish lines and some of the earlier geographical names as found in the land grants. The boundaries of Kingston Parish are those of the present County of Mathews.

TEXT OF MANUSCRIPT SHOWN IN FRONTISPIECE

October the 29th 1655.

This day Pindavako the Protector of the young King of Chiskoyack was at my house intending to have spoken with ..[the].. Governor..[illegible]..then expected to be Heer'd but hee came not, & therefore hee desyred to leave his mind with mee Ma^{ior} Will Wiatt, & divers others, as followeth viz. That. Wassatickon the late King had freely given unto Mr. Edward Wyatt and his heyres, executors administrators or assigns, all the land from Mr. Hugh Gwinns old marked trees to Vttamarke Creeke, including all Pyan[katanck] Chiskoyack Land, being freely given with the consent of all the rest of the Indians. it was also agreed among them all that neither the King nor any other of his Indians should sell, alienate or dispose, of any land belonging unto them without the Consent of Mr. Ed: Wyatt which was the only business that hee had to acquaint the Gover therewith in the behalfe of Mr. Ed: Wyat as wee heere doe testiefy under our hands this present 29th October 1655.

The marke of

ℓ

Pindavako
Protector of the
young King of
Chiskayake

Signed & Delivered in the presence
of all whose names are
heere Subscribed.

John West

WILLM WYATT

John West iunior

Toby West

The marke W of
William Godfrey

The marke IB of
John Talbutt

The marke I K of
John King

[As may be seen from the above text, this land now lies in Mathews County, as it adjoined the land originally granted to Mr. Hugh Gwinn, which is shown by patents as located on the Piankitank River in the vicinity of Queen's Creek. It was most likely the family of this Edward Wyatt (Wiatt) whose names appear in the Vestry Book of Kingston Parish.]

F O R E W O R D

A misconception prevails among many who are interested in Virginia history, both general readers and scholars, to the effect that what has been printed already of the early official documents of Virginia is an exhaustive achievement, entirely sufficient and conclusive for use in constructing an account of the colonial life. The published researches of Dr. L. G. Tyler, Dr. P. A. Bruce, Dr. W. G. Stanard and Dr. R. A. Brock are extensive and enduring, it is true, but these scholars, who devoted their lives to the collection, publication and interpretation of scattered data, lamented the loss of the archives of some of the tidewater counties, and regretted that only a fraction of those documents that survived in county court houses, had been printed. They were aware that the vast reservoir had hardly been tapped.

History is made up of the interaction of individuals, and groups of individuals, in private or official capacity; and in order to interpret it properly we must know about the individuals, where they came from, what their station in life was, what land and how much they owned, what offices they held and how they behaved as officials, what were the details of the estates which they left, whom they married, who their children were, and where these children migrated. The alert and discerning writer on Virginia makes no defence for studying family history, and gathering all the information he can about those who emigrated to the colony, and about their various groups and subsequent group relations. Every addition, therefore, to our knowledge of the persons who settled and built up a prosperous unit of the colony, is welcomed by the sincere and scientific historian. No one will gainsay Mrs. Mason, when she avers in her preface that Gloucester was the most prosperous county in the colony; and may it not also be added that it was the county most typical of the social and political life of the colonial period.

Equally with James City County, Gloucester suffered the tragic loss of all of its court records before 1865. With a supreme devotion to her native soil, and with the utmost patience over a period of ten years, Mrs. Mason has gathered from every conceivable source the fragments of the records of Gloucester and Mathews Counties that survive, and after abstracting them has arranged them in a thoroughly systematic manner in this and the succeeding volume. Many problems will be settled by their perusal and investigators will be most grateful to the author for her initiative and achievement.

E. G. Swem

E. G. Swem

Williamsburg, Virginia
January, 19, 1946

In the tidewater section of Virginia, where we speak of the "lost counties" as those having lost their county records, Gloucester is known as doubly "lost", having twice experienced the loss by fire of all public records. This lamentable destruction first occurred in 1820, when all the history of her colonial past, as recorded in the Clerk's Office, was burned. From copies of old deeds and wills still to be found in a few private homes we learn that, following the 1820 fire, many Gloucester people took their attested copies of legal documents, which were kept for family record, and had them re-recorded by the county clerk. Alas, all of these re-recordings were again lost in 1865 at the burning of Richmond, to which place all of the county records of both Gloucester and her daughter county, Mathews, were taken for safe keeping during the Civil War.

To discover authentic original records of colonial Gloucester that are still existing has for the past several years been the absorbing labor and search of this compiler. It is amazing what a mass of material and information concerning the lands and people of Gloucester has been lying buried for three centuries among the voluminous records of the Colony of Virginia. No search for old relics of any kind can compare in interest with the hunting and the finding of genuine, authentic pieces of human documents, for they are alive with the very personalities and character of the men and women who settled our counties, and who, through the generations, have developed these two counties from the wilderness they found.

Gloucester reached a very high peak of development during the colonial period and was known as the most populous, prosperous, wealthy and influential of all the counties in the colony. This search for Gloucester's past as it is found in existing original manuscripts is confined to the period including that golden era of her history, and covers the one hundred and sixty-five years, beginning with the year of the first grant of her land and extending to the turn of the century in 1800.

The sources where this collection of records were discovered have been numerous and varied, and sometimes most unexpected and surprising. Who would ever expect to find love letters written to a Gloucester girl among the papers and documents of the Society for the Propagation of the Gospel in Foreign Parts? These letters were a thrilling find, furnishing new information on one of the most famous love affairs of the whole colonial period in Virginia. The Society which préserved the letters is the missionary department of the Church of England, and the Library of Congress has many volumes of transcribed and photostatic copies of reports and letters from the colonial files of this Society. By patient searching of these manuscripts, and the hundreds of other volumes in the Manuscript Division of the Library of Congress, there may be found much information relating to Gloucester.

Many deeds, wills and court records of Gloucester people are found in those Virginia counties where the archives have not been lost. Gloucester having been formed out of York, there is a wealth of Gloucester information to be found in the Clerk's Office at Yorktown. There they have a treasure house of records beginning with the year 1633 which have been preserved. The same is true of the neighboring county on the opposite side of Gloucester, Middlesex. But Gloucester material is also to be found in almost any of the counties where colonial record books still exist. For instance, the original deed to Thomas Todd for land of the famous estate of Toddsbury was recorded in Norfolk County, and the ancient document may be seen there to this day.

Nor do we find that all of the sources for Gloucester public records are confined to the State of Virginia. Copies of wills of Gloucester people have been found recorded in England, in Edenton, N. C., in Baltimore County, Md., and in many other places. A copy of a letter written by a colonial Gloucester minister describing his parish at length has been obtained from the manuscripts of the Huntington Library in California. There is also in this California library a manuscript copy of a deed of gift for a large tract of land in Gloucester, on which original paper an Indian king made his mark when he deeded land to a Gloucester white man.

The most fascinating source of all Gloucester history is that to be found in the family records and letters and papers handed down through the generations and tenderly treasured in private homes in both counties. Very few such collections have survived, and the possessors of many of these rare and valuable papers have generously allowed copies to be included in this compilation. More detailed acknowledgment will be made of these when the copies appear.

Many of these accumulations of family papers have been lost sight of, and lie hidden and forgotten in garrets and unused lofts. This was the case at an old colonial home in Mathews, where three bushel baskets full of records relating to numerous family connections were discovered in the unused loft of a little old school house in the yard. The dates on these papers go back to the 1670's. The originals of this family collection have been deposited in the archives of the College of William and Mary at Williamsburg.

The manuscripts in the Library at William and Mary College have been another source of valuable data on Gloucester families, as was also the manuscript department of the Alderman Library at the University of Virginia, and the archives of the Virginia Historical Society.

The Archives Division of the Virginia State Library at Richmond is the largest source in Virginia from which Gloucester's colonial records may be extracted. As the public and private records from all of colonial Virginia which are deposited there are available for searching, a very large portion of the abstracted records included in this Gloucester collection were found in the State Library Archives.

It seemed that the proper place to begin in this piecing together of the lost history of Gloucester was in the Land Office at Richmond. In this office, which is in our Virginia State Capitol Building, there may be seen original books where grants of land were recorded and patented and written in with quill pen and ink. In the effort to put the colonial people back in Gloucester on their lands-as it were - these huge patent books have been searched and researched to discover every acre of land that was ever granted in the county, from the first grant in 1635 down to the very last piece of Gloucester or Mathews land granted and so recorded.

The patents have been abstracted so as to retain every small scrap of information which relates to the landowner or adjoining landowners; all geographic descriptions - names of estates, points, creeks, roads or anything giving the slightest clue of information is included. The original spelling, or variations of spelling, are all shown. The names of all headrights are given with each settler's grant of land, whenever they are shown on the patent record. The names of all these headright settlers, who were brought in, help to swell the index of Gloucester names to voluminous proportions. The right to fifty acres of land was granted to the landowners for every person whose transportation to the colony was paid for by the landowner, and though there is no certain way of determining just how many of these headrights remained in Gloucester, yet we find by searching the index of patents and tax lists that many of the headright names are later found among the landowners.

No history of colonial Gloucester could be told without including the records of her colonial parish of Kingston, which became the County of Mathews in 1791, for this separation occurred fifteen years after the Revolution started which marked the end of the colonial period. Therefore, the whole colonial past of Gloucester is part of Mathews' history, too, and the records in this compilation relating to the colonial people of Mathews can be distinguished as those of Kingston Parish of Gloucester. Men who settled in Kingston Parish represented Gloucester in the Assembly as Burgesses and in the Council and Court of the Colony, and also served the county as Clerks and Justices. Of those who won honors and fame, Mathews can claim many who lived in colonial Kingston Parish during those one hundred and fifty-six years when both counties were of one part, and proudly bore the name of Gloucester.

As it would be impossible to include in one volume the tremendous mass of colonial Gloucester records collected or available, it seems fitting to confine this first volume to the records of the lands and the people who owned them and settled them. Accordingly, Volume I includes abstracts of patents for all lands granted, including headrights' names; the "Rent Role" of landowners in Gloucester's four parishes as reported in 1704 by Lt. Governor Francis Nicholson; the first Gloucester Tax List of 1782, which is combined with a partial earlier roll of 1770; the first Mathews Tax List, when it was formed out of Gloucester in 1791, in which is combined a Tithe List of 1774; all of the tax lists include the property lists showing the number of slaves, carriages, horses and cattle owned. There is also an appendix giving abstracts of land grants described in the patents as Gloucester land, but which lie mostly in the present County of King and Queen; and finally there is as complete a list as can be found of all of Gloucester's colonial Council and General Court members, the Burgesses and other colony officers, as well as the county officers: clerks, justices and sheriffs. This volume is thoroughly indexed, showing, not only the names of landowners and headrights separately, but also every geographical, descriptive or estate name in the text. There are about 3000 family names shown in the index, and including with these the individual names under each family name, the total list of persons is close to 5000.

As soon as conditions permit, the second volume of Gloucester abstracts will be brought out in the same lithoprinted form as this first volume. Included in the second volume will be a miscellaneous collection of wills, deeds, court records and other papers and letters. Many early survey plats of land have been found, copies of which can be accurately shown by planographing or lithoprinting.

These colonial abstracts give many revealing glimpses through those silent years of lost records. The curtain hiding the dim past is slightly lifted with each one, and brought to view are the people who lived their lives and played their parts on the stage of Gloucester's beautiful broad acres. Inasmuch as they are authentic recordings abstracted from originals, they are bare of legend and hearsay. These quoted records, gathered from so many sources, tell the story in the quaint picturesque language of the past - the story of proud personalities and humble character, of humor and pathos, of struggles, disappointments and triumphs. The records speak with authority.

Polly Cary Mason

Post Office Box 720,
Newport News, Virginia.

ACKNOWLEDGMENTS

Perhaps this compilation of Gloucester records might never have been started had it not been first suggested and strongly urged by Mr. Beverley Fleet as a proper task for this writer. Mr. Fleet's own monumental work on numerous other counties and his sincere and consistent interest in this endeavor have been an inspiration.

To Dr. E. G. Swem, Librarian Emeritus of the College of William and Mary, I am indebted for his advice and counsel. That this search was undertaken is largely due to his belief in the need of such a collection of records, and also to his encouraging belief in my ability to do the work.

For their stimulating interest and guiding advice I am most deeply grateful to the Rev. Clayton Torrence, Secretary of the Virginia Historical Society and Editor of the Virginia Magazine of History and Biography, and to Mrs. P. W. Hiden, Virginia Chairman for Restoration and Preservation of Records, Daughters of the American Revolution.

It would be impossible to make adequate acknowledgment of the full indebtedness to Mrs. Nell Marion Nugent, not only for the wealth of information found in her invaluable publication, "Cavaliers and Pioneers", but also for her generous and considerate helpfulness in deciphering the early land patent records which are in her custody.

I am gratefully conscious of the assistance, advice and unfailing encouragement given by my husband, George Carrington Mason, Historiographer of the Diocese of Southern Virginia. It has been a great advantage to have his sympathetic understanding of the task, and his help in reading copy and proof.

To the many persons in libraries, in clerks' offices and in private homes who have so kindly assisted me in the searching, my profound thanks are expressed in this general manner for the many courtesies extended. More definite acknowledgment will be made when the groups of family papers appear.

Polly Cary Mason

CONTENTS

ILLUSTRATIONS

" A nation's attitude toward its own history is like a window into its own soul.........We owe it to ourselves, as one of the great nations of the earth, to study our colonial and Revolutionary periods, not as isolated and provincial phenomena, but as phases of a great forward movement. "

Charles MacLean Andrews.

No legislative enactment has been found ordering the creation of Gloucester County, and the earliest mention of the county name that has ever been found is in the patent dated May 21st, 1651, to James Roe and Peter Richeson. The old calendar year being still observed in Virginia at that time, a few other patents are found mentioning Gloucester and dated in 1651 in the months previous to May, but these would actually fall in 1652 according to our present calendar, as the old calendar year of that time ended on the 24th of March.

Due to this lack of a definite date for Gloucester's formation, there have been differences of opinion as to the correct birthday that may be claimed for the county. Therefore, though county names are not always given in the patents, wherever a county is shown previous to the year when Gloucester first appears, the county name is given herein in capital letters. From these records it is clearly shown that the Governor continued to grant the king's lands, and the Land Office at Jamestown continued to issue patents for the area of the present Gloucester and Mathews, without acknowledging that there was a county named Gloucester until the date above mentioned. This area was first known as a part of Charles River County until that county's name was changed in 1642 to York County, and the colonial government continued to refer to the Gloucester lands as a part of York County in these patent records until May 21st, 1651.

The county name has not been included in these abstracts, after those issued around the year and date of the first appearance of the name, Gloucester, though often - but not always - given in the patents.

....

To preserve as far as possible the quaintness of the ancient original manuscripts, these patents have been so abstracted as to show the queer and varied spellings, the lack of punctuation, and the excessive use of capital letters. Every colorful scrap of information or description, every name of a person mentioned, every geographical location or clue of information has been retained.

....

KEY

FAMILY SURNAMES: It will be noted that family names have been arranged in alphabetical order, and the various spellings of names are given in capitals in the left margin. The first line shown with each name gives the earliest date of the appearance of the family as land owners in the Gloucester area. The first spelling of a family name is the one in which the patents were issued unless another spelling follows the given names.

GIVEN NAMES: The given name of the first of a family to patent land is shown immediately under the surname, and every grant of land patented in the same given name follows in chronological order. For example, the earliest Armistead was William with two patents, both in 1651. The next Armistead land was patented in the name of John in 1674, and there are eight patents in the name of John which follow in chronological order. The other Armistead names of Ralph, Henry and Isaac are given in chronological order as they appear in the patent books.

G. or M. In accordance with the present boundary between Gloucester and Mathews, the county in which the land now lies is shown by the letters - G. for Gloucester and M. for Mathews - in the column under County. It was impossible to determine whether some of the borderline lands were partly or wholly in King and Queen or Gloucester, or in Gloucester or Mathews, and a question mark denotes the uncertainty. Reference to the vestry books of both Petsworth and Kingston Parishes was helpful in settling several such cases.

BOOK - PAGE: The number of the patent book and page number are given for reference, if more complete information is desired. This may be obtained from the Land Office in the Capitol at Richmond.

C. G.: These letters given before the patent book number signify "Commonwealth Grants".

HR: This stands for head rights (see Preface).

D. E.: Deputy Escheator.

P.: Parish, as "Kingston P."

DESCRIPTIONS OF LANDS PATENTED WITHIN THE PRESENT BOUNDARIES OF GLOUCESTER AND MATHEWS COUNTIES, VIRGINIA.

Abstracted from the Land Patent Books
in the Land Office, Richmond, Va.

NAMES	DESCRIPTION	CO.	BK.	Pg.	DATE	ACRES
ABBOTT..ABBOT Christopher	GLOSTER COUNTY- "By the Greate Swamp running E by N. Certificate...granted by... Cort of Gloster bearinge date the 16th of Aprill 1656 but it was soe torn that the names could not be read."	G	4	229	1657 Jan. 20	350
ADLESTON..ADELSTON John	S side of Severne R in Mockjack Bay, adjoining Francis Ceely and George Ludlow, Esq. HR: William Scott, Tho. Ridley, Ed. Emerson, Thomas Cheverell(?), Patt Omallin, Edw. Thomas, Richard Riley, Richard Kirke, Richard Smith, John Cooke.	G.	2	317	1651 May 19	500
ALLOMAINE..ALLOMAN.. ALLAMAN Thomas	KINGSTONE P. Adjoining William Elliott, Wm. Lewis, Lt. Coll. Jno. Armstead, HR: Amory Waine, Mary Arckland.	M.	7	355	1684 April 20	52
AMBREY..AMBERY Ralph	In Poropotank Swamp branches on N side of Coles Branch. HR: Wm. Tassy, Gabriel Michael, Geo. Webb, Samuel Cunny.	G.	5	371	1662 March 18	183
AMBROSE Leonard	WARE P. "Betwixt the Land of Humphrey Mead late Dece'd & the Land of Jno. Wells late Dece'd & the Land of Mr. Ja: Clarke & the Land of Morgan Lewis." HR: Richard Blackwell, Fra. Palmer.	G.	6	559	1675 June 15	60
AMIES..AMISS..AMIS.. AMEE Thomas	Down the maine runn of Dragon Swamp & adjoining the remaining Lands of Saml: Patridge dece'd now claimed by Mr. John Carver by purchase & adjoining Roger Shackelford, Wm. Norman, Charles Roane. Sold to Amiss by Saml: Patridge.	G.	6	666	1678 Nov. 20	295
ANDERSON Richard	Adjoining creek and land surveyed for Robert Hubberd and along York R. SE and NE on Tancks Creek. Granted to Leechman & Bennett 1652, sold to Robert Jones who sold to Anderson.	G.	5	177	1662	200
William	PETSOE P. Adjoining his own land, Major Lewis and John Jebells (?), by five springs and along Nettles' Land. HR: Ja: Bartlett, Jno. Read.	G.	6	601	1675/6 March 11	60
Matthew	Beginning at a corner of Newbottles' Land to an old line of Capt. Anderson's. In consideration of part of a Treasury Warrant No. 114.	G.	22 (C.G.)	295	1790 June 9	8½
ARMEFIELD ________	On Mr. Pate's swamp adjoining John Green's corner, Mr. Peter Knight, Thomas Curles. Sold to Mr. John Pate who assigned to Armefield.	G.	5	153	1663 Nov. 24	400
ARMESTEAD..ARMSTEAD.. ARMISTEAD William	On the head of Eastermost R. in Mockjack Bay on NW side of a small creek on NE side of river encompassing the heads of river to SW side. HR: Elizabeth Price, John Crists, John Lancelott, Richard Gold, Robert Hunly, Wm. Frasey,	M.	2	331	1651 July 1	1231

NAMES	DESCRIPTION	CO.	BK.	Pg.	DATE	ACRES
ARMISTEAD (Continued)	Barbary Frasey, Edward Morgan, Theo. Frasey, John Paptast, James Kittenue, Roger Paynter, Katherine Teye, Thomas Hudson, William Taylor, John Frasey, Jose: Brewster, William Smith, Mary Rekey, Kath. Ayres.					
William	On E side of Eastermost R. in Mockjack Bay above Pudden Creek. HR: James Steward, Thomas Jones, Ann Perry Mary Hall, William Wells, John Owen, Henry Edwards, Tho. Dyer, Danll Forrest, John Hunningford, Tho. Guige, Marg. Brookes. [These rights are written by mistake on Philip Hunley's patent of June 29, 1651]	M.	2	331	1651 July 1	600
John, Capt.	KINGSTONE P. Near head of Creek out of Eastermost R. adjoining X'pr Dickson. HR: John Perry, Jno. Doblander, Jno. Duckenhead, Eliz. Sope, W. Cleaves, Humphrey Jarvis, Tho. Prigg, Samll Curson [Carson], Tho. Davis.	M.	6	536	1674 Sept. 21	440
John, Lt. Coll.	"Upon the head of the Eastermost R. lying between two branches adjoining his own land and Capt. Dudley. Formerly granted Dunken [Duncan?] Bohonon and John Mekin 1667 who assigned to said Armestead & by him deserted & by order of Cort Granted Geo. Seaton who...neglected Pattening... by Council granted said Armestead." HR: Five negroes	M.	6	657	1678 Sept. 21	220
John, Capt.	KINGSTON P. On E side of Eastermost R. to marsh near Mr. Christ'r Dickins plantation, down riverside. Formerly granted to Mr. Wm. Armestead for 600 acs. 1651, due Capt. John Armestead as brother and heire to said William.	M.	6	666	1678 Nov. 20	550
John, Capt.	Same description as above 550 acs. HR: Jno. Wright, Mary Elliott, Abra. Copin, Ma: dutchwoman, Wm. Paine, Han. Waldridge, Walt. Harris, Margery Brookes, Mary Hare, Jno. Roberts, Mary Bradford.	M.	6	674	1678/9 Jan. 31	550
John, Mr.	On S side of Peanketanck R. beginning at a great pine standing on the W side of the mouth of Gwynns Ponds, in the woods SW to Queens Crk. along Queens Crk. side SE to mouth of Kings Crk. up same to the head thereof then NE to pine and Peanketanck R. side, up river to beginning. Land being due by patent to _____ Burton, Sept. 15, 1651, who assigned to Mr. Wm. Armestead 1658, now due Mr. John Armestead sonn & heire of William. Resurveyed by Robt. Beverley, Surveyor of Gloster County, 22nd July, 1670.	M.	7	2	1679 Sept. 25	500
John, Coll: & Mr. John Gwin	Kingston P. Beginning at a small pine "on Eastward side of a Branch near a Chappell...in line of...old Devident of Land formerly taken up by Coll: Hugh Gwin dece'd and sold by the sd Gwin to Mr. Wm. Armstead, dece'd...running SWS to line of Mr. Wm. Elliott, Senr, along Elliotts line to line of Thomas Allamaine to land of Coll: Jno Armstead & so over Gwins Dams to the beginning."	M.	7	532	1686 Oct. 30	202½

NAMES	DESCRIPTION	CO.	BK.	Pg.	DATE	ACRES
ARMISTEAD (Continued) John, Coll:	KINGSTON P. "Adjoining his own land whereon he now lives" and land of George Seaton and Wm. Elliott - beginning at a pine on "the Eastermost side of a small branch not far distant from the Chappell" then to Mr. Wm. Elliotts E line & to corner of George Seaton	M.	7	533	1686 Oct. 30	130
John, Esq.	KINGSTONE P. On S side of a small branch at head of North R. & adjoining "an older devidend of Land lately purchased" down branch to line of John Sares [Saies?] dece'd to the high lands & to Poundsells line. HR: Jno. Turnbull, Jno. Hues.	M.	8	140	1691 April 28	80
Ralph	"At a gum by the path side...being a line tree of Thos. Dyers along Dyers Crk...and crossing same." HR: 1 negro.	M.	6	660	1678 Sept. 26	48
Ralph	Land adjoining above 48 acres, by Dyers Creek side. 48 granted 1678, residue 102.	M.	7	62	1680 Sept. 29	150
Ralph & Robert Cully	E side of Eastermost R. "att head of old Dividend of Land bought by sd Cully of Mr. Mann." HR: Wm. Bastable, Mary Winter.	M.	7	219	1682 Dec. 22	63½
Henry	KINGSTONE P. At a corner pine tree "on Eastermost side of a small branch not far distant from the Chapll" to line of Wm. Elliotts & to Geo. Seaton. Granted Coll: John Armstead 1686 & by him deserted. HR: Tho. Wright, Tho. Mackrill, Henry Dilon.	M.	9	125	1697 Oct. 28	130
Henry	See description Armstead & Gwin, 1686. Deserted by Armestead & Gwin HR: Tho: Croser, Alice Croser, Eliz: Ball, Cornelius Johnson, Wm. Easterley.	M.	9	700	1705 Nov. 2	202½
Isaac	WARE P. Lately property of Robert Bristow British Subject. In consideration of the sum of 8000 pounds. Granted to Isaac Armistead assignee of Thomas Booth who was assignee of John Dixon. Beginning on the Road to Ware Neck and N to George Booth's line & to Back Crk. down the creek to Peter Whiting's corner to Main road and along same.	G.	I (C.G.)	505	1784 April 6	404
ARRUNDELL Peter	KINGSTON P. On Peanketank Bay, at mouth of creek at Narrows of Milford Haven which divides from Jno. Shapley and adjoining Jno. Guyton, Caleb Holder, 200 acs. granted Jno. Congdon 1642, residue 150 acs. HR: Elias Robinson and 3 negroes.	M.	6	479	1673 Oct. 23	350
ASHBOURNE..ASHBURN John	On W side of maine swamp at head of Ware R. by Purton Path and Mr. Francis Taliaferoe.	G.	7	488	1685 Nov. 4	90½
Esther	Widow of John Ashbourne. Escheat Land late in the possession of John Ashbourne. Peter Beverley, Deputy, Richard Johnson, Escheator.	G.	9	238	1699 Oct. 26	104
AXE George	KINGSTON P. On Queens Crk. side at a corner tree of Wm. Elliott Senr. to corner	M.	6	679	1679 May 1	157½

NAMES	DESCRIPTION	CO.	BK.	Pg.	DATE	ACRES
AXE (Continued)	of Armestead by his line to Queens Crk. and along same & adjoining Mr. George Seaton. HR: Ja: Filder, Geo. Gill, Sar. Carter.					
AYLMER Justinian	On E side of Pepper Crk. at the mouth. Adjoining Plummer's land. 300 acres granted Richard Grigson 1651, assigned to William Armestead, and by John Armestead heir of William assigned to Aylmer. HR: Margtt. Jones, Wm. Stevenson.	M.	5	598	1666 April 4	495
BAILEY..BAILY..BAYLIE BAYLEY..BAYLY..BAYLES BEALYE John Bayly	On N side of Charles R. beginning at Indian Quarter Creek. Due by assignment from Wm. Prior of his claime entered Oct. 18, 1641. HR: William Pierce, Robert Fossett, Ann Cock, John Atter, Roger Arteine, William Hopton, Walter Downes, Richard Adkins, Bar. Barnes, John Buck, Corn. Swilliams, Ann Powell, Stephen Sen:, Antho: Gunston.	G.	1 (2)	800	1642 Aug. 10 1641	700
Richard Bayly	Near head of North River & Mockjack Bay beginning at a tree of Wm. Debnams and S-'ly down the river. 200 acs. of which by patent June 8, 1643. HR: Richard Richards, Peter Baker, Richard Newill, Hen. Burnett.	M.	2	357	1651 Jan. 29 1643	400
Richard Bailey	On branches of Hoccadayes Crk. & North R. Mill runns. Adjoining Robert Elliott & Thomas Gaunts land lately purchased of Mr. Wm. Elliott & Conquest Wyatt. HR: James Meridine, Henry Hebe, Soloman Blake, Wm. Harris, Tho. Simson, Richard Hufsey, Jon. Pratt, Issabell Collier, Richard Bailey, Jon Masell, Sara Howard, Henry Herbert, Jon Gibson, George Anderson, Jon Arthur, Anne Hetford,Tho.Harwood.	M.G?	6	439	1672 Oct. 11	882
Richard Baily	On S side of upper Pianketank at Hoccadys Crk. to beaver dams to the Going over or Snellings Path, adjoining Robt. Elliott, Tho: Gaunt, Wm. Elliott, Robt. Beverley & "Mr. Bailys old Divident... at the head of the Valley issuing in to Allins Crk." - along Pianketank R. to Hoccadays Crk. 600 acs. by purchase from Coll: Antho: Elliott 882 by former patent to Bailey, residue being 393 acs.	M.G.?	6	547	1674 Nov. 16	1875
BAKER John	KINGSTONE P. On a branch at the head of Winter Harbour Crk. adjoining his own land.	M.	8	194	1691 Oct. 20	40
BALDING..BOLDING John	PETSWORTH P. Between the branches of Poropotank & Dragon Swamp, adjoining John Norman, Thomas Sadler, William Hall, Soloman Hall. Price 20 Shillings.	G.	32	130	1753 June 6	174
[See BOWLIN..BOWLING..BOLLING]						
BALLARD Thomas	Upon the head of the Pyanketank R. adjoining NW upon the land of Stephen Gill, dece'd. Granted Abraham Moone 1654, who assigned to Ballard. Renewed 1662 in name of Major David Cant, Assignee of Ballard.	G.	4	186	1657 Oct. 15	600
BANNISTER John & Thomas Foote & John Boarham	On S side of Horne Harbour adjoining Mrs. Morrison, Mr. Armestead, Mr. Hall, Henry Singleton, John Teage & Edw. Morgan. 50 acs. assigned from Richard Hull.	M.	3	34	1653	350

NAMES	DESCRIPTION	CO.	BK.	Pg.	DATE	ACRES
BANNISTER (Continued) Mrs. Elizabeth	ABINGTON P. "...for and during her natural life and after her decease unto her sonn John Bannister sonn & heire of John Bannister dece'd...[if] without heirs... to surviving sisters". Land adjoining Major John Scarsbrooke, Edw. Allin, Mr. Wm. Craines, Mr. Debnam, Mr. Stoakes, Cha: Smith, along the Great Road to corner tree of Robert Todd & Edw. Mumford, to John Williams, near house and plantation formerly leased by John Bannister dece'd to John Bell dece'd, and crossing Tindalls Crk. 455 acs. granted Peter Rigby 1651, who assigned to Bannister; 1145 acs. by bill of sale from Coll: Geo: Ludlow to Bannister. HR: ____Moore, Tho. Tole, Wm. Davy, Jno. Hyne, Saml. Mott, X'pr Decus, Griff Loyd, Chas. Gallis, Jos. Oliver, Sa. Swanson, Eliz. Jones, Nat. Spencer, Ja: Fisher, Rob. Walker, Job Whitnell, Rich. Bardly, Fra: Browne, Mary Coleman, X'pr Leucas, Dan'll Oliver, Tho. Mampry.	G.	7	3	1679 Sept. 25	1600
John	Being a neck of land called New Poynt Comfort bounded by New Poynt Comfort Crk. on E & Mobjack Bay on W, adjoining John Gundry. Formerly granted to Wm. Worleigh in 1650, who assigned to Bannister Feb. 2, 1653	M.	7	357	1684 April 20	650
BARLOW Robert	ABINGTON P. Adjoining Christopher Abbot, Dece'd, along by the road to Tyndalls Pt.	G.	7	386	1684 April 26	62
BARNETT..BARNARD..BERNARD						
Mrs. Anna Barnett	700 acs. part thereof at the head of Jones Crk. in the County of Gloster, NE upon Jones Neck E on Rappahannock horse path S on land of Coll: Rich. Lee & Hugh Doudinge W upon a swamp of Jones Crk. opposite land of Samuel Sollace; 300 acs. "abutting NW upon Land of Capt. Lee dece'd SW & SE upon Land of Mr. William Prior, dece'd." HR: Mr. Richard Barnett, Richard Barnett, Mrs. Anna Barnett, Eliza: Barnett, Corderoy Barnett, Ellinor Corderoy, Wm. Corderoy, Edwd. Corderoy, Wm. Ironmonger, Fra. Ironmonger, Eliza: Ironmonger, Eliza: Parry, Isabell Ashton, John Smith, Thomas Feild, Joseph Bacon, Anne Whitelock, John Fuller, Leo. Lett, Henry Fablett.	G.	3	204	1652 July 2	1000
Mrs. Anne Barnett	On N side of York R. adjoining maine swamp upon the head of Johnses Crk. and adjoining Hugh Doodinge, Saml. Sollis, to Rappa Path & to William Thorne who was assignee of Coll: Rich Lee.	G.	3	239	[No date]	900
Mrs. Ann Bernard	Renewal of her patent dated Feb. 26,1653.	G	4	534	1661 Nov. 27	900
Richard Barnard	PETSO. P. Beginning at a white oak standing in the middle of the main Road near Mr. Hansfords mill dam running NNW and on NW side of mill, adjoining Mrs. Pritchetts dower, Jos. Coleman, Mr. Thornton & across dam to beginning. 900 acs. granted Mrs. Annie Bernard Nov. 27, 1661. 190 acs. residue. HR: Andr Teddar, Wm. Harpur, Elias Roy, Mary Ball.	G.	8	98	1690 Oct. 23	1090

NAMES	DESCRIPTION	CO.	BK.	Pg.	DATE	ACRES
BARRINGHAM Richard	WARE P. See Farthingale, Barringham, Forsith & Poole	G.	6	53	1671	800
Richard	Same as above.	G.	6	352	1671	800
BARTLETT John	KINGSTON P. Adjoining William Morgan, including marshes. Granted Wm. Morgan dece'd, patent lost. Assigned Bartlett by Wm. Morgan, heire.	M.	7	218	1682 Dec. 22	50
BATT William	On W side of North R. in Mockjack Bay, at a landing place. HR: Christopher Hooton, Edward Spicer, Richard Cheesome, George Wye, Wm. Smarte.	G.	1(2)	901	1643 Sept. 1	250
BATTIN..BATTEN Ashwell	YORK COUNTY. Upon N side of Yorke R. alongst Perints Crk. which divides from John Perrines. HR: Thomas Williams, Mar. Williams, Judeth Greenwood, Law. Long, Gilbert Fabin, Richd. Woodford, Fayth Webb, Jno. Owine, Tho. Dane, George Lock, Geo. Chiles, Edward Cocks, Edw. Hancock, Wm. Winifield, Richd. Trayillis, James Clarke, John Bell, John Bard, Tho. Nurdon, John Johnson.	G.?	2	324	1651 April 3	1000
Ashwell	GLOCESTER COUNTY. On both sides of Cheesecake path to Mattapony Path between two branches and adjoining Leo. Chamberlaine.	G.?	3	84	1653 Oct. 13	750
BAYLES..BAYLEY see BAILEY						
BEALE..[BELL?] John	On N side of Charles R. 200 acs. assigned by Thos. Jefferyes, 100 acs. by Tho: Deacon, 50 acs. by Tho: Ramsey, 50 acs. by Francis Wheeler. "As also by the names of several people mentioned." HR: Margarett Robinson, John Willshaw, Tho. Jeffers, Morgan Bryan, John Mason, Jon. Chapman, Eliza. Ramsey, Francis Wheeler.	G.?	1(2)	827	1642 Oct. 10	400
BEARD William	KINGSTON P. On a branch which runs by said William Beards house & adjoining Richard Longest, Coll: Dudley, Jno. Waters Plantation. HR: Six negroes, Cha: Stafford, Wm. Farrar.	M.	6	659	1678 Sept. 26	380
BEDLAM William	On N side of Horne Harbour to Winter Harbour, adjoining Fran. Hales.	M.	3	243	1653 July 1	150
BELL..[BEALE?] Thomas	YORK COUNTY. On N side of Charles R. NE on land of Jos. Hayes, SE & SW on land of John Perin. Due by patent to Wm. Hoccaday who assigned to Bell.	G.?	2	302	1651 April 3	200
Thomas	GLOCESTER COUNTY. On Poropotank and NE side of Bennets Crk. adjoining John King and Bennett & Leechman. HR: Thomas Hickman, Thomas Wheely, William Watts, land due for last.	G.?	3	164	1652 Dec. 6	84
Thomas	On Poropotank. 84 acs. granted 1652, residue 50 acs. HR: Wm. Watts (altered to Witts).	G.?	4	82	1656	134
Thomas	NEW KENT COUNTY [and G.?] Additional land adjoining Ashwell Battin. (Total 1100 acs.)	G.?	4	424	1662 Oct. 16	600
BENNETT Richard	Upon the second creek of Milford Haven, adjoining Abraham English. Assigned from Edward Maulson. HR: John Hales, John Binsteed.	M.	1(2)	830	1642 Oct. 13	100

NAMES	DESCRIPTION	CO.	BK.	Pg.	DATE	ACRES
BENNETT (Continued) John	See Leechman & Bennett	G.	3	166	1652	200
Robert	KINGSTON P. Adjoining John Guyton, Jas: Bealye. Formerly granted "Capt. John Armestead 21 of 7br 1674 by him assigned to sd Robert Bennett and his heires forever (alwaies) provided that he die with Issue of his body Lawfully begotten otherwise to return to the said Armestead & heires & to their only use & behoofe which said assignment is for and in consideration that the said land formerly belonged to his father Adam Bennett & the Pattent thereof was lost." HR: Tho Newbery, Jno. Woodroff, Jno. Hardy, Jno. Hadaway, Simon Robson, Jone Fell'ps.	M.	6	554	1674/5 Jan. 26	330
BENSON John	On the head of Beech swamp adjoining Lawrence Smith and Willm Ironmonger. HR: Elizabeth Gilbert, Rich. Wingate, Stephen Cotswood.	G.	6	23	1666 March 15	140
John	On the head of Ware R. adjoining Francis Camfield by the Indian Path that goeth to Cheescake and to Thos. Colles land. HR: Jno. Dunbar, Edward Jennings, Will Grimes, Jno. Harris, Ed. Freman, Jno. Garton, Jno. Cooper.	G.	6	72	1667 April 10	366
John & John Waller	WARE P. Beginning at Mr. Taliafro's land, along Wm. Peach's land to Edw. Trate and X'topr Greenaway's. HR: Eliz. Higgenson, Wm. Hughes, Wm. Johnson, Mary Blury, Jeremiah Upshaw, Jno. Tilson, Tho. Stephens, Robt. Smith, Rebecca Toppin.	G.	6	74	1667 April 10	423
John & Thomas Purnell	On the branches of North R. adjoining Lt. Coll: Elliott. HR: Susan Joyce, Sarah Bew, Jeffry Bew, Dorothy Browne, Jno. Wells, Jno. Grymes, Thomas West, Mary Andrewes, William Clarke, Wm. Portis, John Bennett, John Whitmore.	G.	6	211	1668 Oct. 1	950
BESOUTH James	YORK COUNTY. On N side of York R. near head of Timberneck Crk. HR: "Samuel Besouth his brother & his own personal adventure."	G.	1(2)	886	1643 Aug. 10	100
BEVERLEY Robert	PETSOE P. On path that goes from Wm. Hawwards house towards Mr. Forsiths house.	G.	6	242	1669 Oct. 27	116
Robert	Upon the branches of Hoccadays Crk. & Chiescake Crk. adjoining "Robert Elliott youngest sonne of Lt. Coll: Anthony Elliott dece'd" near Noakes plantation where he now lives to land of Conquest Wyatt. HR: Richard Mounts, Matthew Jones, Samll Cox, Simon Stacey, Elias Robinson, Sara Howard, Wm. Allexander, Henry Herbert, Will. Allen, Jon. Gibson.	M.	6	438	1672 Oct. 10	500
Robert	Upon S side of Pieanketanck R. "neare Noakes his Plantation" and adjoining Robt. Elliott, Conquest Wyatt, George Harper, to Hoccadays Crk. along Pianketank R. to Cheesecake Crk. 500 acs. by former pattent dated Oct. 11, 1672. 1000 acs. residue.	M.?	6	490	1673 Oct. 6	1500

NAMES	DESCRIPTION	CO.	BK.	Pg.	DATE	ACRES
BEVERLEY (Continued) Robert	HR: Jon Ward, Robert Clarke, Anne Lister, Jon Arthur, Tho. Harwood, Geo. Grand, Tho. Lewis, Antho. Beale, Robert Molton, Phill: Surgeon, Jon Rivers, Wm. Finnis, Ann Barr, Ann Herford, Robert Peters, Rich. Long, Tho. Mayor, Wm. Roberts, Geo. Diamond, Peter Russ.					
Robert	On S side of Garden Crk. Former grant to Edw. Lucas 1655, deserted and granted Charles Hill, never seated, since granted Beverley.	M.	6	493	1673 Nov. 6	150
Robert	Between Garden Crk. and Eastermost R. at the head of the dammes. Granted Jon. Hampton 1655, deserted, then to Charles Hill 1658, then to Major Tho. Colie, not seated. HR: Thomas Bramley, John Land, John Poland.	M.	6	494	1673 Nov. 6	150
Robert	On E side of Poropotank adjoining Oliver Greene, to Poplar Spring, to land of John Pate and William Ginsey. 700 Acs. granted Michaell Grafton 1667 and 200 acs. granted to Grafton and then to John Pate then to John Oakham and by them deserted. HR: Thomas Martin, Katherine Power, Joseph Poore, Matthew Tubb.	G.	6	494	1673 Oct. 24	920
Robert, Capt.	WARE P. Lying betwixt and on every point adjoining lands of Mr. William Elliot, Junr, and of Tho: Elliot his brother and lands of Mr. Marke Warkeman Dec'd, Mr. Wm. Marloe formerly pattented by Tho: Collins, "the Lands and lines of the Cheiscake Indians & the Land of Mr. Richd. Bailey and by him purchased of Lt. Coll. Anthony Elliot Dece'd by Land of Mr. Wm. Elliot and Geo Wolley to middle of Warners Meadow...to...the pathside that goes to Hoccadyes Crk. formerly called Snellings path"...to a branch of Wadding Crk. that runs up toward Mr. Tho: Elliots Quarter. 500 acs. purchased of Mr. Wm. Elliott, Junr., deed Sept. 14, 1672, residue 198.	G.?	M.?	6-558	1675 June 15	698
Robert	Betwixt land of Major David Cant & Thomas Dawkins. Formerly granted Robert Moore & Bartholomew Ramsey 1675.	G.	6	666	1678 Nov. 20	300
Robert	"Son of Maj[r] Robert Beverley dec'd". On the Eastermost side of Poropotank Crk. adjoining Maj[r] Robert Beverley, William Ginsey, Mr. John Pate, Land formerly granted to Michael Crafton & deserted, then to John Pate, to John Oakham 1661, to Robert Beverley 1673 but not seated. HR: Jno. Drake, Danl Boss, 1 negro.	G.	8	234	1692 April 29	200
Peter	KINGSTONE P. Adjoining Sands Knowles and beginning "by a path that leads to the head of Eastermost R." Formerly granted unto Mr. Sands Knowles, 1682 and deserted. HR: Thomas Cary, Hester Walker, John Layne?, Thomas Whitnall, Thomas Furman.	M.	9	438	1702 April 25	230
BEW Jeffry	On Ware R. [?] in Mockjack Bay upon the head of Cranie Crk. adjoining Mr. Thomas Breeman on W side of swamp and creek.	G.	3	112	1652 May 13	600
Jeffry	WARE P. To a "valley neare Rich. Trahern-ers house" by Ware R. Swamp and adjoining Wm. Peaches and X'topher Rigault.	G.	6	143	1668 April 4	620

LANDS GRANTED TO JOANE CARELESS, GEORGE BILLOPS AND AUGUSTINE WARNER IN 1653.

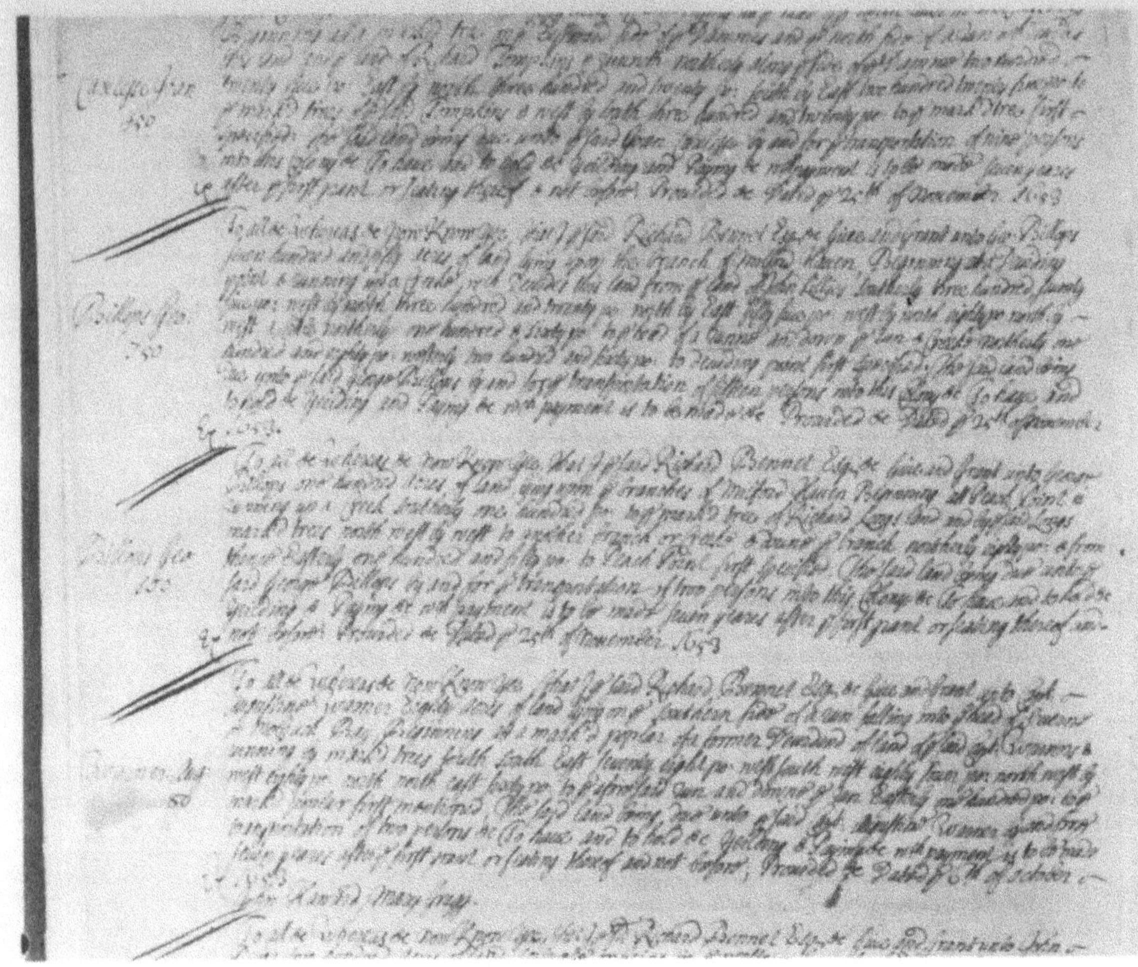

Patent Book 3, page 2, showing patents of Joane Careless for 450 acres, George Billops [Billups] for 750 acres on Milford Haven, George Billops for 100 acres at Peach Point and Augustine Warner for 80 acres near the head of the Severn River.

The Billups land on Milford Haven is still owned in the name of Billups by direct descent.

NAMES	DESCRIPTION	CO.	BK.	Pg.	DATE	ACRES
BILLOPS..BILLIPS..BILLUPS George	Lying upon the branches of Milford Haven beginning at a dividing point and running up a creek which divides this from the land of John Lillies. Renewal of same	M.	3 5	2 167	1653 Nov. 25 1662	750
George	Upon a branch of Milford Haven at Peach Pt. & running up a creek S'ly to a tree on Richard Longs land.	M.	3	2	1653 Nov. 25	100
George	On the S side and head of Garding Crk. opposite Forresters land. HR: Fra. Blagrave, Robt. Severall, Jno. Bayly, Mary Bayly, Hen. Brand.	M.	5	250	1663 Jan. 27	250
George	At the head of Garding Crk. and S side opposite Forrester and along the Bever Damms. Adjoining 250 acs. granted 1663. HR: Ann Crouch, Robt. Harrison, Andrew Grome, Richd. Crittenden, Wm. Budle.	M.	6	514	1674 April 9	500
George	Resurvey of Garden Crk. land. Now adjoining John Calles and Edw. Forrest. 500 acs. formerly granted George Billops dece'd by two pattents 27th Jan.,1663 and 9th April, 1674.Residue 250 acs. HR: Tho. Glen, Richd. Martin, Richd. Hodges, Mary Partan, Wm. Wallis.	M.	7	275	1683 April 16	750
George	KINGSTON P. Renewal of former grant to George Billops dec'd March 18, 1662. Adjoining Richard Billops on head of his land.	M.	7	287	1683 April 16	86
George	Beginning next to the land of John Lilly SW side of Milford Haven, SE to creek that divides from Peter Rigbee SW to woods NW to the head of a creek that divided this land from John Smith. Formerly granted to Abraham Moone 1650, who assigned to Tho. Bourne, who assigned to Geo. Billups. Renewed by order of the Generall Court April 24, 1700. [Resurvey of patent for 750 acs. 1653]	M.	9	283	1700 Nov. 7	500
George	KINGSTONE P. Adjoining head line of Mr. Richard Billops at a corner of Mr. George Billops hundred acres and adjoining John Calles, Marke Foster and Morris Mack a shannock. Formerly granted Richd. Glasscock 1691, deserted, then to George Billops 1705. HR: Seven rights paid for to Wm. Robertson, Clerk of Councill.	M.	9	729	1706 May 2	335
Richard	KINGSTON P. Adjoining former divident of said Billops and Morris Mackashannock. HR: Susanna Emlen, Eliz. Ostler.	M.	7	214	1682 Nov. 22	92
John	KINGSTONE P. Beginning at the mouth of Wrights Crk. Thence N to Mr. Tabbs corner, S along Mr. Tabbs land and along Wrights Crk. HR: Edward Swann.	M.	9	24	1695 Oct. 25,	38
BIRCH Benjamin	See Ralph Harwood & Benj. Birch.	G.	5	350	1663	600
BLACKBOURNE William	Escheat land late in the possession of James Whiteing. Peter Beverley, Deputy Escheator.	G.	9	156	1697 Oct. 28	250

NAMES	DESCRIPTION	CO.	BK.	Pg.	DATE	ACRES
BLUNT Gilbert	On N side of York R. and E head branch of Poropotank adjoining Winfield Webb at Chiskayack path. HR: Gilbert Blunt, his wife, his Brother, William Jackman, Eliza. Wells, Anne Dodson, Ann ___, Wm. Blyth, Jone Blyth. 130 acs. due.	G.	3	94	1652 July 16	320
BOHONO..BOHONON.. BOHANNAN..BOHANNAH Dunkin [Duncan?] & John Mechen	On the head of the Eastermost R. adjoining Mr. Armestead and Capt. Dudley. HR: Tho. Amis, Roger Shackleford, John Blan, John Thomas.	M.	6	102	1667 Dec. 20	220
Dunken [Duncan?]	KINGSTONE P. On Eastermost R. adjoining his own land along the river and Jno. Nevells. Purchased of Mr. Wm. Armestead being part of a greater divident granted Armestead.	M.	6	548	1674/5 March 6	340
Dunken	KINGSTONE P. Adjoining Mr. Richard Dudley, Capt. Knowles, Capt. Wm. Armestead and Aldridge. HR: Wm. Cluny, Harris Temperance, John Smithson.	M.	9	591	1704 April 26	145
BOOKER Richard, Capt.	Escheat land. Formerly in the possession of John Sigismund Cleverous, dece'd. Francis Page, D. E.	G.	7	540	1686/7 Feb. 1	740
Richard	Escheat land, late in the possession of Nicholas Baldwin. Henry Whiteing, Esq. Escheator.	G.	8	376	1694 April 20	180
BORHAM..BOARHAM..BARHAM..BOORUM..BORAM..[BORUM]		M.	2	355	1651	200
John Barham	See Thomas Foote & John Barham				Jan. 26	
John Boarham	See Bannister, Foote & Boarham	M.	3	34	1653	350
John Boorum	On S side of Horne Harbour. Granted Richard Hull 1655 who assigned to Boorum.	M.	4	526	1661 Nov. 20	400
Anne Boram	On Horne Harbour beginning 100 poles from creek side. HR: Rose Davus, Mary Brydon, Payne Harvy.	M.	6	100	1667 Dec. 17	148
Anne Boram	KINGSTON P. Beginning on the west side of a small creek on S side of Horne Harbour. Adjoining Edmund Boram, Ralph Armestead. Renewal of patent of 1667.	M.	7	351	1684 April 20	95
Edmund (Orphant)	KINGSTON P. On S side of Horn Harbour Crk. First granted Mrs. Winifred Morrison 1651 who sold to Richard Hull 1655 who sold to John Boram and repattented 1661.	M.	7	212	1682 Oct. 22	364
BOSWELL Thomas	On N side of Ware R. in Mockjack Bay adjoining Wm. Dudley. HR: Domine Cherrick, Eliza Locker, Fra. Wiggan, Anne Lovell, two negroes, Ann Tabrer, Eliza. Harrage, Jno. Howet, & his wife, Margery Paine, James Kaiton, Miles Moor, John Boswell, Eliza. Wiggs, Jno. Adson.	G	3	42	1652 May 6	800
Thomas	Adjoining Major Curtis and up the river W'ly. 800 acs. granted 1652, residue 172 acres.	G.	4	93	1656 Oct. 8	972
	Renewal	G.	4	560	1662	972
Thomas	The North Point of Ware R. Point including Racoune Island. Adjoining Nath. Fletcher. HR: Mathew Hutson, Stephen Coleman.	G.	5	667	1666 June 10	100

NAMES	DESCRIPTION	CO.	BK.	Pg.	DATE	ACRES
BOSWELL (Continued) Thomas	ABBINGTON P. On York R. side beginning at the mouth of Timberneck Crk. along creek for about a mile from mouth, E to corner of 100 acs. sold to Mr. Booker, SWS to river & along same including all islands to said Timberneck Crk. 1000 acs. "granted to Rich[d] Richards 2nd August, 1645 and from him descended to Hugh Richards who assigned to Thomas Wilson and Richard Jones - Wilson assigned to Rich[d] Jones and from him descended to Cadwallader Jones who conveyed and assigned to said Thomas Boswell 19th March 1679". Residue 100 acs. HR: Wm. Morton, Joseph Thompson.	G.	7	162	1682 April 20	1100
Thomas	WARE P. Resurvey and renewal of former patents for 972 acs. 1656 and 1662 with residue of 128 acs. of land and marsh on Ware R. side adjoining Major Robt. Bristow. HR: John Penride, Richd. Twine, Jno. Sadler.	G.	7	580	1687 April 20	1100
BOWLIN..[BOLDING?] William	First mention of ABINGDON PARISH. Adjoining Coll: Augustine Warner, Edw. Wills, Kerbyes, Mr. Lawrence Smith. 750 acs. granted David Fox 1648, who sold to Bowlin. Residue 137 acs. HR: John Cheney, Hicks, Wm. Preston.	G.	6	131	1668 April 14	887
BOYCE Christopher	In the Peancketank R. 3 miles up the S side at Plumtree Point, and along the river side. HR: Jon Crispe, Christ. Boyce, Mordecay Cooke, Wm. Venice, Jon Johnson, Jon. Tiplad, Jon Fells, Jas. Greenwill, Jon Barlow, Walter Brace, Kath. Lewis, John Williams, Jon Withers, Edmd: Porter & ux(wife), Edmund Porter Junr., Jon Porter Senr., Jon Porter Junr., Marmaduke Atkinson, Mannassa Porter, Thomas Simpson, Elizabeth Flowerdew, Rich. Williams, Robt. Fentrice, Jon Carraway, Robert Fentrice, Georg Harland, Jarman Connaway, Thomas Blatt, Rich. Wooton, Anne Marshall, Tho. Kemp, John Oliver, Tho. Cooper, Thomas Cooper, Thomas Pitcherd, Tho. Correll (?), Joyce Stone, John Cannaday, Wm. Jackson, John Nemo.	M.	1(2)	870	1642 December	2000
BRADBURY James	Beginning at a corner of Oliver Greenes land and running SE. HR: John Coniers, Wm. Marting, Sarah Glover, Wm. Hopes, Jno. Dancy.	G.	5	123	1662 Dec. 31	250
BRADLEY Abraham	ABBINGTON P. Adjoining Danll. Langham, Robt. Coleman, Tho: and Jeffry Graves and Capt. Lawrence Smith along the edge of the high lands and the Roade side. Granted Thomas Seawell 1675 - by him deserted. HR: Jeremiah Rawlins, Robert Smith, John Purvis.	G.	7	163	1682 May 6	150
Abraham	ABINGTON P. On the E side of the "Roade to Tindalls poynt" adjoining land "formerly taken up by Christopher Abbot dece'd". HR: Robt. Barnham, Phill Packer.	G.	7	286	1683 April 16	61
BREEMAN..BREEMO..BREMO..BREAMOR..BREEMORE Thomas Breeman	Lying on S side of a run to Craney Crk in Ware R. Purchased of Richard Kemp Esq[r] Dece'd.	G.	2	308	1650 March 23	500

NAMES	DESCRIPTION	CO.	BK.	Pg.	DATE	ACRES
BREEMAN etc. (Continued)						
Thomas Bremo	GLOSTER COUNTY. A neck of land bounded by Craney Crk. swamp and on NE side by Ware R . continued with another run and swamp. Purchased of Rich. Kemp, esq'r Dece'd.	G .	2	353	1651 Jan. 9	1500
Thomas Breman	Upon the head of another tract of his land near the Beaver Damm. 200 acs. by rights of a Pattent of his in Mobjack Bay purchased by certificate from County of Gloster. (100 acs. residue) HR: David Short, Jone Banton.	G.	3	11	1653 Mar. 11	300
Thomas Breeman	On the N side of the Severne R. bounded by Mr. Robins on the E, S upon the river, W on Capt. Warner and N. upon Lt: Coll: Walker	G.	3	326	1654 Mar.23	600
Thomas Breamor,Capt.	Adjoining his own land	G.	4	106	1656 Dec. 8	300
BRISTOW..BRISTOL..BRISTOE						
Robt., Mr.	On North R. in Mockjack Bay adjoining Thomas Morris, Major Curtis, & Harris, "being parallel with land of Richard Young and crossing Back Crk. mouth to the beginning." 288 acs. granted Mrs. Avarilla Curtis 1661 & part of a dividend of 410 acs., assigned to sd. Bristow her husband.	G.	5	523	1665 Oct. 25	398
Robert	On N side of Ware R. adjoining his own land and land of Harris to an Oyster Shell Pt. HR:: Eliz, Boston, Wm. Browne, John Dowdy, a negro.	G.	5	607	1666 May 7	184
Robert, Major	KINGSTONE P. "On NE side of Mobjack Bay ..neare mouth of North R. on NE side thereof" adjoining Tho: Ryland, Tho: Preston including marshes on bayside. 700 acs. granted Wm. ap Thomas 1652 who sould to Capt. Tho: Todd who sould to Bristow. Residue 230 acs. HR : Wm. Fisher, Wm. Carter, Jno. Whetstone, Henry Charlton, 1 negro.	M.	6	479	1673 Oct. 23	930
BROMLEY. .BRUMLEY..BROUNLEY.. BROWNLEY..BROMELEY						
Archabell Bromley	KINGSTON P. 150 acs. formerly granted Wm. Bedlam 1653 & bounded as in same & in deed of sale from Coll:: Christ. Wormley & Frances his wife to Bromley. 350 acs. lying "betwixt Winter harbour & Horne harbour & the maine bay" adjoining Geo. Peed, John Tillitt, Gyles Vandecasteel, up Horne Harbour to his other land. HR: Tho: Burnett, John Dicks, Elinor Weaver, Phill Stephens, Jno. Craddock, Wm.Thompson, Hester Buckinham.	M.	6	658	1678 Sept. 26	500
Archibald Bromley	KINGSTON P. On N Side of Horne Harbour NE to head of a creek and to S side of Winter Harbour, E down same and W up Horne Harbour. HR: Mary Porteus, Ellinor Gill, Jon Bennet, Hen: Peters, Wm: Henderson, Tho: Bowler, Jon Taylor, John Ayers.	M.	7	161	1682 Apr. 20	400
BROOKIN..BROOKING..BROOKEN						
William & Robert Nettles	PETTSOE P. Beginning at a corner of other land of Brooking & Nettles and adjoining	G.	8	193	1691 Oct. 20	270

NAMES	DESCRIPTION	CO.	BK.	Pg.	DATE	ACRES
BROOKIN etc. (Continued) William & Robert Netles.	land formerly owned by Robert Collis. HR: Wm. Hargrove, Dorothy Hargrove, Geo. Warner, Fra. Prince, Ralph Lisney, Tho. Higden.					
William	PETTSOE P. On a branch at the head of Poropotank Crk. adjoining his own land. 450 acs. granted Thomas Hancks 1663 who sold Owen Kelley July 18, 1665, who sold Robert Callis May 17, 1677, who assigned to Mr. Wm. Brookin Jan. 20, 1689. Residue 67 acs. HR: Edward Shepheard, Eliza. Lost.	G.	8	193	1691 Oct. 20	517
BROOKS..BROOKES George	Bounded by Chesapeake Bay on E, and on S & W by Winter Harbour, on N by Armistead Stuart, Junr. Partly marsh.	M.	75 (C.G.)	502	1827 Feb. 6	100
BROUGHTON Francis	WARE P. Adjoining "Land he now lives oppon" & on Craney Crk. adjoining land of Wm. Roberts late dece'd on W'wd side of Burches Branch to Run of George Poole to Jordans Land.	G.	6	559	1675 June 15	170
BRUMFIELD..BROMFEILD Edward Brumfield, Major, & Mr. Jno Snellinge	On the W side of Hoccadies Crk. of the Peanketank River. HR: Jno. Snellinge, Edward Brumfield, Wm. Simpson, Wm. Feild, John Mutton, Jno. Williams, Hen. Coniers, Geo. Harber, Sarah Mashy, Nath. Ruford, Nath. Pincon, Jno. Abbott, Ann Delue, Rob. Hollaway, Jno. Cranfield, X'pher Hanes, Winifred James, Rob. Fletcher, Tho. a Scott, Thom a Boy, a maid servant, James Hunts wife.	M.	4	159	1657 June 6	1100
BRYAN Robert	On Burts [Burnt?] Crk. [Severn R.?] beginning at a little branch running NW by N.	G.	5	296	(No date)	276
Robert	"a minor son of Robert Bryan late of Gloucester County, dece'd". On the branches of Severne R. beginning at a corner of Valentine & Benja. Lane & along Bryans old line. HR: Two rights paid for to Wm. Byrd Esq. Auditor.	G.	9	439	1702 April 25	57
Robert	ABINGTON P. Son of Robert Bryan dece'd. On a branch of the Severne R. adjoining Valentine & Benj. Laine & land of Robert Bryan, dece'd. HR: John Sanders, Mary Hagaice.	G.	9	614	1704 Oct. 20	60
BUCKNER John & Thomas Vicars	PETSOE P. See Vicars & Buckner for description.	G.	6	144	1667 Feb. 19	517
John	Adjoining the plantac'on he lives on and land of Francis Ironmonger by an "arbour in Mr. Barnards lyne" by Rappa path to lands of Isaac Richardson & Mr. Talliferoe. HR: Wm. Watson, Edward Teale, Tho. Vickers.	G.	6	145	1667 Feb. 19	194
John & Thomas Vicars	On Rappa path adjoining James Bradbury Planta'con & Ginsye. HR: John Morryson, Tho. Johnson, Augustin Cobham.	G.	6	154	1668 June 16	122
John & Thos. Royston	On Chesecake Branches and Chesecake path adjoining Roystons land along Rappa path. HR: John Buckner, Tho. Royston, Eliz. Williams, Valentine Smith, Abr. Smith, Jno. Falkner, Robt. Haniger, Jno. Clay, Edwd.	G.	6	240	1669 Oct. 12	1000

NAMES	DESCRIPTION	CO.	BK.	Pg.	DATE	ACRES
BUCKNER (Continued)	Hewes, Hen. Glover, Jno. Demett, Ann Steed Jno. Colt, Pete Jonson, Jno. Willis, Edwd. ___, Wm. Crump, Hen: Nelson, Pete Burton, Abr. Harman.					
John	PETSOE P. Adjoining and betwixt 200 acs. patented Apr. 1, 1665 by Major John Smith dece'd, on the back of Purton old Dividend, to land of Mr. Francis Ironmonger, to Totapotamie Swamp and to Mrs. Ann Bernard's grant of 300 acs. July 1652, SW along her line to the Smith line.	G.	7	115	1681 Sept. 28	300
John, Mr. & Majr. Henry Whiting	Beginning on the S side of the mouth of a small creek which now parts the lands of Abraham Iveson & Henry Rawlings WNW 640 poles to John Reades old field across Cow Creek swamp thence ESE to a Cove near the mouth of Back Crk. and along North R. to the beginning. 2400 acs. of said land granted Dawber in 1642, conveyed to Mr. Richard Young, now purchased by Buckner & Whiting of "Mr. Samuel Young heire at Law to the aforesd Richard, Dece'd." 273 acs. being found within the bounds of the aforesaid patent. HR: Robert Ellyson, Jno. Walton, Wm. Morgan, Danl. Whitby, Jon Lingson, Joan Cole.	G.	7	212	1682 Dec. 22	2673
John, Mr., & Majr. Henry Whiting	WARE P. Upon WNW side of North R. betwixt land of Edward Dauber and the River side at the beginning place of Daubers patent of 1642 on S side of a creek dividing daubers land from George Levitt thence SSW 600 poles along Daubers land SE to North River & up the Riverside.	G.	7	513	1686 Oct. 30	280
John, Mr., & Majr. Henry Whiteing	On Northermost R. on S side of a creek which divides from George Levitt, extending into the woods WNW, SW and SE unto the River side thence up parallell to the said creek mouth. Formerly granted Edward Dawber 1642, who deserted and since granted to Mr. Henry Wareing 16th October 1686, by him assigned on Oct. 23, 1686 to Buckner & Whiteing.	G.	7	518	1686 Oct. 30	2400
BURGH..BURG..BURGIS George Burgh	KINGSTON P. Adjoining his own land and the old field where Charles Jones now dwells and adjoining John Waters by Gwynns Ridge pathside. HR: Samll Wheeler, Samll Chapman.	M.	7	1	1679 Sept. 5	170
BURNHAM..BURNAM Roland, Gent.	YORKE COUNTY.(By order of Court Oct. 12, Upon the N side of Yorke R. SE on Burnhams Crk. and along the river NW upon John Bayles, NE on Thos. Wilkinson & Robert Norrice. HR: Rowland Burnham his own adventure, Thomasin Knight, James Uteley, Martin Baker, Walter Wood, Tho. Wooldrige, Jon: Mason, Wm. Heyward, Wm. Peach.	G.	1(2)	884	1639) 1643 Aug. 10	450
BURTON Richard	On N side of Queens Crk. near the head at the mouth of Kings Crk. to trees of Edmond Welch. HR: Benj. Mathew, John Lunn, Ann Glouce, John Smith, Eliz. Bristow, Ann Substance, Edw. Harbrough, Andrew WMson [Williamson?] Ann Loyd, Wm. Latham.	M.	3	269	1653 Dec. 20	360

LAND GRANTED TO LEWIS BURWELL in 1654.

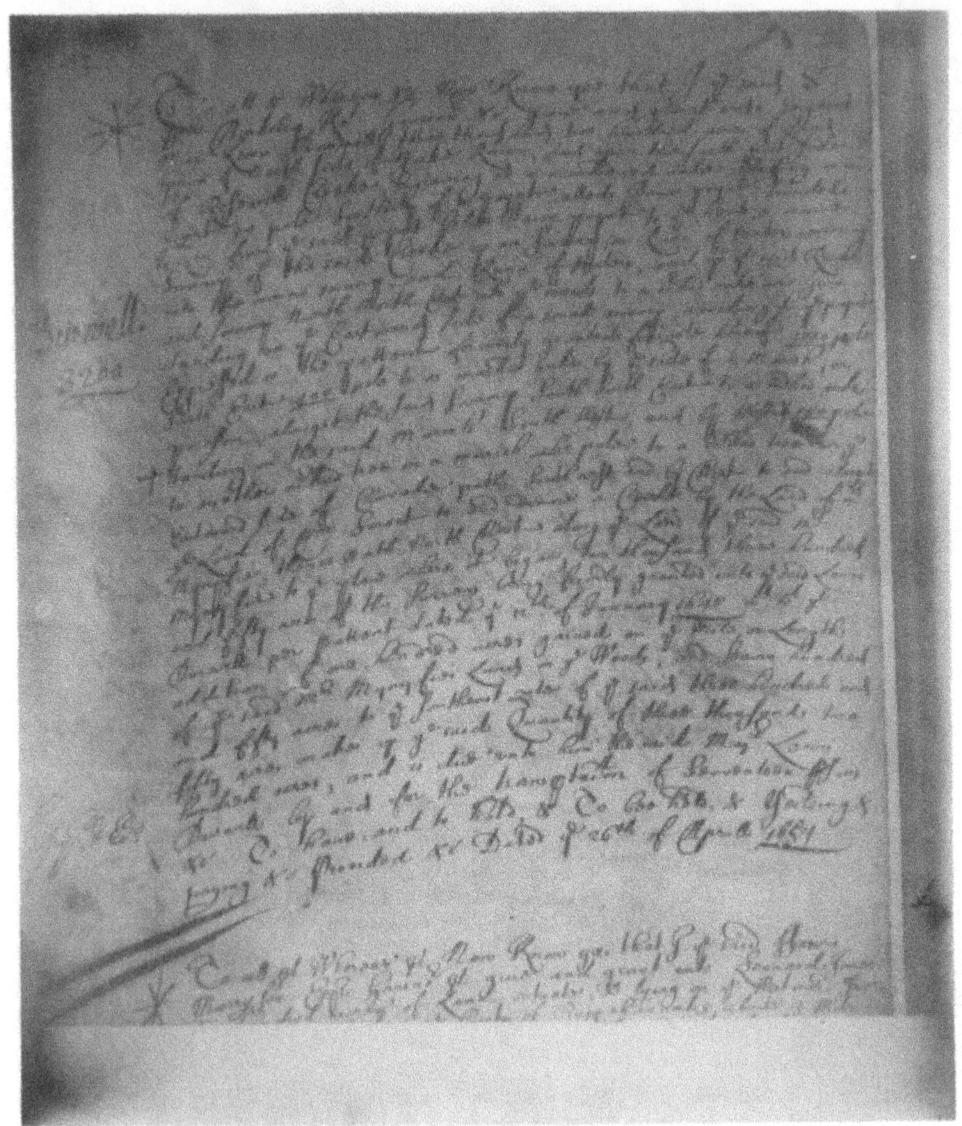

Patent Book 4, page 384, showing patent of Sergeant Major Lewis Burwell for 3200 acres on the North side of York River and upon the southeast side of Rosewell Creek (now Carter's Creek), on the eastward side of Chiscake Path and adjoining George Mynyfie. There was a previous grant in 1648 for 2350 acres to Lewis Burwell, Gent., in this same location.

NAMES	DESCRIPTION	CO.	BK.	Pg.	DATE	ACRES
BURTON (Continued)	John Smith, Eliz. Bristow, Ann Substance, Edw. Harbrough, Andrew WMson [Williamson], Ann Loyd, Wm. Latham.					
John	PETSOE P. Adjoining Mr. Wm. Hansford, Ralph Green, Mr. Benjamin Forcett, Mr. Wm. Haward to the Maine Roade and John Burtons own plantation. HR: Wm. Peircon.	G.	7	588	1687 Oct. 21	31
BURWELL Lewis, Gent.	On N side of York R. up S'd side of Rosewell Crk. to the head swamp and to Bacon Pt. running SSE down the river along the land of Georg Menefy to the land of Wm. Smoot. 900 acs. surveyed by Nicholas Jarnew; 400 acs. by Francis Cartar; 1050 acs. by Symon Bosman. HR: Francis Burwell, Allis Atkinson, Eliza Clap, Anthony Rock, Thomas Vand, Gerrard Hancorne, Robert Throndon, Susan Bayard, Henry Hubberd, William Cromp, Mary Wood, William Webb, Thomas Mase, William Pidd, John Axton, Kath. Key, Edward Croppage, Thomas Lane, Richard Howard, Thomas Reves, John Smith, William Lase (?), James Hume, Robert Deby, Peter Lobbins, Edith Taylor, Adam Finley, Eliza Clapp, Alice Adkinson, George Condell, Gri. Condry, Dow. Cozens, Fra. Burwell, Henry Brake, Wm. Andrews, Nicho. Conell (?), James Tyrrill, Michall Aldrop, Alax. Grey, John Loppham, Mary Frisser, John Cordy, Edward Owley, Ferd. Foster, Ma. Hamilton, And. Adkinson, Hump. Vand.	G.	2	181	1648 June 12	2350
Lewis, Sergeant Major	On SE side of Rosewell Crk. 50 Poles S of Bacon Pt. to E side of Chiscake path, adjoining Mr. Mynyfie & SW along Wm. Smoot. Former grant 1648, 850 acs. additional to SE.	G.	4	384	1654 April 26	3200
Lewis, Major	Beginning at a Mirtle Point on Carters Crk. up creek to head, up NE side of runne, through John Creeds old field & Orchard, adjoining Peter Garlands plantation to Marsh side & Dr. Clarkes cleered ground to Mrs. Bowlins line on edge of high lands, to old quarter field side along Maj^{r} Lawr: Smyths land to main branch of Tymberneck Crk. W to pond and to spring by Mixons Seller so by creek W.....	G.	7	64	1680 Sept. 29	3400
BUTLER Sarah & Alice Saies	WARE P. Sarah, wife of Peirce Butler. Escheat land lately owned by Susanna Smith dece'd, beginning at Debnams line adjoining Wm. Strechers Spring Branch & corner of Thomas Reade, crossing Gridiron Branch to Mirtle branch to Main Road near Debnams & Rows corner along road SW to pond and corner of Simon Stubblefield dece'd and along Willis line. Mathew Page, Esqr, Escheator. Surveyed 1718 by Thomas Cook S. G. C. Price: 2 pounds of Tobacco for every acre.	G.	10	452	1719 Nov. 9	220
CABLE..CABELL..[KEEBLE?..KIBBLE?..KEIBLE?]						
George Cable	On Milford Haven upon Hollowing Poynt running W alongst a creek. **HR:** John Owen, Richard Clothier, Hugh a highlander, Edward Bambas. [See also Keeble..Keible..Kibble]	M..	3	61	1653 Nov. 25	200

NAMES	DESCRIPTION	CO.	BK.	Pg.	DATE	ACRES
CADE Robert	On W side of branch of Cow Creek, of Ware R. HR: Margarett Griffith, Henry Freeman, James Chovell, Tho. Freeman, Samll Walton, Phillip Nicholson.	G.	2	353	1651 Jan. 9	300
[CALLIS]..CALLES..CARELESSE..CARELESS..CARLES..COLLES..COLLIS..COLIS						
Joane Carelesse	At the head of North River of Mockjack Bay beginning on the E side of the Dammes & N side of a run between this and Richard Tomkins.	M.	3	2	1653 Nov. 25	450
Joane Careless	Renewal		4	525	1661 Nov. 20	200
Joane Carles	Resurvey of 200 acs. granted Thomas Morgaine in 1653 who assigned to Richard Wilshin who sold to Careless. Adjoining Andrew Careless.		4	523	1661 Nov. 20	200
Thomas Colles, Merchant	On the head of North R. in Mockjack Bay adjoining Andrew Careless and Lt: Coll: Elliott. HR: Arthur Griggs, Morgan Joanes, Saml. Spendlon, Wm. Colver.	M.	6	91	1667 Dec. 17	200
Thomas Colles	On Deep Branch adjoining Coll: John Walker. HR: Tho. Colles and Sarah his wife, Wm. Powbeney, George Anderson.	M? G?	6	98	1667 Dec. 20	200
John Collis	KINGSTON P. At the head of "the Beaver Damms adjoining Matthew Gayle". HR: An. Roberts, Mary Seayres, Jno. Spragg, Ja: Grencill, Robt. Hall, Jno. Smith, Nich. Glasbe (?), Edward Andrews, Abra. Page, Adam Armstrong, Samll. Carriage, Eliz. Taylor.	M.	6	659	1678 Sept. 26	620
CAMP..CAMPE William	Two islands in York River. Price five shillings	G.	26	540	1748 Aug.20	14 30 po.
CAMPFIELD..CAMFIELD Francis	Beginning at a corner of his own land and adjoining Mrs. Cookes to the head of Crabtree Branch on W side of Indian path road. HR: Wm. Harbry, Jno. Roberts, Rich. Peach, Stephen Pore, Nic. Reinolds, Cha: Gaulter.	G.	6	130	1668 April 10	314
CANNHOE.. CAINHOE..CANHO William, Clerke	On N side of Charles R. & Peanckatanck [Poropotank] Crk. near Mr. Oberts land. [See Wilchin, Hobart and Light patents for this location on the Poropotank.] HR: Reynold Jones, William Lock, John Haddy, Morgan Floreday, William Woodhowse, Edward Blew, Capp Hanna, a negro, Christ Kickett.	G.?	1(2)	829	1642 Oct. 10	400
CANT..KANT	[See Ballard patent 1657]	G.? M.?	4-186		1662 April 2	600
David, Major	Beginning on the west side of Stoare Branch near head of Peankatank R. to Gills corner and adjoining Mr. Ludlowe.	G.? M.?	6-154		1663 March 15	542
David, Major	On S side of Peankatank R. adjoining land of Capt. Stephen Gill, dece'd, 312 acs. adjoining the divident he is now seated on at Stoare Branch and adjoining Ludlow. 600 acs. granted Thomas Ballard in 1657 who assigned to Cant. Residue 312 acs.	G.? M.?	5-300		1663 Oct. 1	912

CANT, etc. (Continued)	HR: Fra: Hart, Wm. Callis, Mary Partin, Tho. Jones, Wm. Crump, Edw. Lewre. [See Gilbert Medcalf patent, 1657]	G.? M.?	4-266		1664 March 25	500
David	"Sonn of Major David Cant, dece'd" Along the Piankatank R. & S side of Store Branch "neere the dwelling house of sd Major David Cant, dece'd" adjoining Geo. Haynes, his plantation, Lambert Moore, Walter Cant, by Knoxs [Noakes?] land to Pianketank. 600 acs. formerly granted to Tho: Ballard 1657, who sold to Major David Cant who bequeathed same to his sonn David. 500 acs. formerly due unto ____Gill & "since purchased by Coll: Augustine Warner Dece'd & by him given & bequeathed unto his grandsonn the sd David". Residue 300 acs.	G.? M.?	6-559		1675 June 15	1400
Walter	"Sonn of Major David Cant, Dece'd". Lying along the S side of the Pianketank R. and to Dragon Swamp. Formerly granted to ____Knox who sold to Major David Cant who bequeathed to Walter Cant.	G.	6	560	1675 June 15	500
CAREY..CARY..CARYE Richard Carey	On S side of Queens Crk. of Pyanketank R. at a tree at the mouth of said Creek, S along the creek dividing from Congdell. HR: Fra. Hayes, Eliz. Smith, Geo. Baines, Wm. Wood, Jon Brown, Derman Tahall, Mary Pomroy, Jarem Cook (?), Robt. Sorrel, Mary Rose, Wm. Mackery, Mary Jefferson, Moses Scarfe, Mary Bland, Tho. Edge, Gilbert Williams, Wm. Carey.	M.	3	5	1653 Oct. 13	1000
	Renewal		4	529	1661	
Richard Carey	On W side of Eastermost R. in Mobjack Bay at a corner of Wm. Armistead and running NW. HR: Sanders Mackell, Jon Burlier, Lewis Burlier, Geo. Adams, Hen: Sudwell, Tho. Scarburgh, Derrick Henn.	M.	3	5	1653 Oct. 13	350
Robert Cary	PETSO P. Adjoining Mr. Wm. Bernard, Jos. Coleman, Mr. Ironmonger and Wm. Fleming. HR: Mich a Scotchman, Francis Jones.	G.	9	90	1697 Oct. 28	90
Wilson Cary	Beginning at the head of the Eastermost head branch of Poropotank R. and up Turks ferry Road. Adjoining Coll: Grimes, Mr. Jno. Royston, Mr. James Dudley, on Pates Swamp and along Purton Road. 1141 acs. granted to Wingfield Webb & Richard Pate, Gentlemen, 1650, and by divers conveyances assigned to Wilson Cary. Price 4 Pounds good and lawful money.	G.	22	188	1744 Aug. 30	1906
CARTER..CARTAR Robert	KINGSTON P. Beginning at a small pine on the E'most side of a branch "not farr distance from the Chappell". Adjoining Mr. Wm. Elliott, Geo. Seaton, Granted Coll: John Armistead 1686, deserted; granted Henry Armistead 1697, deserted. HR: Jarvis Taylor, Wm. Johnson, Wm. Bruin.	M.	9	490	1702 Oct. 30	130
CARVER John, Mr.	PETSOE P. On S side of Maine Draggon Swamp, Adjoining Mr. Charles Roane, Robt. Shackleford, Thomas Amiss, being part of 700 acs. purchased by Carver "of Mr. Richard Wilson and Sarah his wife, sister and heire to Mr. Samuel Partridge, dece'd" 5th of July, 1678. Residue 95 acs.	G.	7	444	1685 April 20	340

NAMES	DESCRIPTION	CO.	BK.	Pg.	DATE	ACRES
CARY	[See Carey]					
CEELY..CEELEY Francis	At a long Cedar Point where the Severne divides. 300 acs. adjoining Thomas Williams. On Sedgy Branch & Creek, around Burnt Point to Ceder Point. HR: Fran. Ceely, John Hills, Carry Fitts, Richard Cooper, Walter Edward, Hen. Stepthorpe, Wm. Waters, Henry Steele, Humphrey Weydon, John Andrews, Ralph Seane, Nathll. More.	G.	2.	155	1648 March 2	600
CHAMBERLAINE..CHAMBERLAYNE..CHAMBERLIN Leonard	On Perrints Crk. adjoining Ashwell Battin & crossing Arracaico Branch. HR: Margt. Lewis, Jon Atkins, Fra. Sharp, Patrick Harper, Mary Green, Jon Williams.	G.?	3	21	1653 Oct 27	300
CHAPMAN John	KINGSTONE P. [First mention of a parish] On S side of Piankatank R. Beginning on the back of Mr. Wm. Armsteads Land adjoining NE to Coll: Gwinns line. Granted to Coll: Humphrey Higgenson 20th day of Sept. 1654 and deserted.	M.	4	304	1657 March 15	250
John	Additional land on S side of Peanketank R. Renewal, Nov. 20, 1661	M.	4 4	314 525	1658 Sept. 15	400
CHEESMAN..CHEESEMAN..CHEASMAN..CHEISMAN..CHISMAN..CHIESMAN. Edmond Cheesman	Upon Garden Patch Crk. issueing from Chisapeyak Bay which bounds it on the E, and bound on the W by a parcell of land bought of Peter Rigby. HR: John Tuffnell. [See Thomas below]	M.	2	262	1650 Sept. 16	50
John, Lt. Col	On S side of a run to Crany Crk. & Ware R. and running S. HR: James Nicholls, Roger Worth, Richard Loude, Jno. Peake, Mary Bind, Edmond Watts, Silvan Prite, John Hill, Wm. Davis, John Jackson, John Haycocks, Simon White, Roger _____, Richard Baines, Thomas Morris, James Robinson, Edw. Everye, Rich. ___, Thomas Williams.	G.	3	117	1652 Sept. 11	943
John Cheesman, Mr.	On S side of Mr. Breeman & E side of Lt. Coll: Cheesman on a branch to Crany Crk. of Ware R. HR: William White, Lewis Roberts, Jno. Clark, Law. Platt.	G.	3	116	1652 Sept. 25	200
Cornelius Cheeseman & Thos. Hanckes	Lying in both Gloucester and New Kent adjoining "Hanckes other lands whereon he now liveth". HR: Tho. Jenkins, Peter White, Wm. Coachman, Mary Haines, Mary Cord.	G.	6	511	1674 April 8	260
Thomas Cheesman	Land and marsh in Milford Haven, beginning near the head of Lilleys Crk. by Forrests line "by agreement...betwixt them both" E and SE to Garden Crk. and Garden Patch, down the creek to the maine bay side, along the bay up to Rigbys Point & Lilleys Crk. mouth including a large tongue of land, marsh and sandy ground with several broad bays of water, gutts and islands, up Lilleys creek to the beginning. 450 acs. granted Peter Rigby 1640, who sold Edmd Cheesman father of sd Thomas Cheesman. 80 acs. residue and overplus found.	M.	7	62	1680 Sept. 29	530

NAMES	DESCRIPTION	CO.	BK.	Pg.	DATE	ACRES
CHRISTMAS Dictoris & Francis Finch	At Finches Crk. & St. Michaells Crk. HR: Dictoris Christmas & Izabell his wife, William Thomason, Carrington Banton, Francis Finch, Joane Glanfeild.	G.	1(2)	831	1642 Oct. 10	300
CLARKE..CLERKE Daniell Clarke	On N side of Seaverne R. of Mockjack Bay and on N branch adjoining Nich. Stillwell. Granted to Abraham Moone 1652 who sold to Clarke.	G.	5	240	1663 March 17	200
Samuel Clerke	On E side of Poropotank Crk. Granted to Peter Knight 1652 now due Clerke "as heire and next of kinne".	G.	6	511	1674 April 8	700
William John Clarke	Land commonly known by the name of Portan. Beginning at a corner of this & land of Catesby Jones, dece'd. S & E 77 poles to road leading to Portan S & E to Halls Swamp corner of Samuel R. Davis dece'd, down the swamp which divides from William Eastwood to a point which is corner of this and Richard D. Leigh's land, NW to Richard D. Leigh's fence, SW along meadow to Broadneck & down the creek to York. R. Bounded by river to Tanks Poropotank or Adams Crk., by the creek to Claborne Coleman's corner, NE to Bookers Branch corner of said Coleman, SE & S and along the branch to the beginning.	G.	101 (C.G.)	382	1849 March 31	1665
CLAW William	On branches of Peanketanke R. adjoining Major Cant & Stephen Gill, dece'd. HR: Jone Jenkins, Anthony Prior, Mary Rason, Wm. Sinett (?).	G.	5	568	1665 Jan. 4	200
William & Cornelius Mathewes	On branches of Peanketank adjoining Coll: Warner and Thomas Royston. HR: Leonard French, Jonathan Catford, Martin Goodwyn, Saml. Sparks, Tho. Jort, Tho. Delune.	G.	6	104	1667 Dec. 20	320
CLEMENTS Benjamin	ABINGTON P. On E side of the roade that goes under the hills and adjoining Major Burwell & Tho. Morrell. Part of 300 acs. conveyed by Wm. Boulding to Rachell his then wife and to Morgan Lewis. Gift by Rachell in 1680 to said Clements for life then to Ann Clements his daughter.	G.	7	290	1683 April 16	150
Benjamin	ABBINGTON P. Description same as above. [Same patent appears to be recorded twice]	G.	7	291	1683 April 16	150
COBSON Elias	At the head of Coxes Swamp and along Rappa path. HR: Eliz. Jenkins, Jno. Champion, Lidda Buttler, Tho. Cooke, Jno. Godwin, Gerard Mart, Marma Shawly, Samll. Turner.	G.	5	405	1664 July 6	300
COLEMAN Robert	On main branches of Burts [Burnt?] Creek adjoining his own land and Daniel Clark and Richard Foster. HR: Gabriell Bradmeed, Tho. Follit, Ann Madden.	G.	5	369	1662 March 18	110
Robert	On a swamp dividing this from land of Daniel Clark & Richard Foster. HR: Jno. Leeth, Francis Bishopp, Wm. Stirkoe, Lanceline Walker.	G.	6	34	1672/3 March 18	200
Joseph	PETSO P. Land adjoining Wm. Pritchett	G.	9	107	1697	344

NAMES	DESCRIPTION	CO.	BK.	Pg.	DATE	ACRES
COLEMAN (Continued) Joseph	Wm. Bernard & William Fleming.	G.	9	107	1697 Oct. 28	344
COLLAINE..COLLAWN..CULLAWNE..COLLONE..COLLAWNE						
William, Junr. Collaine	Adjoining an old devident of land of his father, Wm. Collaine and adjoining Gills. HR: James Rice, Jno. Sop[?], Tho. Grant.	G.	8	148	1691 April 28	140
William, Junr. Collaine	PETTSOE P. Adjoining his own land and Mr. Haines. HR: Gillian Clare, a negro.	G.	8	262	1693 April 29	97
William Collawne	PETSOE P. Adjoining Coll° Warner and Mr. Thomas Whiteing down E side of New Quarter Branch to Ludlow corner and to Richland Swamp. HR: Mary Murritt, Francis Howard.	G.	9	591	1704 April 26	62
COLLES	[See Callis]					
COLLINS George	On E side of Eastermost R. S upon Pudding Creek N on a creek that divides from Robt. Langdall W on the river E one mile into the woods being a neck of land. HR: His own adventure twice, John Brown, Edward Uggins, Grif. Richards, Richard Mort, Thomas Rennells.	M.	3	232	1653 Nov. 25	350
Thomas	KINGSTON P. Upon the Peanketank Ridge by the maine branch of Wadeing Creek up to Mr. Elliotts Quarter and adjoining Mr. Warkeman and Mr. Kemp. HR: Wm. Seaman, Eliz. his wife, Jno. his sonne, John Lee, Samll. Drewer.	M.	6	284	1669 July 19	250
CONNYDON..CONNGDON..CONGDON..CONDEN..CONGLIN..CONGDELL John Connydon	In Pyankatank Bay near land of William English, down the Bay into the narrow on the head of Milford Haven. HR: Transfer of his wife and 3 persons.	M.	1(2)	801	1642 July 1	200
COOKE..COOK Mordecay Cooke	Near the head of Ware R. in Mockjacks Bay. A point of cleared land called Mordecays Mount & running up W side of Cow Creek NW to the swamp and down the NE side of swamp to the river and down the N side of the river to the said Mount. HR: **Edward Bond, his wife, Wm. Sawyer,** Charles King, Henry Cockett, Bart. Lentill, Ann Winn, Thomas Parvoll, Phillip Garner, Mord. Cooke, Richard Viriam, Wm. Geey, Wm. Gillam, Edward Attore, Ja: Banks twice, Alexander Green twice, Jane his wife, Edward Greene.	G.	2	255	1650 Oct. 2	1174
Mordecay Cooke	On N side of a swamp falling into Ware R. opposite land of John Walker. HR: Thomas Seay [?], Henry Norman, Matthew Borrowes, John Gassent, Thomas Cater, Richard Pevvis.	G	3	375	1654 Sept. 7	300
Mordecai Cooke	WARE P. "Beginning on S side of a path that leads to Mr. Francis Campfields plantacōn & adjoining divident whereon sd Cooke now dwells... to Colles branch" by Prices his land to "NE side of the rowling Path &...to North River Path" to Mr. Ironmongers line to Mr. John Smiths line. Within this survey 140 acs. belonging to Mr. Tho: Colles, dece'd.	G	7	63	1680 Sept. 29	1000

NAMES	DESCRIPTION	CO.	BK.	Pg.	DATE	ACRES
COOKE (Continued)						
Mordecai Cooke	Escheat land late in the possession of Alexander Murray. Deputy Escheator, Wm. Jones. Matthew Page, Escheator.	G.	9	542	1703 April 24	1200
John Cooke	On W side of a run falling into Cow Creek & Ware R. adjoining Robt. Cade. HR: John Cooke, Alice Little, Danl. Farbuth, Margaret a maidservant.	G.	3	137	1652 Dec. 6	200
Thomas Cook	Formerly granted to Edward Davis in 1700. Upon the Islands & marshes of New Point Comfort, into Dyers Creek. Lapsed. HR: Andrew Spencer, Anthony Prosser, Wm. Jernian, Watkin Price [?], John Beacham, Perrie Reyan.	M.	10	122	1713 Nov. 13	300
Thomas Cook	PETSOE P. Formerly granted to William Heyward in 1691. Adjoining Cook's former land & along the land of Mr. Edward Porties, NW &c to a branch that falls into a swamp belonging to the head of Capahosick Crk. by a whitemarsh side and a path, & by a plantation belonging to said Heyward. HR: Thomas Dickinson, Isabell Banks, Eliza. Brown, Isabell Cutter [?].	G.	10	123	1713 Nov. 13	156
CORBELL Henry (Hy.)	On N and S side of a path leading from the now plantation of Coll: Richard Lee, Esqr., to plantation of Mr. Thomas Breeman and adjoining Jeffrey Bew. HR: John Wrightwell, John Hudson, John Coheane, Henry Elmore, Richard Baragan, Mary Bansworth, ___Littlefield, ___Follards.	G.	3	56	1653 March	600
Henry	Renewal of above.		5	168	1662	
CORBETT John	KINGSTON P. Beginning at the head of Ducking Pond Crk. and adjoining Isaac Plumer, Ralph Armstead, Thomas Dyar. HR: Jon Moyo, Richd Ball, Wm. Martin Jon Wayne. Tho. Thorne, X'pher Wyn, Wm. Tyton, Jon Copeland.	M.	7	354	1684 April 20	400
John	Land and marshes on Island of New Poynt Comfort. Beginning at a creek "that runs through marsh to Dyars Crk. which divides from Maine land, down Mobjack Bay to the utmost poynt & up the maine Bay". HR: Richd Cooke, Fra. Bick, Richd Bick, Alice Watkins, Alice Johnson, Eliza. Johnson.	M.	7	359	1684 April 20	300
CORBIN Gawin	PETSO P. Adjoining Wm. Upshaw, Mr. John Grimes, crossing Noxes [Knox?] Swamp to Dragon Rode. HR: Seven negroes.	G.	9	90	1697 Oct. 28	61
CORDEROY William	On swamp at head of and on S side of Craney Crk. to Ware R. adjoining Jeffry Bew. HR: Daniell Cadbaty & his wife, Ann Younge	G.	3	320	1654 March 6	150
William	Renewal of above		4	262	1658	
William	On ESE side of Poropotank adjoining land of Nich. Jarnew, Samll. Sollis, SW on Tottopottomoyes Crk. Granted to Oliver Greene 1653 who assigned to Edw. Corderoy who sold to William.	G.	5	175	1662 March 18	120
William	By cross path to Mr. Buckners to a poplar	G.	5	59	1664	400

NAMES	DESCRIPTION	CO.	BK.	Pg.	DATE	ACRES
CORDEROY (Continued) William	on first branch on NW side of Totto-pottomoyes Swamp and running by Purton Path. HR: Anthony Stevens, John Jones, Thomas Towers, Wm. Draper, John Browne, Francis Cooper, Wm. Cooke, Alice Swan.	G.	5	59	1664 Feb. 1	400
COUCH Robert	Adjoining Abraham Ivesonn along a path-side and a swamp. HR: Thomas Cloutson, John Trevillian.	M.?G.?	8-258		1693 April 29	77
COX Richard	On Cow Creek swamp in Ware R. adjoining Joseph Gregories. 700 acs. granted Henry Peasley 1650, who assigned to Cox. Residue 109 acs.	G.	4	201	1657 June 5	809
Richard	On branches of North R. Mill Damms. 809 acs. thereof due by Patent of Oct. 26, 1666 the other 243 acs. residue adjoining aforesaid tract and the land of John Benson, John Reed, Coll: Ant. Elliott. HR: Five negroe servts by assignment of Jno. Carter, Attor. of Mr. Gilbert Metcalfe.	G.?M.?	6-331		1670 Oct. 19	1050
CRAFTON	[See Grafton]					
CREEDLE..CREADLE..CREDLE..CRUDLE- Richard	On North River side adjoining and beginning at Thomas Tabbs corner "to a corner ash at the head of the branch by the Chappell being also a corner tree to Tomkins formerly Turners land" which branch divides this and the land of Tomkins, down the branch and along the river. 200 acs. due by patent to said Creedles father 1643. Residue 20 acs.	M.	7	1	1679 Sept. 5 ... 1643	220
CRIMES..GRIMES..CRYMES..GRYMES- William	On Poropotank adjoining Capt. Richard Dudley, Geo. Haynes, Spencers land in Dancing Valley along Curtis Path, Richland Swamp & adjoining Majr Richard Lee. Formerly granted Mr. Jas. Stubbins, 1674, and deserted. HR: John Hill, John Dyer, Joan Homes, Ann Roberts, Jno. Wragg, Robt. Hall, Nich. Glass, Abra. Page, Mary Seayres.	G.	6	646	1678 June 5	450
CRIPPS Zachary	At the head of a branch falling into Ware R. adjoining Capt. Breeman and Mr. Mordecay Cooke.	G.	4	53	1655 March 24	300
Zachary	In Ware neck adjoining his land & Mr. Peach & Mr. Mordcai Cooke. Residue 500 acs. HR: Charles Grimes, Ralph Danby, Rich. Stone, Tho. Faulkner, Jno. Woodgeare, Jno. Willoughby, Ann Hegnone, Jno. Workeman, Jno. Elcock, Mingo a negro.	G.	4	159	1657 June 6	800
CROSHAW Richard	On the N side of York R. called by the name of the Stayres, SW, NNW & W upon the river NW on Timothy Lodell SW & S upon Sunken Lands and by a swamp issuing out of the river. HR: Richd. Finch, Mary Finch, Elizabeth Finch, John, William & Mary Finch, Richard Saeton, Wm. Coote, Tho. Laramore, Ja: Clarke, John Elly, Wm. Pountney, Jno. Bucherin, Mart. Lear, Walt. Gealter. [It is not certain that the land described above was in Gloucester. A later patent shows that Richard Croshaw owned land called "Stayres" in King William County. Yet	G.?	2	202	1649 Feb. 27	750

NAMES	DESCRIPTION	CO.	BK.	Pg.	DATE	ACRES
CROSHAW (Continued) Richard	cross references in the index show that Richard Crowshaw did own land on the Poropotank in Petsoe P. at a later date.]					
CULLY Robert & Ralph Armstead	On E side of Eastermost R. "att...head of ...old Dividend of Land bought by sd Cully of Mr. Mann".	M.	7	219	1682 Dec. 22	63½
CURTIS..CURTICE Thomas	"Situate lying and being in Mockjack Bay beginning in Ware River in a bay called Brownes bay...along marked trees dividing from the land of John Harris...runs into the woods...thence E & S unto the head of Curtis Crk. down the creek unto Ware River and up Ware River unto... where is begun." HR: John Lether, John Roberts, James [?] Berry, John Dyas, Tho. Peirce, Ellen Powell, Edward Marsam, John Jarre.	G.	1(2)	795	1642 Aug. 15	400
Thomas, Mr.	In Mockjack Bay beginning at the head of a branch of Blackwater Creek near Thomas Sayes land.	M.	1(2)	804	1642 Aug. 15	700
Thomas, Mr.	At the head of Fordes Crk. and down Mockjack Bay. HR: John Yates, Margaret Yates, Henry Bourne, Dorothy Dile, Thomas Moore, Tony & Basse 2 negroes land due for last negro.	G.	2	182	1649 July 16	300
Thomas, MR.	On S side of North R. beginning at a lone pine and running S by the bay side to a branch & up same to the E corner tree of Basses Creek devident & along same W to the Back Creek down said creek to the river & northerly 168 poles to the lone pine first specified. HR: Elizabeth Beiry, one man servant, one maid servant, Eliz. Love, John Harmor, Miller Turton, Millison Biggs, Kath. Scarburgh, Jane Knapton, Tony & Lawrence Negroes, & two Negro women.	G.	3	107	1652 Sept. 20	670
Thomas, Mr.	On Blackwater Creek, North River, on NW side of Phesant Crk. up said creek NE to head of Dividing Crk. down same and over Blackwater to the beginning. 700 acs. granted Aug. 15, 1642, residue 450 acs. HR: Patrick Forgeson, Walter Michell, Alexander Marke, John Allen, William Knotts.	M.	3	107	1652 Sept. 20	1150
Thomas, Mr.	On Ware R. adjoining his land. Resurvey of former grant on E side of Brownes Bay to the head of a branch in Basses Crk. and down same to the mouth and up the river to the first place. 400 acs. granted Aug. 15, 1642, residue 142 acs. HR: John Trace, Joseph Pye, Annie Parry.	G.	3	209	1652 Aug. 15	542
Thomas, Major.	Resurvey of Brownes Bay and Ware R. land, "by marked trees dividing this from the land of Mr. Thomas Boswell" to Ware R. and up the river. 542 acs. granted Sept. 20, 1652 residue 88 acs. HR: Elizabeth Boston, Hannah Blackwell.	G.	4	84	1656 Oct. 8	630
Thomas, Major.	Resurvey of Brownes Bay, Ware R. land. 542 acs. by patent 1652. Residue 188 acs. HR: Wm. Browne, Jno. Dowdy, Wm. Harman, and his wife Alice.	G.	4	135	1657 June 3	730

NAMES	DESCRIPTION	CO.	BK.	Pg.	DATE	ACRES
CURTIS (Continued)	Renewal of grant of Sept. 20, 1652.	M.	4	535	1661	1150
Thomas, Major	" " " " June 3, 1657.	G.	4	535	1661	730
John	Beginning at the head of Back Creek in North R. in Mockjack Bay by Major Curtis marked trees, W by Mr. Harris line, N & NE to Whites [Whiting's?] Crk. E & S to mouth of Back Crk. and up the creek to the first place. HR: Silvanus Wood, John Snell, 5 Negroes.	G.	4	97	1656 Oct. 18	350
John	Adjoining Thomas Purnell, John Benson, and Coll: Elliott on branches of North R. HR: Thomas Williams, Griffith Hewes.	M.	6	241	1668 Oct. 27	160
Avarilla, Mrs.	Upon the head of Back Crk. in North R. adjoining Major Curtis and Mr. Harris to the head of Whites [Whiting's?] Creek S to the mouth of Back Crk. 350 acs. granted to Mr. John Curtis 1656, who assigned to Avarilla.	G.	4	464	1661 April 3	410
George	On Blackwater Crk. beginning at a White marsh and down dividing Crk. Granted to Thomas 1642 for 700 acs. 400 additional acs. HR: Leonard Parker, Wm. Beard, Simon Gold, Patrick Forgeson, Sander Murray, Mary Rownd, Rich. Gibbs, Anne a negroe.	M.	6	97	1667 Dec. 20	1100
George	KINGSTONE P. On S side of Pianketank R. betwixt a creek called Pianketank alias Colo: Kemps Crk. & Wadeing Crk., beginning at the mouth and at the side of Pianketank R. to the mouth of Wadeing Crk. and up said creek, adjoining Coll: Kemp, Wm. Marloes, Mr. Thos. Palliser, to corner of Lady Skipwiths land, down the main branch of Pianketank Crk. which divides from Coll: Kemp to the mouth. Purchased from Edw. Wyatt.	M.	6	552	1674/5 Jan. 26	800
DAVIS..DAVIES John Davis	On both sides of Chescake path [that goes] to the Mattapony R. adjoining Leonard Chamberlaine. Granted Ashwell Batten 1653 who sold to Davis.	G.?	5	291	1664 May 24	750
Edward Davis	KINGSTONE P. At the head of Ducking Pond Crk. which divides from Isaac & Thomas Plumer, adjoining Ralph Armistead & Thomas Dyer. Formerly granted to John Corbett 1684 and deserted. HR: Richd. Smith, Fran. Woosell, Abra. Roane, George Walter, Richd. Harford, Humphrey Hunt, Hen. Green, William Atwood.	M.	8	262	1693 April 29	400
Edward Davis	Land and marshes upon the island of New Point Comfort beginning at the mouth of a creek that runs through the marshes into Dyers Crk. betwixt the island and main Land & running down Mock Jack Bay to the point upon the main Bay. Formerly granted to Mr. John Corbett 1684, and deserted. HR: John Butler, Mary Butler, John Castle, Edward Browndell, Thomas Purdy, Grace Taylor.	M.	9	282	1700 Nov. 7	300
DAWBER..DAUBER Edmond	On the Northermost R. of Mockjack Bay beginning on the S side of a creek dividing this from the land of Geo. Levitt. By Court order	G.	1(2)	866	1642 Nov. 28 1640	2400

LAND GRANTED TO JOHN DEGGE [DIGGS] IN 1678.

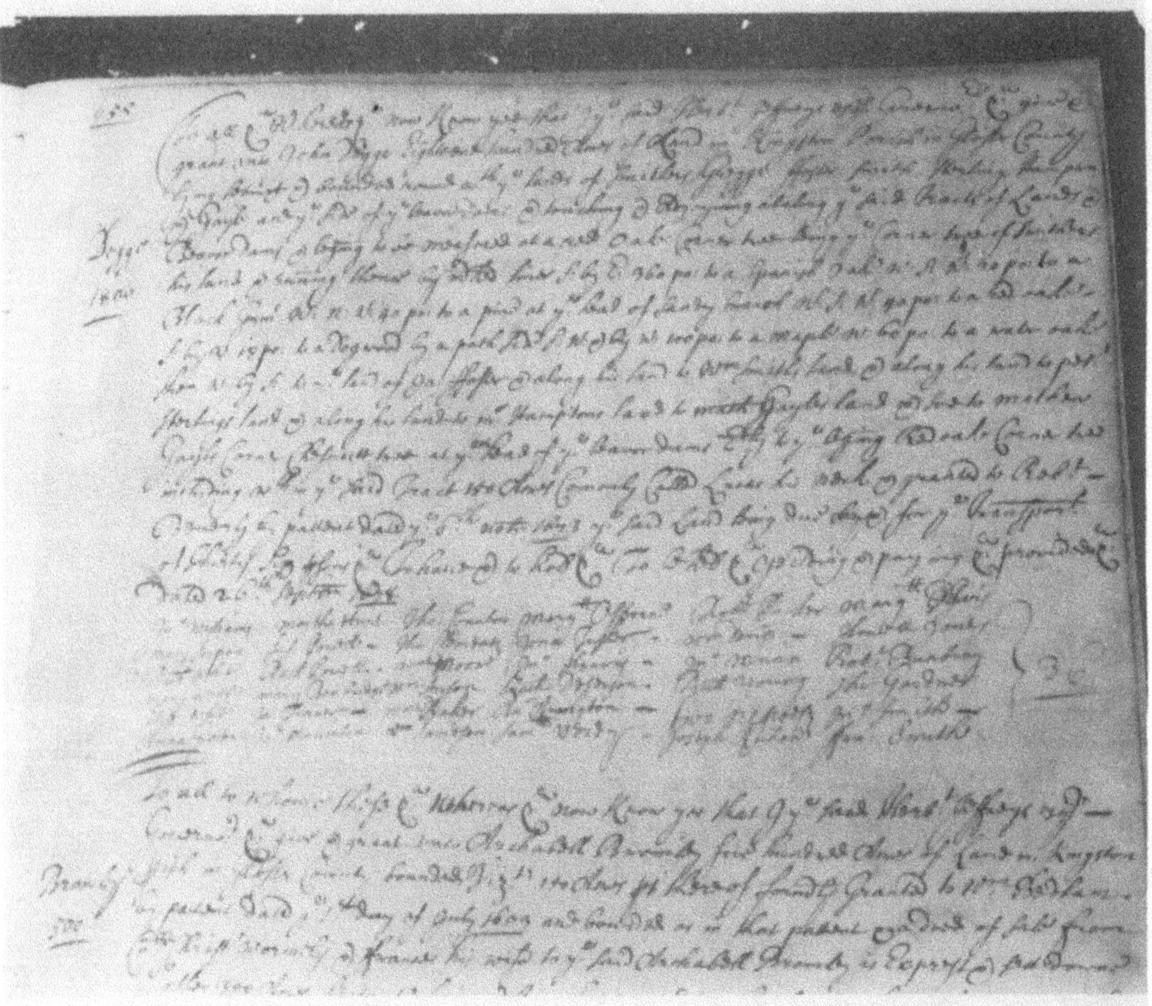

Patent Book 6, page 658, showing patent of John Degge [Diggs] for 1800 acres near the Beaver Damms and giving the 36 head rights brought in by Degge. Small tracts of this land are still owned by Diggs' descendants.

Part of a patent in the name of Archabell Bromley for 500 acres is also shown.

NAMES	DESCRIPTION	CO.	BK.	Pg.	DATE	ACRES
DAWBER (Continued) Edmond	On N side of Mockjack Bay upon Seasand Crk. which divides same from land of Thomas Curtis. By Court Order June 1640. Renewal of both of above patents 1649.	M.	1(2)	867	1642 Nov. 28 1649	1600
DAWSON Samuel	WARE P. Adjoining Mr. Burches and along the "Roade to Mr. Willis land". 345 acs. by purchase. Residue 50 acs. HR: Anne Potter.	G.	7	580	1687 April 20	395
DAY John	On SE side of Poropotank Crk. adjoining Isack Richeson, Willm Kinsey and Wm. Bayley. HR: Mary Hockett, Elizabeth Hockett, Mary Clover(?), Fra. Jacob, Tho. Lake, Thomas Clarge [Clarye], Judith Laton, Ann Field.	G.	3	52	1653 Oct. 19	400
Lewis	On SE side of Poropotank Crk. and along Isaac Richeson & Wm. Kinsey [Ginsey] to a white marsh on the head of Tottopotomoys Crk. Due said Lewis "as sonne of John Day, dece'd".	G.	5	411	1664 Sept. 12	400
Lewis	PETSOE P. On Tottopotomoys Swamp near John Boothes plantation. Former grant to John Day in 1653. Due Lewis Day as son & heire of John Day, dece'd.	G.	6	557	1675 June 15	400
DEACON Thomas	"P'cell of land...sd land being formerly given by...Thomas Bremor unto Margarett Breamor his wife...by last will and testament" lately found to escheat. Miles Cary, Esqr. Escheator for Gloucester.	G.	6	381	1671 Oct. 5	______
DEBNAM William	Along Craney Crk. of Ware R. adjoining Thomas Breman, and land formerly belonging to George Worleich. HR: Pollardary Pritchard, Francis Hemsley, ___Dickinson, Isarell Gore [?], Geo. Jyllings, Roger Williams, John Winter, 2 negroes.	G.	3	91	1652 May 6	600
William	On a branch one mile from the Severne R. beginning at a marked tree of Geo. Ludlow Esq., through Cedar Island to the Bay, to Shaws Crk., including all marshes and Oaken Island. HR: Robert Woodstock, John Butcher, Geo. Marton [?], Samuel Stephens, Bennedick Gracewood, John Harvey, John Gurrington, Rowland Jones, Nicho. Botcham, Thomas Passe, Robert Griggs, Henry Walby, Wm. Crane, Thomas Warbeton, Wm. Kempton, Thomas Lane, X'topher Boone, Thomas Cure, James Hurst, James Rouse, Thomas Saker, Thomas Parry, Henry Noakes, Fra: Willoughby, Jno. Hamwood, Alice Curnock, Wm. Ashwell, Tho. Hedges, Richard Hobson, Wm. Booes. Renewals of both of above	G.	3	55	1653 Dec. 26 4-441-442,1661	1500
DEGGE..DEGG..DEGGS..[DIGGS] John	KINGSTONE P. "Track of land and beaver dams...lying betwixt and bounded round with the lands of" Smithers, Ia. Foster, William Smith, Peter Sterling, Mr. Hampton, Mathew Gayle, to the head of Sandy Branch and including 150 acs. "commonly called Lucas his neck & granted to Robert Beverley in 1673". HR: Jno. Williams Mary Scipon, Rich White, Eliz. White, Mary Webb, Anna Gibson, Martha Hunt, Sus. Powell,Mary Benbridge, James	M.	6	658	1678 Sept. 26	1800

NAMES	DESCRIPTION	CO.	BK.	Pg.	DATE	ACRES
DEGGE..[DIGGS] etc.(Continued) John	Turner, Jos. Manniton, Tho. Counlow [?], Tho. Clements, Wm. Moore, Wm. Anson, Wm. Baker, Wm. Davidson, Margt. Osborne, Jonna. Tucker, Jno. Harris, Zach. Deserson, An. Amington, Samll. Verdy, Robt. Parker, Wm. Davis, Jno. Munn, Rich. Young,Margtt. Davis, Howell Jones, Robt. Banbury, Thos. Gardner, Jno. Smith, Fra. Smith, two negroes Joseph & Richard,	M.	6	658	1678 Sept. 26	1800
John	KINGSTONE P. Beginning to be measured at a corner of Richard Ripleys land and adjoining Mark Thomas, Henry Singleton to Mr. Plummers line. HR: Jno. Degg, Abra. Buckley, Edw. Davis, Ja: Bradock.	M.	6	659	1678 Sept. 26	200
John	KINGSTONE P. Beginning to be measured as in first patent above, and resurvey of same shown adjoining Mathew Gale, John Garnett, Mr. Hampton, dece'd.	M.	7	279	1683 April 16	1425
DENNIS Humphrey	On S side of Kings Crk. near Poropotank. HR: Mary Smith, Tho. Bourne, Tho. Thraile, John Bootwright.	G.?	3	322	1654 July 6	200
DEYNES..DEINES..DAINES..DAYMES..[DAVIES?] William	On S side of a creek in the Northermost R. of Mockjack Bay which divides from Geo. Levels and along the river. Granted Dawber 1642 and deserted.	G.	3	32	1652 March 19	2400
DICKINS..DICKINSON..DICKSON..DICKENS..DIXON Christopher Dickins	KINGSTONE P. Additional land adjoining his own plantation & Mr. Humphrey Toy "then by a new line of young Phillip Hunleys" land. HR: John Hill, Jno. Dyer, Jonna. Holmes.	M.	6	659	1678 Sept. 21	160
Christopher Dickens	KINGSTONE P. Beginning at Humphrey Toys & the said Dickens corner on a small point on the S side of Benits Crk. & along the land said Dickens now lives on & up Eastermost R. to Benits Crk. HR:Wm.Giles.	M.	10	219	1714 Dec. 23	20
DICKSON..DICKENSON..[DIXON?] Mary Dickson	Escheat land formerly in possession of Edw. Titterton. Coll: Phill. Ludwell, Escheator.	G.	6	591	1675 Feb. 24	930
John Dickenson	Escheat land formerly granted to Mary Dickenson als. Titterton, Dece'd. Capt. Francis Page, D. E.	G.	7	688	1688 Oct. 20	930
DIXON..[DICKSON?..DICKENSON?] John Dixon	Escheat land "formerly owned by William Major who was attainted of murder". Lying on the branches of Poropotank in both King & Queen and Gloucester adjoining Dixons own land & Kemps, near Charles Waldens spring to the Ridge path to Dillards corner to Crittendens corner. Price 2 pounds of Tobacco per acre.	G.	37	46	1767 July 10	481
DIXON John Dixon, Clk.	Escheat land formerly owned by William Major who committed a murder. Beginning at Livingstons corner to Rainers Swamp to Carys line to Poropotank Crk. adjoining Alexander Weatherspoon. Supposed to contain 1335 acs. - survey shows 493. Price 2 pounds of Tobo. per acre.	G.?	37	48	1767 July 10	493

NAMES	DESCRIPTION	CO.	BK.	Pg.	DATE	ACRES
DOBSON Edward	On S side of Severne R. and E side of Burnt Pt. adjoining Mr. Ceeleys and including Cedar Island. HR: Edward Dobson, Fra: his wife, John Snellings, Wm. Dorcye, Elizabeth Dodberye, Richard Hagan, Richard Baker, John Broune[?] Anne Kinge, Danl. Mackell, John Smith twice, Joane his wife, Richard Moseley, John Powell, Cor. Peterson, Wm. Townsend, Jane Haslewood, Alexander Anderson, 30 acs. due for last name.	G.	3	53	1653 July 10	920
	Renewed above		4	524	1661	
Edmund, William & John	ABBINGTON P. "Sonns of Edward Dobson, dece'd". Beginning at the mouth and E side of Burnt Crk. bounded by Mobjack Bay and Severne R. including marsh and islands to the mouth of the Severne R., up Severne to Burnt Crk. Due by will of father and patent of 1653. Residue 230 acs. HR: Ed. Linkitts, David Wooley, Ann Gwyn, Abra. Amiss, Jno. Rogers.	G.	6	649	1678 June 5	1150
DUDLEY..DUDLY Richard	On E side of North R. of Mockjack Bay beginning at Curtis land on the river side near Blackwater Crk. HR: William Morksley, Fr. Halliard, Wm. Mash, Mary Andrews.	M.	3	94	1652 Sept. 24	200
Richard	On E'ward side of North R. at a small creek within Blackwater Crk. mouth called Pine Poynt Crk. and along the land of Mr. Peter Ransone SW on Blackwater NE to woods S & W along land of said Ransone to a tree on North R. which divides from Ransone. 140 acs. granted to Major Thomas Curtis 1642, 200 acs. granted Dudley 1652, residue 299. HR: John Emerilla [?], Tho. Kinge, John Bolton, John Cooper, Tho. Reyland, Edward Smith. Renewed above 1662.	M.	4	377	1659	639
Richard	On E side of Eastermost R. and NW side of Pudding Crk. NW along the river to a creek dividing from Robt. Landall, and adjoining Philip Hunley. 350 acs. granted to Collins 1653. Residue 105 acs. HR: Wm. Story, Peter Oliver, Andrew Jones.	M.	5	479	1665 Sept. 4	455
Richard	On Gwins Ridge HR: Jane Bartlett, Issabel ___, Tho. Cobb, Jno. Bolton, Jno. Cooper, Edward Smith.	M.	6	103	1667 Dec. 20	300
Richard	At a creek dividing from Edward Welsh, Deced. HR: John Mechan, John Snow, Rich. Phillips, Saml Powdry, Jno. Walton, Jno. Whaley.	M.	6	104	1667 Dec. 20	300
Richard	On Poropotank adjoining John Green, Peter Knight, Spenser, to Parradise Path, down Chiscaike path to Mr. John Pates corner. 400 acs. granted to Wm. Armefield 1663 sold to John Pate who assigned to Dudley. 544 acs. residue. HR: Edw. Holland, Rich. Perkins, Jno. Dance, Jno. Holmes, James Griffin, James White, Wm. Evans, Margaret Milburne, Franc. Hilyard, Mary Wilson, Francis Sale.	G.	6	172	1665 Oct. 28	944
Richard	On Poropotank Crk. Formerly granted 1665 and deserted by Dudley. Upon petition granted	G.	6	442	1672 Dec. 15	944

NAMES	DESCRIPTION	CO.	BK.	Pg.	DATE	ACRES
DUDLEY (Continued) Richard	Peyton in 1670 and by him assigned to Dudley. HR: John Prichard, Rich. Preston, Jno. Roberts, John Mathram, Wm. Ward, Rosse Allen, Nich. Moore, Walter Chapman, Geo. Pritley, Jno. Basse, Anne Devenport.	G.	6	442	1672 Dec. 15	944
Richard	Resurvey of Poropotank land. 944 acs. granted 1665, residue 36 acs. HR: Robert Yellow.	G.	6	512	1674 April 9	980
Richard, Colo:	KINGSTON P. On E side of North R. & on Blackwater Crk. at mouth of Piney Poynt Crk. adjoining Mr. Presson to a path to Mr. James Ransons land, to mouth of the dividing creek. 490 acs. by former grant 1659, residue 212. HR: Wm. Matthews, Cha: Clarke, Ed. Clarke, James Clarke, Ann Page.	M.	7	352	1684 April 20	704
Richard, Coll:	KINGSTON P. On E side of Gwins Ridge near Lawrence Parrott. 250 acs. granted 1667, residue 31 acs. HR: Geo. Arkland	M.	7	356	1684 April 20	281
Ambrose	Part of a patent to Coll: Richard Dudley 1684, Deserted. Paid Wm. Byrd Esqr. Auditor for five rights.	M.	9	621	1704 Oct. 20	212
William	On W'ward side of North R. of Mockjack Bay, on head of Ginger Crk. and including Five Pine Island. Due to mistake	G.	3	198	1652 Sept. 20	400
	Patent reissued:- assigned to Augustine Horth. (R. Huberd, Clk.)	G.	4	572	1652 Sept. 20	350
DUVAL William	PETSWORTH GLEBE: beginning at Thomas Baytops line to John Kinninghams corner to and along the road from Gloucester Court House to Poplar Spring Church to said Duvals own land & adjoining Robert Lemmon.	G. (C.G.)	51	124	1802 Dec. 4	266 & 56 P.
DYARS..DYER..DYERS Thomas	KINGSTON P. On W side of Dyars Crk. Formerly granted to John Gundry 1650 who sold to Dyar.	M.	7	353	1684 April 20	100
EDWARDS Thomas & John P. Minter	Island at the mouth of Milford Haven, to the Thoroughfare, which is another mouth of said Haven.	M. (C.G.)	91	513	1841 July 31	110
ELLIOTT..ELLYOTT..ELLYOT..ELIOT Anthony Ellyott	Lyeing on the NW side of North R. in Mockjack Bay on the NE side of a creek dividing from Thomas Chapman and running up same to Mr. Holdens land & SW down the river 125 poles. HR: William Loe, Pet. Pet. Dowland, Tho. Peare, Rich. Nevil, Tho. Jarvis, Ralph Mines [?], Ann Masie, Alice Toomes, Mary Cartar, Wm. Carney, Wm. Baskett, Tho. Hensett, Jno. Bertram, Xtopr. Hughes, Jno. Steed, Bryan Skarfe.	M.	2	284	1650 March 20	1150
Anthony Ellyott	On NW side of North R. adjoining Abraham Iveson. HR: Overner Shadwell, Edward Skinner.	G.?	2	284	1650 March 20,	100
Anthony Elliott, Lieut. Coll:	At Ware Point and Mockjack Bay adjoining Mr. Boswell & Wm. Dudley to and including all the marshes. HR: Andr: Frimer, Wm. Morgan, Henry Pawlett, Barnaby.	G.	2	358	1651 Jan. 29	200

NAMES	DESCRIPTION	CO.	BK.	Pg.	DATE	ACRES
ELLIOTT, etc. (Continued) William Elliott, Senr.,	Planter of KINGSTONE P. On Queens Crk. near the head adjoining Richard Cary to Shaking Bridge to Dirty Branch to Mr. John Armsteads saw pitts and adjoining John Seaton, and Thomas Sellars.. 900 acs. granted Edmond Welch 1654 who assigned to Thomas Boswell, Sen'r, 1663, who sold to Elliott. Residue 200 acs. HR: Joseph Fellowes, Danl. Ware, Richard Browne, Ellinor Anderson.	M.	6	428	1672 Oct. 8	1100
William Elliot, Mr.	"Sonne of Lt. Coll. Anthony Elliott Dece'd" On N side of North R. Mill runne adjoining Mr. Peter Starling, Dece'd, Tho. Gaunt, to Hoccadays Crk. to S side of North R. Mill runne & now Mr. Ivesons Quarter to Corner tree of Coll: Anthony Elliott dece'd. HR: Wm. Alexander, Wm. Allen, Mathew Jones, Simon Story, Sara Howard, Henry Herbert, Jno. Gibson.	M.	6	475	1673 Oct. 23	340
ENGLISH Abraham	At a point at the mouth of Milford Haven on SW side as you enter out of Chesipiacke Bay to a creek dividing from Rich. Bennet, to English Crk. and down Milford Haven. HR: For transfer of himself and wife, John Temperance, Dennis Cicann [?], James Stanks [?], Wm. Neesum.	M.	1(2)	799	1642 July 10	350
William	In Peankatanck Bay near land of John Conden & Mr. Barland and down English Creek. HR: Henry Williams and Joane English.	M.	1(2)	825	1642 Sept. 19	100
EVANS Thomas	Of King & Queen. Escheat land late in the possession of John Kelly dece'd. Peter Beverley, D. E.	G.?	8	401	1694 Oct. 26	220
FALKENER Thomas	On the Eastern R. formerly granted Thomas Todd "the s^d Todd dying w'thout heire or otherwise disposing thereof by will" found to escheat.	M.	6	374	1671 Sept. 26	140
FARTHINGALE Richard & Richard Barringham George Poole & James Forsith	WARE P. Beginning at Henry Corbells corner, Formerly granted to Henry Corbell 1653, and assigned to above.	G.	6	53	1671 April 7	800
Richard etc. [same names as above]	Adjoining Henry Corbell. 600 acs. formerly granted Henry Corbell 1653 and by him assigned to above. HR: Charles Hatcome, Charles Bostock, Jno. Gregory, Eliz. Wood.	G.	6	352	1671 April 7	800
FENTRY Stephen	KINGSTON P. "On Queens Crk. side" adjoining Jno. Curtis, James Lindsayes and part of a greater divident purchased of James Cary.	M.	6	549	1674/5 March 6	300
FINCH Francis & Dictoris Christmas.	See Christmas					
FITCHETT John	In Mathews County, beginning at Palisters corner and adjoining Curtis, Mahon & Callis.	M.	69 (C.G.)	174	1820 May 12	51..
FLEET..FLEETE John	On N side of York R. adjoining Mrs. Frances Jones relict of Mr. Rich. Jones, dece'd and SE on land of Robt. Todd. Granted Col. Rich. Lee, March 20, 1653, sold to Rich. Beadle who sold to Fleet.	G.	5	177	1662 March 18	300

NAMES	DESCRIPTION	CO.	BK.	Pg.	DATE	ACRES
FLEMING William	PETTSOE P. Adjoining Capt. Lightfoots plantation "Wm. Cooke & Wm. Prichett both dece'd" and adjoining Joseph Coleman, Francis Ironmonger of whom Fleming purchased 200 acs. of this land, to the W side of path to Purton and adjoining land formerly belonging to Mr. Pryor dece'd, 200 acs. taken up by one Edward Williams dece'd 1642; 1651, held- "by Edw. Williams son & heir & Abigall Davis Relict of Edw. Williams dece'd now wife of Richard Davis of Dorssettshire in the province of Maryland" sold to Fleming Sept. 4, 1685. 200 acs. granted Francis Ironmonger 1665 who sold to Mathew Miller, Mariner, who sold Fleming 1685. Residue 200 acs. HR: Wm. Buckner, Jeffery Phillips, Eliza. Standley, Jno. Rosse.	G.	8	144	1691 April 28	600
FLETCHER Nathan	80 acs. marsh on Ware Point on North R. and Ware R. adjoining Thomas Boswell Sen'r on old line and Augustine Horths. 200 acs. granted Lt: Coll: Antho: Elliott 1651 and by him assigned.	G.	6	253	1670 April 22	240
FOOTE Thomas & John Barham & John Bannister	On S side of Horne Harbor, 320 poles along the creek. 50 acs. assigned from Richard Hull. HR: Humph. Kirby, Alice his wife, James Kirby.	M.	2	355	1651 Jan. 26	200
FORREST..FORRESTER Henry (Hy.)	On Milford Haven Creek and Garden Creek. NE on John Lilly down Garden Crk. to land of Edward Cheisman. 150 acs. granted Abraham Moone who assigned to Thos. Borne who assigned to Geo. Billipps who assigned to Forrest. 550 acs. due. Renewed above HR: Alexander Hall, Richard Batchelor, John Butcher, John Cavelery, Edward Forrest, Rice Aldcock, Henry Forrest & his wife Elizabeth.	M.	4	314	1658 Sept. 25 1659	700
John	On N side of Garden Crk. including 50 acs. marsh. Beginning near the head and E side of Mr. Lillies Crk. up the branch SW to head and to line betwixt Edmund & John Forrest "according to their Fathers last will & testament", down green branch SE to Garden Crk. & along same to poynt of land near mouth which adjoins Mr. Thomas Cheesman. 350 acs. formerly granted Mr. Henry Forrest 1658. Residue 170 acs. HR: Wm. Bremor, Hen. Jones, Richd. Slovnal [?], John Hackley.	M.	7	351	1684 April 20	520
Edmund	KINGSTON P. Beginning at the corner of Mr. John Lilly and Mr. George Billops & SW down holly bush branch to Garden Crk. up Green Branch to head along John Forrests land according to last will of their father Mr. Henry Forrest dece'd, to head branch of Mr. Lillies creek. 350 acs. formerly granted Mr. Henry Forrest 1658. Residue 155 acs. HR: Annie Turkley, An Matthews, Alice Croxon, Wm. Anderson.	M.	7	358	1684 April 20	505
Anne	KINGSTONE P. Part of 430 acs. granted Abraham Long. Beginning at a corner of	M.	9	588	1704 April 26	200

LAND GRANTED TO HENRY FORREST IN 1658.

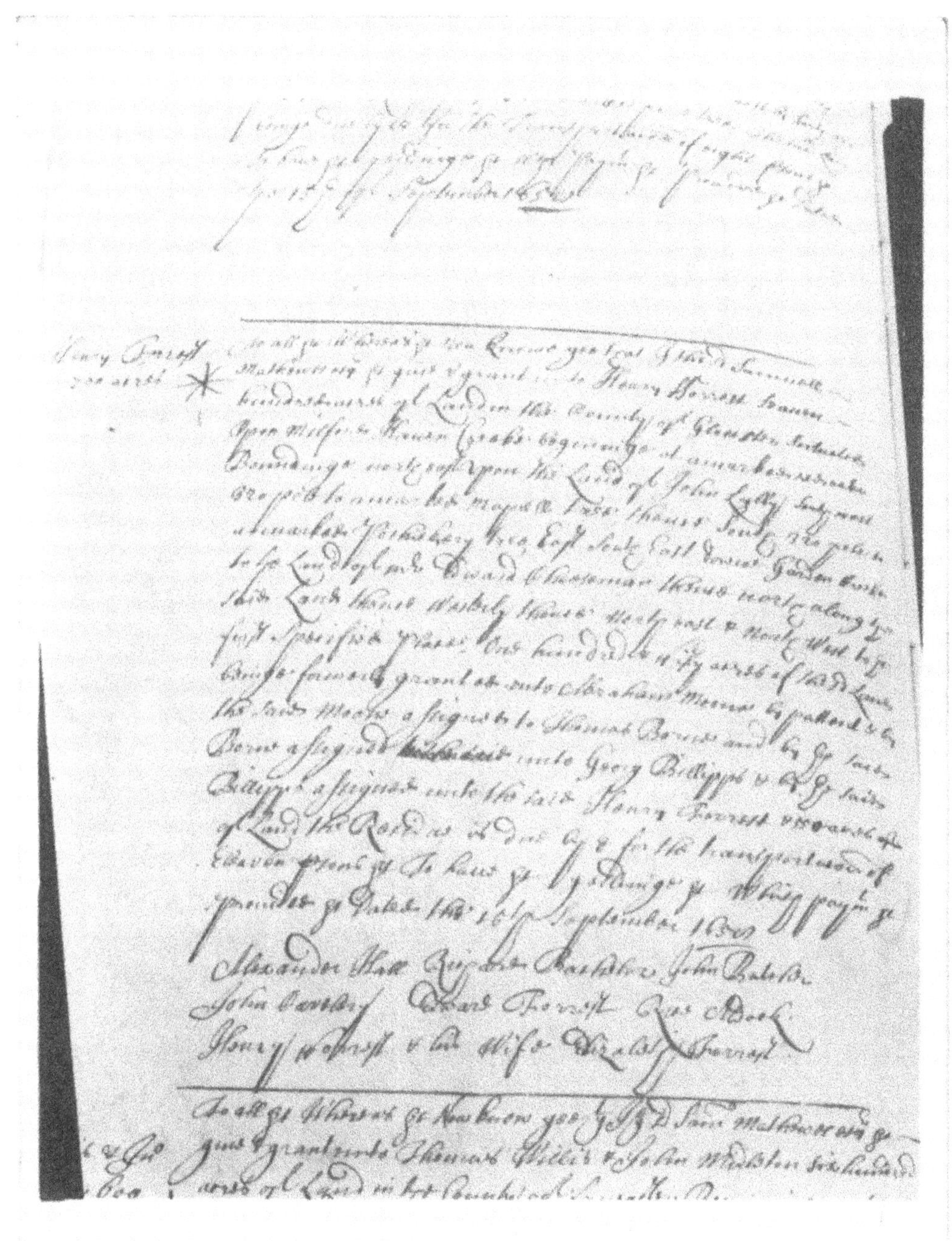

Patent Book 4, page 314, showing patent of Henry Forrest for 700 acres lying between Garden Creek and the land of John Lylly in Milford Haven. Part of this land is still owned by a direct descendant of Henry Forrest, though not in the male line. The Lilly land is still owned in the name of Lilly by direct descent.

NAMES	DESCRIPTION	CO.	BK.	Pg.	DATE	ACRES
FORREST (Continued Anne	Charles Hunley & billops and adjoining Garretts line. "Given s[d] Anne Forrest by the last will...of her brother Abraham Long." Will proved in Gloucester Court 17th May 1703.	M.	9	588	1704 April 26	200
FORSITH..FORSYTH James	WARE P. See Barringham, Farthingale & Poole " " " "		6 6	53 352	1671 1671	800 800
James, Mr.	PETTSOE P. On the path from Hawards to Forsiths & adjoining land he lives upon. HR: Tho. Hill, Jno. Phillips.	G.	6	243	1669 April 13	116
James	PETSO P. Adjoining James Forsith, Sen'r, James Burton, Thomas Cook by the road, and along old Hopkins & across a swamp. HR: John Sterne, Tho. Gillet, Mich. Murrey.	G.	9	114	1697 Oct. 28	135
FOSTER Mark	At head of Pudden Crk. and along same adjoining Philip Hunley. HR: Rich: Rose, Ann Jonson [Iveson?]	M.	3	268	1654 June 6	100
Mark	On the E side of Pudden Crk. in Eastermost R. adjoining Goodman Halliard. HR: Grace Farrwell, Eliz. Sternell, Robt. Read, Jno. Correld, Robert ___, Silvester Wells, John Mackdaniell, Geo. Burt, John Ham, Wm. Ableck.	M.	4	355	1658 March 6	500
Mark	Renewed in the name of Mark Foster, the son.		4	355	1661	
Mark	KINGSTON P. On Pudding Crk. side, E/S 320 poles, NE 250 poles, NW 136 poles to Philip Hunleys land SW 150 poles to Pudding Crk. down same creek to the beginning. Renewal of 1661 patent.	M.	7	62	1680 Sept. 29	475
Richard	On the head of the southard creek in Severne R. of Mockjack Bay, on Coll: Ludlows line. HR: Ellen Foster, Mary Foster, Sarah Davis Robert Bynam, Fra. Bignall, land due for last. Renewal	G.	3 5	336 262	1655 April 1 1662	200
FOX Henry	"Son and heire of Mr. John Fox, dece'd". Lying partly in New Kent and Gloucester. Formerly granted Hanckes & Garret, 200 acs. having been purchased by Mr. John Fox of Mr. Thomas Hankes. Adjoining Wm. Anderson Coll: John Lewis, his quarter, Wm. Lynes. Residue 100 acs. HR: Robert Seale, Tho. Lee.	G.	7	245	1682/3 Feb. 28	300
GARNETT..GARNET..[GARDNER?] John	Along the S side of Garden Crk. adjoining John Smither, John Degge, 180 acs. purchased of Humphrey Toy June 15, 1676. Residue 80 acs. HR: Elizabeth Tindal, Tho. Combs.	M.	7	289	1683 April 16	260
GAYLE,.GALE Matthew	KINGSTONE P. Adjoining the back line of Philip Hunley. HR: Wm. Blake, James Paine, Mary Bullock, Tho. Harwood, Anne Herdford, John Arthur.	M.	6	429	1672 Oct. 8	284
GILL Stephen	"At the head of Rosewell Crk. at a point called Peach Pt. where Mr. Menefies land ends" said creek divides this from the land of Nicholas Jornian [Jarnew]. HR: John Dawson, John Chambers, Jon. Mills, Jon. Hunter, Eliz. Maior, Edward Fisher, Jon Grundich, Thomas Kembell, Hen. Shone-	G.	1(2)	819	1642 April 24	1000

NAMES	DESCRIPTION	CO.	BK.	Pg.	DATE	ACRES
GILL (Continued) Stephen	lock, Jon Cartright, Hen. Huntley, Jon Bennington, Wm. Chappell, Rich. Wade, Jon Herring, Wm. Smithell, Jon Trollock, Rich. Burgeyny, Jon Shuttleworth, Hen. Smithfield.	G.	1(2)	819	1642 April 24	1000
Stephen	YORK RIVER COUNTY. Bounding ESE with Rosewell Crk. on SSW of Mr. Minifie on WNW with Burnhams Crk. to head of Rosewell Crk. 1000 acs. part thereof by former patent. HR: Wm. Walters, Stephen Gill, Rich. Hanly[?] Hen. Avery, Ann his wife, Eliza.____, Tho. Rodgett, Hen. Tappin, Jon Wright, Peter Shinger, Edward Plunket, Tho. Watts, Eliz. Garrett, Mr. Jon. Sheppard, Ann his wife, Sara Hanly [?], Sara Bond, Cornelius ___, Wm. Jenkins, Wm. Jackson, Peter Roberts, Hen. Line, Joseph Barnett, Jon. May, Maude Richard,Bedford Francis, Mary Foster, George Turner, Gilbert ___.	G.	1(2)	873	1642 Nov. 18	2500
Stephen, Lieut.	YORK COUNTY. On N side of Charles R. adjoining Rosewell and Burnhams Creeks. Due by former patent of 1649.	G.	2	160	1649 April 30	25
Stephen,	YORK COUNTY. On N side of Yorke R. up Rosewell Crk. part being a neck of land within said creek. W adjoining his own land and S on Mr. Gouch. HR: Francis James, Wm. Thomas, Jno. Hart, Tho. Hollowell, Richd. Smith, Sarah Smith, Robert Cartar, Andrew Cobb, James Hunt, Edward Harvey, Wm. Roberts, Fra. Smith, Ja: Winchett, Edw. Parr, Robert Pinn, Tho. Hackery, Edw. Nessum, James Wilson, Wm. Frost, Wm. Wright, Ralph Jarret, Alex. Downes, Peter Sterkey.	G.	2	163	1649 April 30	1150
Stephen	Resurvey of land patented by Stephen Gill, dece'd, Nov. 18, 1642, on the W'ward side of Rosewell Crk. beginning at the creek-side and adjoining land formerly belonging to Mr. Minifree, but now belonging to Mr. John Man & running NW to the E side of Claybank Crk. Crossing said creek & NNE to the corner of Mr. Wm. Hansford then NE to a corner of Mr. Thomas Cheesman ESE above Creeds Spring SSW to Mill dam at head of Rosewell Crk. across dam & down creek to beginning. Said land surveyed at request of several purchasers.	G.	7	482	1686 Nov. 4	2369
GINSEY..KINSEY..GINSIE..GINSYE.. William	On SE side of Poropotank adjoining Isaac Richeson & John Day. HR: Patrick Criste, James Johnson, Anne Burton, Gabriell Coox, Thomas Williams, James Engler.	G.	3	203	1652 Sept. 9	302
GLASSCOCKE..GLASSCOCK..GLASSCO..GLASCOCKE..GLASCO Thomas Glascocke	1½ miles up the S side of the Peanketanke R. adjoining Christopher Boyce and 100 poles along the river. HR: Thomas Glasscocke, Jane his wife, William Charles, James Allen.	M.	1(2)	903	1643 Aug. 30	200
Richard Glasscock	KINGSTON P. On the head of Richard Billops 100 acs., and adjoining John Colles, Marke Foster, Morris Mackachacock. Formerly granted Edward Cassell [Lassell?] and deserted. HR: Francis Right, John King, Mary Browne, Tho. Jones, Luke Burkins, Ann Noades, Andrew Reward.	M.	8	206	1691 Oct. 20	335

NAMES	DESCRIPTION	CO.	BK.	Pg.	DATE	ACRES
GOHON..GOWIN Daniel Gohon	KINGSTON P. "Adjoining said Gohons plantation" and Mr. Henry Preston. HR: Mary Hare, Ralph Rand.	M.	6	679	1679 May 1	100
Daniel Gowin	Adjoining Mr. Henry Preston, Ambrose Dudley, Capt. Ransone, Thomas Ryland.	M.	9	147	1698 April 26	52
GOODSON John	On S side of North R. Mill runn adjoining Henn. Jeff & his own plantation & Mr. Abraham Iveson. HR: Dorothy Bywater, Jno. Jones.	M.	6	470	1673 Oct. 20	100
GRAFTON..CRAFTON Michael Grafton	On E side of Poropotank Crk. bounded on W on Mr. Jarnews land & S adjoining Wm. Ginsey and N on Mr. Pate.	G.	4	330	1658 Nov. 2	200
Michaell Crafton	On E side of Poropotank Crk. beginning at the mouth of a small branch that divides this land and Oliver Greens, and adjoining John Pate on E'most creek of the Poropotank to a Poplar by a Spring. 614 acs. formerly granted to Nich. Jarnew July 3, 1652, who sold to Crafton. HR: John Barthes, James Wince, Robert Colter.	G.	6	83	1667 Oct. 8	720
GRAVES Thomas	Betwixt the Severne R and the Indian path. HR: Edward Lasley, Sam. Claton, Philip Soloman, Judith Haselwood.	G.	4	212	1657 March 20	240
Thomas	One mile beyond the head of Timberneck Crk. adjoining Christopher Abbott. HR: Phillipp Stevens, Thomas Feard.	G.	4	211	1657 March 20	55
	Renewals of above		4	523-530-1661		
Thomas & Jeffrey	ABBINGTON P. Adjoining Robert Coleman near the dwelling house of Jeffry Graves to the "Greate Roade to Tindalls Point". 200 acs. formerly purchased of Danl. Clarke by Thomas Graves Sen'r, 240 acs. by patent of 1661. "The whole now...due sd Tho: & Jeffry Graves by last Will & testament of their Dece'd father Thos. Graves, Sen'r... In their Presence Divided by Capt. Lawrence Smith & Capt. Robt. Beverley."	G.	6	548	1674/5 March 16	440
GREEN..GREENE Ralph	Being a neck of land on the N side of York R. within Bennetts Crk. HR: Gilbert Mace, George Turner, Mary Turner, Mary Foster, Thomas Williams.	G.	2	265	1650 July 8	300
Ralph	At the head of Jones Crk. on the back of Jones land. HR: Mary Gardner.	G.	2	265	1650 July 8	50
Ralph	At the mouth of Jones Crk. ESE on said creek dividing from Coll: Richd. Lee & adjoining Wm. Thornes land assigned by Col. Lee. HR: Wm. Coldham, John Cranford, John Roberts, Rich. Rithstroote, John Glass, Henry Elcher, John Griffin, Richard Johnson.	G.	3	369	1653 Feb. 16	400
	Renewal of above		4	79	1656	
Ralph	On N side of York R., from Jones Crk. to a creek dividing from Col. Richard Lee, NW to a creek and Wm. Thorne's land. 400 acs. granted 1653, 700 acs. additional. HR: Wm. Turner, Henry Jones, John Haies, Edward Pinton, Geo. Foster, Jane Young, Robert Bellfinn, Roger Collins, John Logg, Andrew Pight, Rich. Foster, Jas.Green,Wm.Stiplee.	G.	4	312	1658 Aug. 31	1100

NAMES	DESCRIPTION	CO.	BK.	Pg.	DATE	ACRES
GREEN..GREENE (Continued) Ralph	Renewall of 1100 acs. above		4	577	1662 Feb. 10	
Oliver	On the E side of the Poropotank adjoining Nicholas Jarnew, Saml. Sallis, & on Atapotomays Crk. HR: William Davis, Walter James.	G.	3	16	1653 July 24	120
Oliver	Behind the land of John Day and on both sides of a swamp which runs into Mobjack.	G.	4	122	1657 March 30	450
Oliver	On N side of Ware R. swamp to a branch dividing from Edward Trate & adjoining James Bradbery. 400 acs. granted March 30, 1657. HR: John Collins, Tobias Hurst, Anna Ashley, Jno. Caterett, Robert Henley, Elizabeth Thomasett, Stephen ___, Henry___.	G.	6	26	1666 March 16	770
John	At head of Poropotank Crk. adjoining Mr. Blunt. Granted Henry Hubberd 1655 who assigned to Green.	G.	4	407	1661 Jan. 13	350
John	PETSOE P. On the branches of the Poropotank adjoining his own land and Henry Sheldrake [?], and Saml. Clarke. 350 acs. granted 1655, renewed 1661.	G.	6	551	1674/5 March 16	600
GREENAWAY Christopher	Adjoining Mr. Rigault in Peaches swamp. HR: Alexander Anderson, Jno. Horne, Edward Hawkins, Jno. Heyward, Robt. Fargar, Hen. Browne, Francis Sterne, David Sterne.	G.	6	142	1665 Oct. 28	370
Christopher	WARE P. Beginning at Regault line in Peaches swamp & adjoining his own land & John Waller dece'd. 370 acs. granted 1664. HR: Abraham Stanton, Grace Holmes.	G.	8	17	1689 Oct. 20	445
GREGORY..GREGORIE..GRIGORIE Joseph	On a branch of Cow Creek adjoining Rich. Dunninge and Henry Peasley. HR: Alexander Mackarle, Za. Cripps, Mich. Smith, Alice Hewitt. 300 acs. by surrender of a patent.	G.	3	136	1652 Dec. 6	500
Anthony	On a branch falling into Cow Creek and Ware R. adjoining Richard Daving, and Henry Peasley. Formerly granted Joseph Gregory father of Anthony in 1652. HR: Robert Manhood, Hugh Macfarline, Tho. Parsons, Wm. Hulb [?], Wm. Burgridge, Richd. Mishards [?], Jane Goodhand, John Ashford, Jack and Robin negroes.	G.	7	662	1688 April 30	500
Anthony	KINGSTONE P. Adjoining Charles Jones, Henry Wareing, dece'd, "to land formerly belonging to Mr. Roberts but now to..Mr. Todd." HR: Ezekiel Reynolds, Jonathan Cocker.	M.	9	46	1696 Oct. 29	70
GRIGG..GRIGGS..GREGG..GREGGS Robert Gregg & Edward Wyatt	KINGSTONE P. On Garden Crk. extending from creek to the Bay SE and adjoining John Smithy [Smither?]. HR: Mary Jones, William White, Jno. Tappin, Andrew Mayle, Jane Carter, Stephen Godlad, Wm. Hankin, Antho. Grigson.	M.	4	439	1662 April 19	370
Robert Griggs	On Winter Harbour beginning at the Bay side, running W and adjoining his own land and Charles Sallace. Granted to Walter Prichard 1654. Assigned to Griggs.	M.	4	640	1662 June 1	250

NAMES	DESCRIPTION	CO.	BK.	Pg.	DATE	ACRES
GRIGSON Richard	In Mockjack Bay and E side of the mouth of Pepper Crk. HR: Florentine Paine, John Grinfield, Rob. Gilford, Fra. Smith, Marg. Haseldine, Grace Lovell.	M.	2	336	1651 Sept. 13	300
Richard	Adjoining the above location. HR: Thomas Todd, Joane Backer, Richard Ford.	M.	2	336	1651 Sept. 13	150
GRIMES..GRYMES..CRIMES..CRYMES [See Crimes]		G.	6	646	1678	450
GUNDRY John	On E side of New Point Comfort Creek. HR: John Gundry, John Gundry his brother, John Gundry Jun'r.,Eliza. Gundry.	M.	2	228	1650 Aug. 13	200
GUTHRY..GUTHRIE John	On S side of Kings Crk. near Poropotank. Granted to Humphrey Dennis 1654, deserted. HR: William Thomas, Jno. Humphreys, Jane Humphreys, Sarah Johnson.	G.?	8	158	1691 April 28	200
GUYTON..GYTON..GYLON..GRITON [?] John	On the head of Green Branch of Milford Haven, adjoining Peter Arrundell, Thomas Puttman. HR: Ann Ellis, Nathan'll Giles, Jno. Jackson, Richd. Mounts.	M.	6	449	1672 March 19	188
John	Adjoining his own land and the land of John Armestead. 188 acs. by former grant, residue 125 acs.	M.	6	549	1674/5 March 6	313
GWIN..GWINN..GWYN..GWYNN..GWYNNE- Hugh Gwin, Gent.	By order of Court: "Beginning at Gwins Pond lying in a bay short of the mouth of ______[Piankatank?] River parallel and due West to an island called _______ thence SSW by the creek nine ______...320 poles to a branch thence SE 426 poles thence NE & E 206 poles thence down the creek unto the mouth." [Record incomplete. Later patents of surrounding lands refer to this as Hugh Gwin's grant in the "Main" - meaning mainland. Reference will show that it is for land on the Piankatank River in the vicinity of Queens Creek.]	M.	1(2)	806	1635 Dec. 19	1000
	Patented: [This above patent for land granted by order of court in 1635 is the earliest grant of land to be found for the area of the present Gloucester and Mathews Counties]	M.	1(2)	806	1642 Aug. 10	1000
Hugh Gwyn, Gentl'm[n]	Near the mouth of the Pyankatanke R. Beginning at a sandy point on Chisopeiake Bay up Milford Haven Bay to the narrow bounded by a great bay called Stengra Bay being due E from said River mouth, parallel to Rappahannocke Bay & S'ly parallel to Chisopeike.200 acs. marsh. HR: Christo. Higginson, twice, William Parker, Francis Chambers, Rich. Bennett, Mrs. Ann Gwyn, Tho. Taylor, Jon Knight, twice, Rich. Ingram, James Haire, Jon Mills, Jon Bradley, Sarah Allison, Tony a Negroe, Nich. Raynolds, Antho. Carr, David Jankin, Ashwell Bird, Arundell Parris, Allen Luddington, Nich. Gibson, Richard Kirby, Wm. Loyd, Hugh Gwin, Tho. Dodd, Jon. Avery, Hen. Thacker, Nath. Webster, Henry Crosby, Howell Powell, William Deane, Eliza. Higgenson, Margarett Bivens, Isabell Richerson, Thomas Hartley, Nicholas Jones alias Bonds.	M.	1(2)	865	1642 Jan. 17	1700

NAMES	DESCRIPTION	CO.	BK.	Pg.	DATE	ACRES
GWIN, etc. (Continued) Hugh Gwyn, Col.	On the W side of Gwyns Island being surplusage, SW upon the Narrows, S on Deep Crk. HR: John Cookeley, Nathan'l Walters, Mary Joyce, Robert Wison al Wisson, George Pletsoe, Banja. Sarrow, Peter Cade, Humph. Higgins, Susan Parker, Susan Hillary, negro woman. Land due for last five.	M.	3	120	1652 Dec. 6	300
Hugh Gwin, Col.	On a narrow ridge which runs through the land, SW of Edw. Clercifull [Percifull?] on Milford Haven Creek. HR: four negroes Antonio, Domingo, Calentia, Mamia.	M.	4	236	1657 March 11	165
	Renewal of above:		4	530	1661	2000
Edmund Gwinn	Escheat land formerly granted Capt. Tho. Bremore dece'd then to William Court. Coll: Phillip Ludwell, Escheator.	G.?	6	622	1678 April 4	80
Edmund Gwyn, Mr.	Escheat land "W'ch Thomas Breeman late of s[d] County dyed seized of". Francis Page D.E.	G.	7	360	1684 April 20	200
John Gwin, Mr. & Coll: John Armstead	KINGSTON P. "...on Eastward side of a Branch near a Chappell...in line of trees belonging to an old Devident of land formerly taken up by Coll: Hugh Gwin dece'd." [See Col. John Armstead for further description]	M.	7	532	1686 Oct. 30	202½
Henry Gwyn (Harry)	KINGSTON P. Beginning at Mr. Hughes corner and adjoining Armistead to the road side, thence to the Wolf Trap & to Palissters line. Price, fifty shillings.	M.	32	47	1753 March 20	462
HAINES..HAYNES..HANES John	PETSO P. Adjoining Coll: Warner, Wm. Hall, Coll: Lee, Mr. Wm. Crymes, Wm. Cullawnes, Thomas Dudley. HR: John Batey, John Dashwood.	G.	9	101	1697 Oct. 28	260
HALE Francis	On N side of Horne Harbour at the head and to the S side of Winter Harbour. HR: Francis Hale, John Steere, John Turner, Anne Watson, Nathaniell Parmeton John Parmeton, Elizabeth Sadler, Sara Palmeton.	M.	3	34	1653 Nov. 25	400
HALL William	PETSOE P. Adjoining Mr. Haines, Rich. Lee, Esq., Mr. Brookin, Dudleys line and to the Main Road. HR: Margaret Younge, John Young, Edmond Day, Geo. Proud, Christian Boros.	G.	8	195	1691 Oct. 20	220
William	PETSOE P. Beginning on Coles Branch of the Poropotank near fork and to Coll: Lees corner "along the Main road that leads to Dragon Bridge" and to Mr. Wm. Brookins land. Formerly granted Charles Roane 1691, deserted. HR: John Bayley, John Dashwood, Tho. Greenwood, Joseph Ranson, Patrick Ferguson.	G.	8	429	1695 April 21	278
William	PETSO P. At a marsh on Peanketank adjoining Mr. Thomas Buckner, Mr. John Grimes and along the road. HR: Christopher, Roger, Joseph.	G.	9	145	1698 April 26	140
William	PETSTO P. Adjoining Thomas Poole, Wm. Norman, Mr. Nettles. HR: Tho. Tyler, Jack, Cicily, Robin.	G.	9	145	1698 April 26	149
William	PETSOE P. Escheat land formerly in the	G.	10	219	1714 Dec. 23	149

NAMES	DESCRIPTION	CO.	BK.	Pg.	DATE	ACRES
HALL (Continued) William	possession of Owen Caley, dece'd. Beginning at Brookings corner near Bakers Bridge & adjoining Dawkins, Thomas Dudley and Baker. Part of a former grant to Thomas Hanks, 1663. John Lewis, Esq., Escheator, Thos. Cook, Surveyor. Price: 2 pounds of tobacco per acre.	G.	10	219	1714 Dec. 23	149
HALLIARD..HILLIARD..HELLIARD Thomas	On Eastermost R. adjoining Philip Hunley & along the river to Mark Fosters. HR: Thomas Halliard, Alice his Wife, Fran. Spencer, Joell Gibbs, Adam Horne, Edey ___, Patr. James, John Hatt, Dor. Kemerley.	M.	3	131	1652 Nov. 1	450
HAMPTON William	On the E side of the Eastermost R. on the S side of a creek. HR: Thomas Smith, Richard Cary, Hugh Bromley, Wm. Boreman, Jeremy Edes, Philad. Hampton, John Ash, John Longford, Wm. Yateman, Wm. Davis, Symon Vaughan, Wm. Boreman, John Wattkins, Ailce Walker.	M.	2	311	1651 March 25	700
William, Mr.	KINGSTONE P. Beginning by the Road in the lower line of patent to said Hamptons father, to a creek and along same to the head, and adjoining land that was Robert Culleys. HR: Richard Oliver.	M.	9	126	1697 Oct. 28	42
William	On the Eastermost side of the Eastermost R. & along Mr. Wm. Hamptons old Patent. HR: Tho. Tyler, Jane, Will.	M.	9	138	1698 April 26	148
John	Beginning at the head of the beaver dams between Garden Creek and the Eastermost R. Assigned from Lt. Coll: Walker. HR: Edmund Walch, Abraham Barreb, Teage O'Moulins.	M.	3	347	1655 July 14	150
HANKES..HANCKES..HANCKS..HANKS Thomas	On branches of Peanketanke Swamp & Poropotank adjoining his own land & Coll: Lee, S to the Rappa Path & to Poropotank swamp. HR: Edward Roe 2 tymes, Hannah Wilson, John Law, Edward Roper, Francis Tersell.	G.	6	84	1667 Oct. 8	300
Thomas	In New Kent and Gloucester. Adjoining Samuel Huckstep & on the Dragon Swamp. HR: Robt. James, James Buglaste, Mary Huttson, Wm. Sineton, Jon. Wan.	G.	6	472	1673 Oct. 23	264
Thomas	On Poropotank Swamp adjoining his own land & Charles Roane, Tho. Dawkins, Lambert Moore & Huckstep. Resurvey of patent.	G.	6	476	1673 Oct. 26	500
Thomas & Cornelius Cheeseman	In New Kent and Gloucester. Adjoining "Hancks other lands whereon he now liveth" and also adjoining Thomas Jenkins.	G.	6	511	1674 April 8	260
HANSFORD..HANSFOARD Tobias	On Deepe Crk. of Ware R. Adjoining Edw. Willis [Wills?]. Formerly granted to Edward Wills 1652, who assigned to Hansford.	G.	4	559	1662 Feb. 27	200
Tobias	WARE P. On the E side and mouth of Deepe Crk. & down the Bay adjoining Christopher Robins, to Finches Crk. and to Coll: Augustine Warner. 150 acs. granted Coll: Jno: Walker 1652. HR: Richd. Jones, Jno. Bennett, Tho. Dowler, Tho. Brummfield, Jno. Howell, Saml. Coldbrook, Susan Titole, Jno. Yewin.	G.	6	138	1666 Jan. 8	324

NAMES	DESCRIPTION	CO.	BK.	Pg.	DATE	ACRES
HARPER George	"Between the bounds of Chiescake Indian Lands &...Conquest Wyatt." HR: George Anderton,Dorothy Jones,Simon Stacey.	G.? M.?	6	438	1672 Oct. 10	133
HARWOOD Ralph & Benjamin Birch	On SW side of Craney Crk. near Geo. Pole [Poole?] & Edward Freman. Granted Jeffry Bew in 1652, who assigned to Harwood & Birch.	G.	5	350	1663 Feb. 5	600
HAWARD..HOWARD..HEYWARD..HAYWARD..HAYWOOD..[HEYWOOD] William Haward	At Bennetts Crk. by four small springs to the Mobjack path. 200 acs. purchased of Col. Rich. Lee, Esq. 1653. HR: Anne Excell [?], Antho. Haines, Alex. Kimrose, John Page.	G.	3	7	1654 June 5	400
	Renewal		5	172	1662	
William Haward	PETSOE P. Beginning on the path that goes from Hawards house & Mr. Forsiths to the Rappa. Road and then to Robert Lees line. HR: Joseph West, John Gunson, Elizabeth Browne, John Fryser.	G.	6	137	1668 April 1	164
William Howard	PETSOE P. "betwixt Bennets Crk...and his other land...at the pitch of the Oyster Shell poynt by Oyster Shell Branch...near mouth of Bennetts Crk...to a corner tree in Cappahoshack att Capt. Jenings his path". HR: William Powell, Martha Cockett, Tho. Killerson.	G	6	411	1672 Aug. 14	108
William Heyward,Mr.	PETTSOE P. Adjoining his own land and along the land of Edward Poeties, NW & W 180 poles to a branch of swamp of Capahosack Crk. to a white marsh. HR: Richard Jackson, Wm. Hoagarth, Wm. Widdon, John Driver.	G.	8	194	1691 Oct. 20	156
Mary, Elizabeth & Anne Howard	PETSOE P. "daughters of Mr. Thomas Howard, dece'd". Beginning at the "head of a branch called little Ease" adjoining land of Mr. Wm. Howard, dece'd. 88 acs. formerly taken up by Ralph Green who sold to Mr. Thomas Howard, dece'd, 1673. Residue 92 acs. HR: John Williams, Jane Porter.	G.	7	643	1688 April 23	180
HAYES..HAIES Joseph, Gent.	YORK COUNTY. On N side of York R. beginning on the W side of Bennetts Crk. dividing this and the lands of John Bennett & Thomas Litchman, WSW to Thomas Bell, SE to John King. Assigned by Abra. Moone and Thomas Bourne. HR: Henry Newby, Thomas Allen, James Miller, Sarah Leeman, Richard Goode, Walter Oliver.	G.	2	304	1651 April 3	300
Thomas	On E side of Eastermost R. beginning at James Callis corner and adjoining Matthew Gale, Alexander Cray, Henry Knight to Pools line to Jos. Billups corner. Price: 20 shillings.	M.	28	240	1747 Oct. 1	168
HIGGENSON Humphrey, Col. & Thomas his sonne	"...One of the Council of State". On S side of Pyanketanke R. at a creek dividing from land of Col. Hugh Gwin now in possession of Wm. Armestead and along the head of Armesteads land. 500 acs. by assignment from Col. Ludlow's patent of 2000 acs.	M.	3	304	1654 Sept. 20	800
HILL Charles	Between Garden Crk. and Eastermost R. Granted John Hampton 1655, deserted.	M.	4	370	1658 March 15	150

NAMES	DESCRIPTION	CO.	BK.	Pg.	DATE	ACRES
HILL (Continued) Charles	HR: Roger Smith, Tho. Allen, Wm. Jorden.	M.	4	370	1658 March 15	150
Charles	Same description as above. Formerly granted Edward Lucas. HR: James Hill, Wm. Rogers, Mary Jones.	M.	4	370	1658 March 15	150
HOBART..OBERT..[HUBARD?] Bertram	On N side of Charles R. in Peanpetanke Crk. [Poropotank?] adjoining Mr. Vaus E to great creek and Oyster Shell Banck. HR: Bertram Hobart himselfe twice, Sarah his wife, Francis Pepper, Francis a Negroe, Tho. Austin his wife and 2 children, John Tredescant, Jon Eyres, Edward Goldborne, Tho. Bawcock.	G.?	1(2)-	827	1642 Oct. 10	650
HOCKADAY..HOCKADIE..HOCCADY..HOCCADAYS..HOCCADYES William	On S side of Pyanketanke R. on the W side of a creek called Hockadays Harbour. 350 acs. due by assignment for transfer of himselfe and eleven servants.	M.	1(2)	811	1642 Aug. 11	1100
William	SE of Chiskiake side at the head of Arthur Price and adjoining his former divident on a creek dividing from George Read. HR: James Drapp, Richd. Moores, Fra. Pett, Tymo Turton, Eliza. Avile, Joan Cannon, Fra. Crave, Tho. Inarnold [?], Edward Tybotts, John Pye, Peter Coge [?], Thomasin Drew, Richard Spence, Benja. ____, Mary Aswell, Robert Hill, Wm. Nurton, Fra.Rowland.	M.	2	168	1649 June 6	900
HODDIN..HODIN..HOLDER..HOLDEN..[HOULDER?] John Hoddin, Mr.	On a creek on NW side of Mobjack Bay & up the river. HR: Thomas Morrey, Charles Sallett, Sanders Murrey.	M.	1(2)	919	1643 Oct. 17	150
John Hoddin	At the head of North R. upon the NW side of maine dammes and adjoining his own land. HR: Mary Thomas, John Thompson, Humphrey Gum, Christian his wife, his own adventure, Martin Skinner, John Barnes, Tho. Poynter, Tho. Fletcher, Jon Fletcher, Wm. Blare, James Taylor, Sanders Allen, John Burnham, John King, Tho. Hopkins, Tho. Tompson, Henry Thomas.	M.	1(2)	920	1643 Oct. 17	950
HOGGEN William	KINGSTON P. Adjoining Mr. Gregg on a branch at the head of Winter Harbor Crk. NE to John Degge. HR: Michael Thompson.	M.	7	214	1682 Dec. 22	15
HOLDER..HOLDEN..HOULDER..[See also HODDIN] William Holder	On Horne Harbour Crk. on a branch. HR: Richard James, Richard Jones.	M.	2	228	1650 Aug. 13	200
William Holder	On N side of Ducking Pond Crk. in Mockjack Bay & a small creek dividing from the land of John Watts. HR: Hugh Inman, John Cabboe [?], Edw. Roberts, Elizabeth Grant.	M.	2	229	1650 Aug. 13	200
HORTH Augustine	At Five Pine Island & Ginger Crk. Granted William Dudley who assigned to Horth.	G.	4	572	1652 Sept. 20	350
Augustine	WARE P. Land and water beginning 100 poles from Lone Pine on W'ward side of North R., S down the river to Five Pine	G.	8	17	1689 Oct. 20	441

NAMES	DESCRIPTION	CO.	BK.	Pg.	DATE	ACRES
HORTH (Continued) Augustine	Island & adjoining James Morris. Residue 91 acs. HR: Matthew Hudson, Eliza. Desormane [?].	G.	8	17	1689 Oct. 20	441
HUBERD..HUBBERD..HUBBARD..HUBARD..[HOBART?] Robert Huberd	On the W'ward side of Bennets Crk. adjoining Thomas Bell, John King, Bennett & Leechman. Granted Joseph Haies April 3, 1651 and deserted.	G.	3	375	1654 June 6	300
Henry	On Poropotank Crk. at the head adjoining Mr. Blunt. HR: Robert Long, Jammay Long, Emma Brett, Thomas Nash, George Mutford, John Harrison, Nich. Bridges.	G.	3	362	1655 Aug. 25	350
Henry	At the fork of the Poropotank adjoining his own land & Mr. Knight. Granted Gilbert Blunt & deserted.	G.	4	38	1655 March 17	250
HUGHES Thomas	CHARLES RIVER COUNTY. NNW upon Tymber Neck Crk. and adjoining Richard Richards. HR: George Burford, Sen'r, George Burford, Jun'r, William Cox, Mary Cox, John Shell, Tho. Tapp, Wm. Thorpe.	G.	1(2)	907	1643 Sept. 28	400
John L.	Forest land six miles from the Court House & adjoining Blassinghams. Escheat land of which George Duncan a free man of colour died seized & Possessed.	G. (C.G.)	78	53	1825 June 11	41
Henry	This land to Mr. Henry Hughes.				1829	
HULL..[HALL?] Richard	Within Pepper Creek on the N side & adjoining Wm. Morgan. HR: Richard Bundick, Temperance Hyer, Charles Williams, John Williams, Henry Church, John Paul.	M.	2	232	1650 Aug. 13	300
Richard	On N side of Pepper Creek at the mouth in Mockjack Bay adjoining Thomas Foote. Patent for 300 acs. surrendered, same head rights named. [Note: name altered may have been written Hall]	M.	2	355	1651 Jan. 26	250
Richard	On S side of Horne Harbour, granted Winnifred Morrison 1651, assigned to Hull and renewed.	M.	3	393	1655 Oct. 9	400
HUNLEY..HUNDLEY..HUNLY Phillip	Along the Eastward of the Eastermost R. in Mockjack Bay beginning at a small creek within Budden Crk. HR: Elizabeth Hunley, Eliz. Bacon, James Beck, Flor. Jones, Charles Spratt, Matt. Lee, Thom. Bacon, Thom. Clapps, Jane Davis, Mary Blive [?], Sil. Marston, Ralph Marton, [These rights were entered by mistake on William Armestead's patent]	M.	2	330	1651 June 29	613
Philip	On W side of Budden Crk. in Mockjack Bay running 320 poles S down the creek. HR: Sanders Blacke, Sanders Mackdowell, Wm. Mack Loyd, Wm. Morrison, Mackin Mackloyd, Andrew Trumbell. Renewed	M.	4 4	269 527	1658 June 11	300
Philip	KINGSTON P. Beginning at Philip Hunleys landing place on Pudding Crk. adjoining Richard Long & Mark Foster. 300 acs. by a former patent, 160 acs. additional. HR: Thomas Garwood, Edward Hayes, Thomas Haverfinch, Bridget Derrell.	M.	6	414	1672 Aug. 19	460
Phill., Jun'r	KINGSTON P. Adjoining his fathers land &	M.	6	660	1678	200

NAMES	DESCRIPTION	CO.	BK.	Pg.	DATE	ACRES
HUNLEY..HUNDLEY..HUNLY Phill., Jun'r	(Continued) beginning at his fathers landing on Pudding Crk. adjoining Mr. Dickins and along pudding crk. HR: Mary Bald, George Gwynn, Hum. Gwynn, Geo. Buckingham.	M.	6	660	1678 Sept. 26	200
Phillip Hundley	On the N'ward side of Pudding Crk. adjoining his own land and the "Gleab land".	M.	7	522	1686 Oct. 30	89
HERST..HURST..HUST William	PETSOE P. Adjoining Tho: Royston to Rappa: path, to Richard Irelands Plantation, and David Munorgan, by Bryery Branch. Part of Thos. Roystons grant 1667 who sold to Herst.	G.	6	448	1672/3 March 18	363
William	ABINGTON P. Adjoining Mr. John Robins, dece'd, Coll? Augustine Warner, dece'd, SSW & E 280 poles to the land of the Free Schoole. HR: Jeffery Powers, Nicho Dale, Mr. Nicho Coffin, Tho. Burbage, X'pher Young.	G.	7	357	1684 April 16	300
IANSON George	On North point of Ware R. running to a small creek in marsh of Ware R. Point, around point NNE including Racoune Island to line of Nathaniel Fletcher to Ware R. Formerly granted Thomas Boswell 1666, deserted. HR: Thomas Edward, Hugh Morris.	G.	9	695	1705 Nov. 2	100
IRONMONGER William	At the head of a branch of Ware R. and Beech Swamp adjoining Coll: John Walker. HR: Henry Peasley [Peasly] twice, Jeremy persons, Jno. Hall, Martha Robertson, Thomas Knight, Jno. Lincolne.	G.	5	407	1664 June 3	350
Francis	At a corner tree of Major John Smith & Wm. Corderoy and adjoining Richard Barnard along the back line of Purton Divident & near the head branches of Totopotomoys Creek.	G.	5	194	1665 Aug. 21,	660
IVESON..IVESSON..IVESSONN Abraham	On SW side of North R. in Mockjack Bay adjoining land of Thomas Chapman along the river to Geo. Leavitt, dece'd. 250 acs. by patent Aug. 15, 1642; 200 acs. by assignment from Richard Bayley & Thomas Wright patent 1640. 205 acs. residue	M.& G.	2-	327	1651 June 10 / 1642	655
Abraham, Sen'r	On North R. side to branch of North R. Mill Swamp adjoining Richard Cox, to the Horse path and down along the river. 655 acs. granted Iveson 1651, 100 acs. granted Coll: Anthony Elliott and assigned to Abraham Iveson, Jun'r. 230 acs. residue. HR: An Key, Mary Jones, Wm. Steward, Peter Hart, Anthony Jackson.	M.& G.	5-	586	1665 Oct. 10	985
Abraham, Jun'r	At above location. Granted Lt: Coll: Anthony Elliot 1650. Renewed 1662.	M.	4	34	1656 March 26	100
JARNEW..JARNIAN..JERNEW Nicholas	On N side of York R. joining Warranuncock Island, SW upon the river & sunken land N upon the island, SE upon a swamp, 1½ miles into the woods. Patent relinquished, and new one issued as of HR: Paule Chiffton, Timo. Worldridge, 2 negroes, Henry Smith, Francis Jernew, Eliza. Blanchett, Francis Coote, Edmund & wife, Elinor Thomas, Masser William, Ann Burton, Wm. Wells.	G.	2	207	1649 Feb. 27 / 1650 Oct. 18	1000 / 900

NAMES	DESCRIPTION	CO.	BK.	Pg.	DATE	ACRES
JARNEW, etc. (Continued) Nicholas	On E side of the Poropotank adjoining Oliver Green, Mr. Webb & Mr. Pate. HR: Richard Wright, Eliz. Thomas, Rob. Hendley, Tho. Williams, Fra. Morgan, Thomas Wood, James Hinde, Henry Tomkins, Wm. Moore.	G.	3	104	1652 July 3	614
JARVIS..JERVIS Francis	KINGSTON P. On the E'ward side of the Eastermost R. beginning at Robert Lendalls corner by Henry Prouse plantation & along the river. HR: Margtt. Ashon, Hen: Webb, Sar Muskett.	M.	6	681	1679 May 1	150
Francis	KINGSTONE P. Adjoining Humphrey Toye, Christopher Dickins at the Eastermost R. Part of 200 acs. granted Henry Prouse 1667 and purchased by Jarvis.	M.	7	63	1680 Sept. 29	131
JEFFERSON Robert	On N side of Crane Neck Creek adjoining Mr. Regaults to Bay path. HR: Wm. Powell, Martha Cookett, Tho. Killerson.	G.	6	131	1668 April 3	92
JEFFS Henry	WARE P. Adjoining Peter Starling, Dece'd Jeffs own land & "One Goodson", and along Cooleys land. HR: Robert Davis, Eliza. Allen,Mary Priory.	G.	8	18	1689 Oct. 20	143
JOHNSON..JOHNSTON.. Jacob	KINGSTON P. On E side of Queens Crk. adjoining James Lindsay along the crooked line of John Curtis, along the Roade, adjoining Wm. Elliott Senior, by Dirty Branch to head of Queens Crk. & corner of Richard Cary & Wm. Elliott. 440 acs. purchased of Rich. Cary. 300 acs. now taken up.	M.	6	551	1674/5 March 6	740
JONES John	On N side of the Charles R. between two creeks & NW upon the island. HR: "Himselfe & 2 persons".	G.	1(2)	810	1642 July 20	150
Robert, Gent.	On the E side of Poropotank Swamp beginning by a Beech Spring ESE and above the maine swamp.	G.	4	6	1655 Nov. 24	450
Thomas	Upon the branches of Tottopottamoys Swamp adjoining Michael Grafton, Samuel Sollis, Edward Corderoy. HR: Mary Stoakes, Rebecca Shatten.	G.	6	74	1667 April 20	130
Charles	Escheat land "w'ch Joane Careless late of the County dyed seized of". Mr. Francis Page, D. E.	M.	7	361	1684 April 20	650
KEMP Richard, Esqr	"Secretary of State for this Colony" On Mockjack Bay in Ware R. 3000 acs. running from the mouth of the Snare Crk. into the woods W 1120 poles, N 600 poles SSE 420, NE 440, NNW 718, SE 460, SE & S 490 to a fresh run of water at the head of Ware R. then down the river parallell thereto on SW side & soe downe by the branch of s[d] river crossing the mouth of Creans [Craney?] Crk. to the beginning. The tract called by the name of Hunting Dale. 500 acs. at a creek dividing from John Terry, 320 W & N & 250 poles SW to the bounds of Dictoris Christmas, due E to St. Michaells Crk. Tract called the Meadowes. Assigned by Capt. Ralph Wormeley.	G.	2	174	1649 May 29	3500

NAMES	DESCRIPTION	CO.	BK.	Pg.	DATE	ACRES
KEMP (Continued) Richard, Esqr.	HR: Mr. Ralph Wormeley, Mrs. Agatha Wormeley, Coll: X'topher Wormeley, Mrs. Mary Wormeley, Mr. Wm. Littlewood, Richard Lewis, Robert Cheaning, Wm. Buttler, Teague Bryan, Doctor French, John Blacke, Robert Browne, 14 negroes, Nicholas Clarke, Nicholas Jarnew, Ryon Fletcher, Simon Byle, Robert Huett, A frenchman John Losway, Cornelius ___, 4 Negroes, Hugh Gwyn, John Thomas, Henry Marshall, Thomason a maid, Jenkin Williams, Morris Prower [?], Henry Hewes, William Watts, Charity his wife, Daniell Gale, Nicholas ___.	G.	2	174	1649	3500
Matthew, Coll:	KINGSTONE P. At a corner of this & Mr. Palliser near the Road path adjoining Joanna Pounalls near Coll: Kemps Quarter. 400 acs. granted John Chapman Sept. 15, 1658, who sold Coll: Matthew Kemp. Residue 173 acs.	M.	6	552	1674/5 Jan. 26	573
Mathew, Mr., Jun'r.	KINGSTON P. Adjoining Thomas Palliser, Coll: Mathew Kemp & and along the Pianketank River. HR: Jno. Stephens, Eliz. Packwood, Ann Sargent, Margrett Banks, John Greene.	M.	6	550	1674/5 March 6	229
Peter	On S side of the Pyankatank R. Betwixt the mouth of Allens Crk. & up the maine branch & & along supposed Indian Lyne to Wadeing Crk. Adjoining Thomas Amee. Said land granted Coll: Mathew Kemp Esqr dece'd by Lease by King of Cheesecake 1671, recorded in Gloster Court. Surveyed by Lawrence Smith in obedience to an Order of Governor & Council held at Greenspring 22nd day of May 1683. HR: Wm. Newton, Tho. Mugg, Robt. Mershouse, David Davis, 9 negroes.	M. & G.?	7-618		1687 Oct. 21	638
Peter	PETSWORTH P. Beginning by the Rappa Path S along Campbells patent to line of Hanks patent, to corner of Mr. Rones land to Fork of the Roads & along Mrs. Ambris' church path to Partridges line & adjoining Vicaris Nettle Marsh.Price 15 Shillings.	G.	32	83	1753 May 9	153
Matthew W.	WARE P. Adjoining Richard Johnston to a corner of Mary Bohannan & John C. Dare and to Thomas Jackman and along old County Road to Frederick Weedon.	G.?	M.?-79-289 (C.G.)		1830 Sept. 18	61½
KERBY..KIRBY..KERBYE John	WARE P. Adjoining land whereon he lives. HR: Wm. Fleet, Jno. Wurrett, Peter Spraggy.	G.	6	75	1671 April 22	130
KIBBLE..KEEBLE..KEIBLE.. George	[See CABLE..CABELL] On S side of Peanketanke R. a mile or more from river to S side of certain ponds, and near to Rappahannock path. 300 acs. granted April 1,1655.	M.	3	384	1656 June 4	740
	Renewal		5	251	1662	
	HR: Charles Leach, Robert Filkin, Peter Leach, Peter Garland, Robert Thompson, Robert Smith, Thomas Hansen, John South.					
Mary	Daughter of George Kibble, Dece'd. Granted to Robert Beverley "the day before this date...& sett over by deed to Mary Kibble". On branches of Hoccadayes Crk. adjoining Robert Elliott son of Anthony Elliott. Beginning at a corner by a valley side near Noakes plantation to corner of Conquest Wyatt's.	M.	6	438	1672 Oct. 11	500

NAMES	DESCRIPTION	CO.	BK.	Pg.	DATE	ACRES.
KING John	YORK COUNTY. On the N side of York R. at the mouth and W side of Poropotank NE on Kings Crk. HR: Robert Lester, Geo. Littleton, Tho. Lomans, Thomas Mansfield, John Boshoe, John Daniell, Morgan Joanes, John Williams, Henry Thompson.	G.?	2	192	1649 Nov. 19	500
John	GLOSTER COUNTY. On NW side of Poropotank and NW side & head of Bennetts Crk. adjoining Litchman & Bennett. HR: Alice Kelley, Walts Mander, Francis Williams, James Town.	G.?	2	345	1651 Oct. 10	200
KINGSTONE PARISH	"to the Vestry belonging to". Lying upon the N side of Puddin Crk. and adjoining upon the Gleab land of the parish to the mouth of the creek & adjoining Philip Hunly Jun[r]. HR: Thomas Cornish	M.	8	390	1694 Oct. 26	40
KNIGHT Peter	On S side of Poropotank in York R. adjoining Coll: Richard Lee. HR: William Uert [?], Robert Young, Godfrid Nixen, Wm. Evans, Lawrence Evans, Humphrey Hawoods, John Fulcher, John Knighthill, John Farmer, Wm. Chamberlin, Mathew Bradford, John Lastly, James Foster, Ursela Smith, William Wright, John Smith, Thomas Jervis, Stephen Collin, Thomas Powell, Eliza. Monke.	G.	3	95	1652 July 16	1000
Peter	Towards the head & E side of Poropotank Crk. adjoining Mr. Blunt & Col: Richd. Lee. HR: John Ball, Alex. & Rich. Weston, John Henton, Thomas Cobb, Thomas Taberer, Richard Lathberry, James Clarke, Margery Chamber, Thomas Miller, Kath. Huse, Arthur Carpenter, John Simson, Saml. Clarke.	G.	3	197	1652 Aug. 25	700
Peter	Resurvey showing 574 acs. instead of 1000 acs. as by patent of 1652. Adjoining Mr. Fra. Ironmonger, Fra. Morgan & corner of Purton Dividend.	G.	6	137	1668 April 3	574
Peter, Mr.	One mile below Oliver Green "at a marked poplar by a Great Swamp w'ch runns by Mr. Cookes land". Formerly granted Wm. Newman 1657 and part sold by him to Elias Cobson who assigned to Knight.	G.	6	333	1668 March 2	400
Guy	On Milford Haven and known by the name of Eagles Nest adjoining Abraham English up the Western Branch Crk. to land of John Smith. HR: Sam Bridges, John Begg, Will Martin, Will Groves, Thomas Stint, Hugh Row, Thomas Monke, Jno. Stores.	M.	5	648	1666 Aug. 27	400
Guy	On Milford Haven, & Western Branch adjoining Abraham English, Dece'd, along haven and Bay adjoining Tho. Putnam, Jno. Shaple. 400 acs. granted 1666, residue 23 acs. HR: Geo. Anderson.	M.	6	476	1673 Oct. 23	423
KNOWLES Sands	KINGSTON P. Adjoining land belonging to Knowles beginning by "the side of the path that leads to the head of the Eastermost R." HR: Richard Phillips, Sam'll Southworke, Margery Watkins, Isaac Sterlinge, Wm.Wood.	M.	7	223	1682 Dec. 22	230

NAMES	DESCRIPTION	CO.	BK.	Pg.	DATE	ACRES
LANDER..[SANDER?] John	Escheat land late in the possession of Geo: Burgh. Wm. Jones, Deputy Escheator to Hono[bel] Mathew Page, Escheator.	M.	9	595	1704 April 26	250
LANGHAM Daniel	ABBINGTON P. Adjoining Robert Coleman. Granted to X'pr Abbott in 1657 due "Langham by marrying Mary daughter of s[d] X'pr Abbott".	G.	6	549	1674/5 March 6	350
LASSELL Edward	KINGSTON P. Joining the head line of Mr. Richard Billops & adjoining Mr. George Billops' 100 acs. also adjoining Jno. Calles, Mark Foster, Morris Mackashannuck. HR: Henry Dawson, Edwd. Lassell jun'r, Jno. Duffy, X'pher Starton, Moses Baker, James Sanderling, Ann his wife.	M.	7	222	1682 Dec. 22	230
LAYNE..LANE Henry	At the head of the Upright Crk. of the Eastermost R. 100 acs. granted John White 1653, 50 acs. additional. HR: Wm. Miller.	M.	4	161	1657 Oct. 10	150
LEE..[See LEIGH] Richard, Gent.	On the N side of the Charles R. called by the name of Indian Spring in Poropotank Crk. adjoining Francis Morgans land, along Freshwater Crk. By assignment from Mr. Thomas Hill, Florentine Paine & Mr. Freeman. Rights for 150 acs. assigned to Mr. Dixon. HR: Due for own personal adventure, his wife Ann, John Francis, Joane Pickering, Thomas Hackett, Florentine Paine twice.	G.	1(2)	797	1642 Aug. 10	1000
Richard, Gent.	On N side of the York R. being land formerly owned by John Bayles & Geo. Knight, wanting heir devolved to his Majesty. "Opposite Poplar Neck on the S side". 400 acs. sold to Ralph Green; 400 acs. to Geo. Austin; 50 acs. to Anthony Savage. HR: Wm. Crawford, Henry Hed [?] Wm. Batchelor, Nicho. Merror, Mathew Lee, John Farror, George Way, Chris. Feathergill, Edward Dicks, Wm. David, Joane Pealeys [?], John Lyne, Elizabeth Reds, John Hunt, John Thomas, James Ware, Mary Martin, Peter Parchmore, GeorgeLight, Fra. Newton, Geo. Lee, Tho. Kidd, Henry Cloyd, John Permeter.	G.	2	153	1648 Dec. 21	1250
Richard, Coll: Esq[r],	"Secretary of State". 350 acs. adjoining W boundary of Lees other tract & 200 acs. on the W side of a branch of Bennetts Creek.	G.	2	314	1651 May 21	550
Richard, Coll: Esq[r]	GLOCESTER COUNTY. At the head branches of Poropotank Swamp S & N on the Mattapony path, on Spring Valley, bounded on the E, S & E by Spring Valley. HR: Mathew Peacock, Eliza. Hurrs, Roger Ashby, Robt. Kemp, John Gray, John Smith, John Bright, William Mathews, Edward Haward, John Charles.	G.	2	338	1651 Oct. 18	500
Richard, Coll:	SW & southerly upon Yorke R. NW & WNW upon the land of Richard Jones, dece'd, now in possession of Frances Jones, relict, E & SE upon the land of Robert Todd.	G.	3	27	1653 March 20	300
Richard, Col.	Bounded on NE & E by Henry Corbell, on SE by Wm. Haward, S & SW on his own land W on Dogwood Spring Branch N & NW by Thorne. HR: Cormack O Mally, Teague Flanny,	G.	3	337	1655 May 17	200

NAMES	DESCRIPTION	CO.	BK.	Pg.	DATE	ACRES
LEE (Continued) Richard, Col.	Richard O Harratt, Giles Peirce.	G.	3	337	1655 May 17	200
Richard, Col.	Towards the head of Poropotank Crk. "Whereon the store of the s^d Col: Lee stands". Part of a divident granted Peter Knight, merchant, 1652, now deserted. HR: 1 servant, Morris Plummor.	G.	4	47	1656 June 4	5
Richard, Mr.	PETSOE P. In Beech Spring Valley to a poplar in bridge swamp, adjoining Charles Roane to Coles Branch. HR: Rich: Lee, Abra. Good, Silvester Ison, Geo. Jennings, Wm. Winfeild, Nath. Dent, Sarah Ingram, Geo. Henry, Jno. Horton.	G.	6	243	1668 Jan. 29	450
Richard, Major	Resurvey and renewal including residue of 140 acs. "Knowne by the name of Paradise beginning at the mouth of a branch issuing out of Poropotank maine swamp...called the Bridge Branch runing... up the branch to Spring Valley upp that Valley...passing Beach Spring...including same...to Rich land branch or swamp ...Colemire Branch...to Mr.John Lewis his line...to Mr. Lee his branch called Horse-pasture Branch". 1000 acs. by two pattents, residue of 140 acs. found to lie betwixt the two. HR: Tho. Mason, Mary Woodward, Wm. Butler.	G.	6	523	1674 July 22	1140
William & Hancock	"sonns of Col. Richard Lee" In Peanketank Swamp. 500 acs. granted to John Woodward, Atty. of Coll: Lee, 350 acs. residue. (Note: Deserted by Wm. & Hancock Lee and regranted to Thomas Brereton.) HR: Roger Sheely, Jno. O Leally, Patrick O Crahan, John Mathew, David Mahoone, Denny Carby, Richd. Joy, Dermot O Farne.	G.	4	47	1656 June 2 1662	850
Robert	Adjoining his own land and along Mr. Thorntons path, SE to Col^o Lees horse path, SW to the barrens & WNW to Dogwood Valley. 200 acs. formerly granted Col^o Richd. Lee 1655, and assigned to Robert Lee 1657, residue 342 acs. HR: John Bucknell, Eliz. Williams, Valent. Smith, Abra. Smith, Jno. Folcner, Tho. Roulston, Robt. Haniger, Tho. Clay.	G.	5	333	1662 Dec. 23	542
Robert	Renewal, described as above and "to a Poplar by the dogwood branch to Robert Lees plantation". 200 acs. being formerly granted Coll: Richd Lee 1655.	G.	8	215	1662 Dec. 23	542
LEECHMAN..LITCHMAN..LEITCHMAN..LEACHMAN Thomas & John Bennett	On the N side of York R. On the SE side of a creek dividing from Robert Huberd, NE on Tankes Creek. HR: William Jones, John Clerke, Richard James, Henry Lodwell, "Wrong enter'd- instead Wm. Porter, Robert Dorfield, Rob. Lane, Richd. Wilkins".	G.	3	166	1652 Jan. 13	200
LEEKE John, Mr.	At Tindalls Point adjoining Robert Todd, along the Road and by "a great hole dug in the ground...to the corner of Furbush his fence...along York River". Purchased of Alexander Huspie.	G.	6	542	1674 Sept. 21	83-
LEIGH..[LEE?] William, Capt.	On the N side of the Charles R. in Poropotank Crk. adjoining Capt. Wormeley.	G.?	1(2)	802	1642 Aug.___	1000

NAMES	DESCRIPTION	CO.	BK.	Pg.	DATE	ACRES
LEIGH (Continued)	"Transfer of himself his wife Mary Daughter Mary and 17 persons."	G.?	1(2)	802	1642	1000
LEITHERMAN..LEITHERMORE	See John Thomas for description.	M.	3	138	1652	400
LENDALL..LANDALL..LANGDALL..LENDELL Robert	On N side of the Eastermost R. [Record incomplete.] HR: Joan Maning, Ann Moseley.	M.	3	173	1652 Oct. 18	150
	Renewal: Beginning at Mr. Armisteads tree on the river...running N & S to a creek down the creek S to the river and W up same.		4	529	1661 Nov. 20	150
Robert	KINGSTON P. Renewal: "adjoining Hum. Toys land formerly Mr. Armisteads land." From Toys corner to the Eastermost R. side and up the river. Resurvey.	M.	6	661	1678 Sept. 26	150
LEONARD..[LENNALLS?] Roger	On the E side of the Eastermost R. adjoining Adam Bennett, Henry Prouse to Asmole Creek. HR: Elizabeth Lag, Isaac Remnant, John Book, John Morgan, Wm. Combes, Mary Harwood.	M.	6	100	1667 Dec. 20	300
LEVITT..LEAVIT..LEVELL..LEAVITT..LEVETT..LEVEL Georg	Near the head of the North R. of Mockjack Bay near land of Richard Bayly & John Hoddin & along the NW side of the Otterdamms which divided from John Hoddin. HR: His own personal adventure twice, Alice his wife, John Jenings, Robert Tibaults, Elias Degaris, Tho: Tabb, Franc. Cherry, Jone Hobbs, Daniel Thorpe, Willi. Tompson, Theodor Moyses, Jon Weeks, Nath. Wilsonn, Jon Jones, Richard Cooke, Geo. Wharton, Mary Fowler, Eliza. his wife, Robert her sonn.	M.	1(2)	930	1643 Oct. 19	1000
LEWIS Jon, Mr.	At the head of the Poropotank on a branch of Lewis Crk. formerly Totopotomoys Crk. and adjoining Capt. Francis Morgan, Sam'l Sally. HR: John Lewis, Lidia Lewis, Wm. Lewis, Edwd. Lewis, Jon Lewis, jun'r.	G.?	3	4	1653 July 1	250
John, Jun'r	On Poropotank adjoining Coll: Rich. Lee to Beech Spring fork & up same.	G.	4	9	1655 Dec. 29	250
John	At head of Poropotank Crk. on both sides to land of Mr. Major NE to lands of Thomas Hanckes, George Austin, up Coles Branch SE to Col. Richard Lees land &c to the bridge swamp. 120 acs. granted to Timothy Lowdell & Thomas Broughton 1651; assigned to Lewis; 1000 acs. patented by Howell Price 1656 and assigned to Lewis. Residue 600 acs. HR: David Jones, Mary Crow, Peter Brookes, Richard Foxon, Peter Story, Edw. Thonall, Tho. Arnoll, Symon Groves, Geo. Edmonds, Wm. Thompson, Henry Hunt, Wm. Webb.	G.?	5	229	1663 Nov. 22	1700
John, Mr.	"In Gloster & New Kent"; on both sides of the Poropotank Swamp adjoining said Lewis plantation by Old Womans Poynt & adjoining Rich. Major, Timothy Lowdell, Geo. Major, John Fox, Rich. Lee, Jno. Chamberlin, to the mill. 80 acs. purchased of Timothy Lowdwell; 1000 acs. of Hoel Prise; 600 acs. by patent Nov.23,1663; 920 acs. residue.	G.	6	171	1667 Aug. 16	2600

NAMES	DESCRIPTION	CO.	BK.	Pg.	DATE	ACRES
LEWIS (Continued) John, Mr.	HR: Wm. Jones, Morgan Kennett, James Stephens, Tho. Page, Sarah ___, Robt. Rosse, Henry ___, Ann Smith, Robert Wilson, Isabell Wilson, Mary Bowly, Jeremy Nouson, Israel Jormy, Peter Armstrong, MaryMeredith, Tho. Brough, Tho. Moose, Roger Ingerson, Robert Morris.	G.	6	171	1667	2600
John, Esq[r] & John Smith of Purton, John Washington, of Westmoreland.	Beginning at a chestnut by the roade. Surveyed for George Warner, dece'd, and granted to above heirs to said Warner. HR: John Phipps.	G.	10	13	1711 April 28	46½
John, Esq[r]	ABBINGTON & WARE Ps. Adjoining Jacob Hurst along Warners line to Dorrills corner. For ten shillings of good & Lawful money.	G.	10	419	1719 July 11	58
Nicholas	"Upper end of PETSWORTH P." Beginning on the east side of the road adjoining his own land & John Dillard. Price: 5 Shillings.	G.	41	253	1773 March 1	23
Nicholas	Near the Dragon & on the road from the Dragon Ordinary to King & Queen, adjoining his own land and John Dillard, John Dixon & Thos. Hall. "In consideration of the ancient composition of five shillings Sterling."	G.	B (C.G.)	404	1780 July 15	44
LIGHT George	On W side of Poropotank on a creek dividing from Leechman & Bennett. Part of a grant to Mr. Cainhoe & purchased of John Underwood who married the relict of Cainhoe. Deed Oct. 6, 1650.	G.?	3	199	1652 May 13	200
LIGHTFOOT Phillip	ABBINGTON P. Adjoining land of Edward Momford on one side & York R. on the other & also adjoining Mr. Richard Booker (lately Mr. Reynolds' [land]), Mr. John Bannister & on fourth side along the river. This land "formerly due unto Capt. John Lightfoot by purchase from the widdow Fleet & John Cooper & his wife & since for a debt due from the said Capt. John Lightfoot to Mr. Phillip Lightfoot." 60 acs. being overplus.	G.	6	557	1675 June 15	150
Phillip, Coll:	IN WARE & PETSOE Ps. Adjoining at the corner of Coll: John Cheeseman's land by Mr. Wm. Hansfords path along "Walter Gracowitts Plantation" adjoining Robert Spinks, John Burton, and by Jonathans Pond.	G.	7	567	1687 April 20	269
LILLY..LYLLEY..LILLIE..LILY..LYLLIE..LYLLEY John Lylley	On the SW side of Milford Haven being a neck of land near the land of Peter Rigby & Edward Peirsifull. HR: For transfer of himself, wife, & 5 servants: William ___,Thomas Steele [?], John Leake, Eliza. ___, Ellen Brown.	M.	1(2)	800	1642 June 20	350
John Lyllie	Betwixt Garden Creek & Milford Haven adjoining Mr. Edmd. Forrest, George Billops and John Callis. HR: X'pher Trow, Sarah Sparrow, Joan Godden, Isaac Hopkins, 1 negro.	M.	7	213	1682 Dec. 22	234
LINDSAY..LINDSAYE..LINDSEY James	KINGSTON P. "At Queens Creek syde" adjoining Jacob Johnson, Stephen Fentry.	M.	6	549	1674 March 6	390

NAMES	DESCRIPTION	CO.	BK.	Pg.	DATE	ACRES
LINDSAY, etc. (Continued) James	Part of a grant to Richard Cary who sold to Lindsay.	M.	6	549	1674 March 6	390
LITTLEFIELD Robert	& Thomas Viccars. [See Viccars]	G.	6	284	1669 Aug. 16	550
LODELL..LOWDELL..LOWNDELL..LOWDWELL Timothy	YORK COUNTY. On the N side of the Yorke R. adjoining Crowshaw. HR: John Worker and 9 negroes.	G.?	2	209	1649 Feb. 22	575
LONG..LONGE Richard	On Milford Haven on W'ward side of a branch dividing from George Billops. HR: Edward Dymont, Henry King, Robert Maysfield, Hannah Cotton, Mary James, Thomas Hale, Lt. Col. Griffith, Ann his wife.	M.	3	135	1652 Dec. 6	350
Richard	Same location, record incomplete. Renewal: 1661	M.	3 4	60 560	1653 Nov. 25	430
Sara Long & Mary Shipley	Daughters of Abraham English dece'd & according to ancient bounds of grant to English, lately found to escheat. Capt. Philip Ludwell D.E.	M.	6	250	1669 July 4	350
LONGEST Richard	KINGSTONE P. Adjoining Jacob Johnson & Capt. Armestead along branch by Wm. Beards plantation & adjoining Coll: Dudley, John Waters and Mr. Wm. Elliott. HR: John Territt, Rich. Whitehead, Alice Baserman, Jno. White, Mary Bridge, Geo. Wilcock, Eliz. Alliborne [?], Jno. Wright, Jno. Sheppard, Abra: Capin, Jane Bedy, Wm. Paine, Jno. Lacy, Walter Harris.	M.	6	661	1678 Sept. 26	680
Richard	KINGSTONE P. Lying near the head of Eastermost R. adjoining Capt. Wm. Armistead & his own land. HR: Wm. Tunley, Wm. Pritchard, Wm. Gordon.	M.	10-219		1714 Dec.23	130
LUCAS Edward	On SW side of Garden Creek. HR: John Morraine, Kennet Morraine, Jno. Shallamine.	M.	3	352	1655 July 14	150
LUDLOW George, Col Esq[r]	One of the Counsell of State. On the S side of the Pyanketanke R. between Wading Crk. & Gwins Crk. and adjoining Col. Gwin. Due by exchange with King of Chiskyeake. Allowed by Governor & Council.	M.	3	23	1652 March 12	2000
George, Coll:	Record incomplete. Mentions Pyanketanck and Wading Crk.	M.	3	32	1652 March 12	
George, Coll: Esq[r]	[Land described in first patent seems to be repatented] On S side of Pyanketanke R. opposite land of Thomas Trotter, dece'd, along the river WNW to a branch near the head. Beginning at the mouth & WNW side of Gwins Crk., along the river WNW & from the W side of Wading Crk. to the land of Col. Gwin. Due by exchange with the King of Chiskyacke, acknowledged before Governor & Councell. HR: Wm. Wilcock, Fran. Taverne, Pater Thunder, Michael Wilcox, Eliza Harris, Eliza Trevill, Ann Playstoe, Sen'r, Ann Playstoe, Gabriell Ludlow, Thomas Ludlow, Katherine Ward, Elinor Buckster [?], Grace Wilcoxe, Joane Cullin, James Field, John Richards, John Covide, Roger Perkins, 4 negroes, John Rumsden, Saml. Carrington,	M. & G.?	3	116	1652 Oct. 25	2000

NAMES	DESCRIPTION	CO.	BK.	Pg.	DATE	ACRES
LUDLOW (Continued) George	Bened. Grint, Wm. Edwards, Sen'r, Wm. Edwards Jun'r, John Rop [?], Wm. Labor, Mary Woodnut, Tho. Fabin, Archeball Douglas, John Githred, John Pase, Antho. Grant Robert Wilson, Robt. Stuart, Wm. Dinglas, Danl. Hamilton, Tho. Joanes.	M.& G.?	3	116	1652 Oct. 25	2000
MACHEN..MACHIN..MECHEN..MEACHEN..MEKIN John Mechen & Dunkin Bohono	See Bohono for description.	M.	6	102	1667 Dec. 20	220
John Machin	Kingston P. Escheat land formerly owned by Henry Preston, dece'd, on the W side of the Eastermost R. adjoining land of John Cary, ___Dudley, to Gowins line, along the river front several courses NE 401 poles. Thos. Mumford Surveyor, John Robinson Escheator. Price: 2 pounds of Tobacco per acre.	M.	32	645	1754 Sept. 10	606
MACKASHANOCK..MACK A SHANOCK..MACKACHACOCK Morris	KINGSTON P. Beginning at a pine near the head and on the E side of Peach Point Crk. out of Milford Haven adjoining Richard Billops. 40 acs. sold by Mr. George Billups dece'd to Mackashannuck. Residue 100 acs. HR: Wm. Norton, Tho Hallier.	M.	7	220	1682 Dec. 22	140
MACKENNY William	E side of the Eastermost R. adjoining Phillip Hunley & Mark Foster. Granted Thomas Helliard 1652 who assigned to John Singleton who sold to Mackenny.	M.	4	527	1652 Dec. 3	450
MAJOR..MAIOR Richard	[Very likely King & Queen land] On N side of Charles R. NW & N on Perringes Crk. adjoining Ashwell Batten, Tho. Bell,John Major, James Holding and his own land. 400 acs. granted John Perrin 1651 who assigned to Major. HR: Tho. Parker, Robt. Wherry, Jon. Garrett,Jane Bowden, Jane Moss, Ann Hinshaw, Rich. Tidderson, Kath. Goodman,Mary Hinshaw.	G.?	3	8	1653 March 20	1000
John	Adjoining Joseph Haies & John Perine. 200 acs. assigned from Thomas Bell's grant of 1651. Renewed	G.?	4	203	1657 Dec. 28 1663	300
MAN..MANN John	On E side of the Eastermost R. at Chestnut Crk. adjoining Wm. Holden. Granted Thomas Todd 1653 who assigned to Man.	M.	4	531	1661 Nov. 20	600
MARCHANT Richard	KINGSTONE P. Adjoining Mr. Long and Thomas Puttman. HR: William Oakley, Susana Mann.	M.	8	273	1693 April 29	84
MATHEWES..MATTHEWS..MATHEWS Cornelius & William Claw.	For description see Claw.	M.	6	104	1667 Dec. 20	320
MEAKES.[MACKIE?] John	On the S side of the S branch of the Severne R. in Mockjack Bay on Meakes Crk. HR: For transfer of himself and 3 servants: Richard Carter, Robert Peircifull, Mathew Chapman.	G.	1(2)	809	1642 Aug. 20	200
MEDCALF..METCALF..METCALFE Gilbert	Along Peanketanke R. adjoining Abraham Moone. Patent to John Woodward dece'd 1655 & assigned by Joseph Woodward brother & heire; deserted and renewed in the name of Major David Cant 1664.	M.-G.?	4	266	1657 March 15	500
Gilbert	London Merchant. 650 acs. on Peancke-	M.	5	455	1664	810

NAMES	DESCRIPTION	CO.	BK.	Pg.	DATE	ACRES
MEDCALF, etc. (Continued) Gilbert	tancke R. side at John Chapman's by survay made 1663; 250 acs. purchased of Mr. Edward Wyatt, adjoining Wm. Armestead along old marked trees of Col. Hugh Gwin in the Pinnace Neck "including a neck of land most of it Indian feilds, as will appeare by bill of sale in Gloster Records." HR: 9 negroes & Mary Vaughan.	M.	5	455	1664 Sept. 25	810
MILLER Thomas	PETSOE P. Adjoining Isaac Richardson, John Dayes, Richard Barnard, Thomas Vicars, Thos. Wisdome and near the Rappa Road. HR: Tho. Beale sen'r, Tho. Beale jun'r, Twice, Alice Beale Thrice, Jno. Pope, Jno. Temple.	G.	6	159	1665 Oct. 28	390
Thomas, Mr.	PETSOE P. On the E side of a branch "that runs into the Poplar Spring Branch adjoining Isaac Richardson, along Rappahanock Road, and adjoining land formerly taken up by Mr. John Buckner, Dece'd", Mr. Barnard, Dece'd, Mr. Thomas Vicarrs along a swamp to a branch dividing from land of Tho: Wisdom dece'd...& adjoining John Easter. 390 acs. by former patent 1665, residue 270 acs. HR: Jno. Cownell [?], Jno. Wornam, Phil: Thomas, Wm. Lewell [?], Ja: Batchley [?], Fra. Simson.	G.	9	58	1696 April 29	660
William	PETSWORTH P. Escheat land lately owned by Isaac Richeson, dece'd, on the head branches of Atapotamoyes Swamp near John Days land down the swamp to the mouth of Vicarys & Millers branch adjoining Capt. Thomas Buckner, John Day, down branch & Poplar Spring Run. John Lewis, Escheator. Thomas Cook, Surveyor. 2 pounds of Tobacco per acre.	G.	11	59	1720 Feb. 21	430
MINIFYE..MINIFIE..MINIFEE..MINIFREE..MENEFY..MYNYFIE Georg, Esq'r	One of the Council of State. On the N side of the Charles R. beginning at the creek upon the W side of the Indian Fields ..opposite Queens Crk. and down the river to Timberneck Crk. "To be doubled when sufficiently peopled and planted..Transfer at his cost of 60 persons." HR: Benjamine Pixley, Thomas Greene, John Chapman, Henry Martin, John Burgis, Mathew Ward, Thomas Prince, James Sheers, Richard Turner, 4 negroes bought of Mr. Oldis, 2 Negroes bought of Randall Holt, William Menifie, Francis Garrett, Thomas Sharples, James Sherbourne, Robert Williams, William Jones, John Wilkinson, Joane Wilkinson, Thomas Waggatt, Georg Kennon, John Kennon, John Richards, Edward Andrewes, Francis Young, James Hawkins, Joseph Willis, Francis Blacke, Thomas Morter, 9 negroes bought of Mr. Constable, John Brooke, Thomas Howler, Humphrey Dennes, John Tabor, Henry Ashwell, Robert Mason, Thomas Hearne, John William, Thomas Holmes, Adam Key, Saml1. Walker, Stephen Leech, Julian Reed, William Hill, William Munday, Adam Coote, William Powell, Humphrey London.	G.	1(2)	704	1639	3000

NAMES	DESCRIPTION	CO.	BK.	Pg.	DATE	ACRES
MINTER	Thomas Edwards & John P. Minter See Edwards for description.	M.	91 (C.G.)	513	1841 July 31	110
MOGSOM..MOGGSON John	ABINGTON P. Near head of Cedar Bush Crk. on W side adjoining Mr. John Mann, Major Lewis Burwell, Lawrence Smith, across Cedar Bush Crk. along Capt. Richd. Bookers line. 125 acs. bought by Wm. Mogsom dece'd of Francis Wheeler dece'd, 1652. 300 acs. formerly sold by Major Lewis Burwell, dece'd to Mathew Hawkins of Queens Creek, Nov. 17, 1651, who sold to Wheeler by deed dated April 1, 1652, who sold Mogsom Sept. 4, 1652. HR: Andw. Robinson.	G.	7	359	1684 April 20	433
MOONE..MOON Abraham	Next to the land of John Lylley on the SW side of Milford Haven running SE into a creek that divides this from the land of Peter Rigby, SW into the woods NW upon a creek which divided from the land of John Smith. Assigned to Thomas Bourne by Moone May 26, 1652. Witnesses: Edward Wyatt & John Jackson. Recorded Lancaster Court 6th day of February 1653. Teste - John Philips,Cl.Cur. Assigned to George Billips by Thos. Bourn 5th of Feby. 1657. Recorded: Feby. 6,1657. Thomas Morris, Cl.Cur. [Gloucester] Witnesses: Humphry Gwyn, Edward Bullock, Thomas Morris. "At a Gener[l] Court held at James City the 24th day of Aprill,1700 The above patent together w'th Abraham Moones & Thomas Bournes assignm[ts] thereon upon the petition of George Billups is admitted to record and a new patent to issue in the s[d] Billups his name for the same land. Nov. 7th, 1700.... Teste C. C. Thacker Cl Genl Cur."	M.	9	245	1650 June 6	500
Abraham	On the S side and head of the Pyanke-tank R. Adjoining Capt. Stephen Gill. HR: James Morth, John Phillips, Peter Worth, Richard Heler, William Bryan, William Jones, Thomas Box, Mich. Floyd, James Harren, William Newark, David Williams, Richard Parrinter.	G.?	3	326	1654 Nov. 1	600
MOORE..MORE Diana	"the relict of Jno. Axford"[Oxford?]. Escheat land formerly granted to John Axford, Dece'd. Phill. Ludwell D.E.	G.?	6	250	1669 Oct. 24	100
Lambert & Bartholomew Ramsey	Betwixt the lands of David Cant, dece'd & Thomas Dawkins. HR: Ellin Forman, Jno. Savage, John Norrich, Elias Paine, Jon. Howard, Robt. Lane.	G.	6	429	1672 Oct. 8	350
MORGAN..MORGAINE William	Lyeing upon Mockjack Bay which is the W'rn boundary for one mile... on the N side of Pepper Crk. & by a gut which divides this and the land of Richard Hull. HR Henry Moore, Michaell White, Henry Hamond, Robert Grey, Wm. Bilsbrough, Robert Dye.	M.	2	270	1650 Oct. 26	300
William	Adjoining his own land [above location] to Henry Singleton's line. HR: Wm. Bilbrough, Robert Dye, Hen. Moor, Murael White, Hen. Hamond, Robert Grey, The husband of Eliza Adison,Eliza Adison herself.	M.	3	10	1653 Feb. 25	550

NAMES	DESCRIPTION	CO.	BK.	Pg.	DATE	ACRES
MORGAN (Continued) William	On the E side of Mockjack Bay adjoining Walter Morgan. HR: Anne Disford.	M.	6	99	1667 Dec. 20	50
William	KINGSTON P. Adjoining Walter Morgan "formerly granted Wm. Morgan Dece'd since his death Patt lost...Due to William as Son & Heire".	M.	7	214	1682 Dec. 22	50
Francis, Capt.	On E side of Poropotank Crk. adjoining his own land and on to Atapatamoies. HR: Robert Borden, Eliza Parry, Eliza. Smith, Geo. Court, Jno. Parker, Ro. Dorfield, Rob. Lane, Richd. Wilkins, Wm. Porter, Hen. Wilson, Richard Parker.	G.	3	194	1652 July 27	510
Thomas	At the head of North R. in Mockjack Bay adjoining Andrew Careless. HR: Jonathan Harris, Joane Careless, John Grey, Elizabeth Williams.	M.	3	60	1653 Nov. 25	200
Edward	John Teage & Edward Morgan. See Teage.	M.	4	211	1657 March 16	150
Walter	KINGSTON P. Beginning on the W side of the mouth of Pepper Crk. Granted Wm. Morgan Dece'd...pattent lost. Due said Walter as heire to William. HR: John Smallwood.	M.	7	220	1682 Oct. 22	201
MORRELL Thomas	ABINGTON P. On the maine run to the Seaverne R. neare a spring "that belongs to said Morrels Dwelling house" adjoining Major Lewis Burwell, Mr. Benj. Clements on the Maine Roade, and Maj. Lawrence Smith. Being part of 300 acs. conveyed by William Boulding [see Bowlin] to Rachell his then wife for her life and to one Morgan Lewis his heirs &c by deed dated March 14, 1670. Recorded in the Court of Gloucester. "Said Morgan Lewis made his last will...dated 6th daye of Jany. 1675 ...did bequeath the s[d] land to Rachell... who by indenture of sale...dated 1681... did convey to the above Morrell."	G.	7	289	1683 April 16	150
MORRIS Thomas	On a branch of Milford Haven to the mouth of Green Branch adjoining Richard Long. HR: Joyse Echoll[?], John Preston, William Blades, John Blades (Sonn).	M.	3	135	1652 Dec. 6	200
Thomas	Adjoining his own land [at same location as above], assigned to James Foster who assigned to Capt. John Smith, Oct.8, 1656.	M.	3	1	1653 Nov. 25	400
Thomas	On the S side of North R. in Mockjack Bay beginning at a Lone Pine, S by the Bay side to the E'ward corner tree of Basses Crk. dividend, W & N to Back Crk. down same to the river and to the beginning. Granted 1652 to Mr. Thomas Curtis and by said Curtis and his wife Avarilla assigned to John Curtis who assigned to Morris.	G.	4	415	1661 Feb. 13	670
Thomas	In Ware Neck on Bassetts [Basses?] Creek adjoining his own land and Mr. Boswell, to Turtons fence. HR: Richard Spragg.	G.	5	508	1665 Oct. 11	50

NAMES	DESCRIPTION	CO.	BK.	Pg.	DATE	ACRES
MORRIS (Continued) James	On the side of North R. beginning at a place called "the loane Pine" running down North R. SE & SW to the mouth of a Gutt & up same WNW 300 poles then SSW 169 poles to Mr. Thomas Boswells line along his line WNW 378 poles & so to Back Crk. and along the creek to North R. southerly down North R. to the beginning. 670 acs. formerly granted Mr. Thomas Curtis 1652, residue 80 acs. HR: John Easterfield, James Huzzy.	G.	7	520	1686 Oct. 30	750
Christopher S.	PETSOE P. Adjoining Thomas C. Anthony and crossing the road leading from the Dragon Ordinary to the Court House and adjoining Mr. Paget and Dawson Soles.	G.	71 (C.G.)	392	1822 Nov. 1	100
MORRISON..MORRYSON Winefrid, Mrs. Widdow	At the head of Pepper Crk. and along the S end of Richard Hull's land one mile to Town Harbour [Horne Harbour?] and adjoining the land of Richard Grigson. HR: Major Francis Morrison twice, Thomas Jackson, Wm. Thorpe, Robt. Noble, Ann Darby.	M.	2	232	1650 Aug. 13	300
Winefrid	On S side of Horne Harbour. 300 acs. due by patent of Aug. 1651 and 100 acs. for transfer of 2 persons. Assigned unto Richard Hull 1655. HR: Major Richard Morrison, Ann White.	M.	2	356	1651 Jan. 26	400
MOSELEY George	On the E side of the Severne R. adjoining Lt. Col. Walker, Jno. Robins, Thos. Breman, Capt. Warner. HR: Ann Ryalls, Sarah Ryalls.	G.	3	338	1655 May 17	100
MUMFORD..MOMFORD Edward	One mile above Tindalls Point beginning at Fishing Point by the Road and adjoining Robt. Todd, to and along the York R. 68 acs. high land in the right of Mary his wife & daughter of Jos. Watkins who purchased of John Fleete. 12 acs. Island. "this day measured and taken up by Mrs. Elizabeth Bannister, Widd:...and by her sould...immediately to Mumford". HR: Jack.	G.	7	4	1679 Sept. 25	80
Edward	A small island in the York R. part marsh, next to his other island "called Oak Island". HR: Jon Badworth.	G.	7	230	1682 Nov. 22	25
MUNORGAN..MONORGAN David	On the head branches of the Ware R. at a corner of Will Culmans [Collaine?] & near Thomas Royston and Rich. Renshaw on Bryery Branch. HR: John Danies, Tho. Hoton, Doko Hast, David Parker, Rich. Hickson, James Ambrose, James Tredings, Nath. Lomber, Wm. Wood, Barth. Clarke, Jno. Collmer, Jno. George, Jno. West, Wm. Lewis.	G.	6	42	1667 Feb. 2	696
MURRAY..[MORAY?] Alexander, Mr.	On the E side of Beach Branch of Ware R. adjoining Coll: Walker. 200 acs. being granted Coll: John Walker and deserted. Residue 1000. HR: John Trott, Wm. Phillips, Peter Crow, Alexr. Whitloe, James Barkin, Tho. Primm, Jeffrey Miller, Tho. Fisher, Tho. Hill, Jno. Cradock, Humphrey Hellier, Richd.	G.	6	366	1671 June 14	1200

NAMES	DESCRIPTION	CO.	BK.	Pg.	DATE	ACRES
MURRAY (Continued) Alexander	Johnson, Wm. Penroe, Jno. Keat, Hen. Hockley, Mary Dumond, Eben[r] Joller, Jno. Hart, Wm. Symes, Tho. Braddy.	G.	6	366	1671 June 14	1200
Alexander	On and near Chesecake path and on Beech Spring of Ware R. adjoining Thos. Colles, Maj[r] John Smith, Mr. Cooke, Mr. Campfield. HR: Winnifred Alfred, Peter Stout, Ann Scott, Ja: Whittaker, Wm. Garland, Agnes Rose, John Seaward, Nicholas Harper, Peter Loyd, Jeff Bewston, Jno. Adams, Jno. Skinner, Tho. Stroud, John Ashby, Mary Fry, James Trott.	G.	6	60	1672 Nov. 13	704
NEEDLES John	Near Horne Harbour adjoining Mrs. Morryson. HR: John Needles, John Wiseman, Joane Curle, Abbalto a Negro, John Cooke, Eliza his wife, John Cooke his sonn. Land due for last right.	M.	3	190	1652 March 10	300
NETLES..NETTLES Robert	PETSOE P. See Brookin. & William Brookin	G.	8	193	1691 Oct. 20	270
NEVELLS..NEVELL..NEVILL John, Infant	KINGSTON P. On Easterne Riverside adjoining Dunken Bohannan, Richd. Cary, Jno. Armestead. Purchased by Dunken Bohannan of Mr. Armestead and sold to the father of infant John "now due as sonne & heire of his dece'd father".	M.	6	549	1674/5 March 6	100
NEVETT Hugh	"At a fork of a branch issueing from the head of a white marsh creek,... into the head of Dividing Crk. and down the same...& over the Blackwater & the white Marsh Creek". 940 acs. purchased of Geo. Curtis Feb. 16, 1668, 230 acs. residue. HR: 1 Negroe, Robert Ballard, Martha Brentfar, Ann Hartwell, Jonath King.	M.	6	383	1671 Oct. 6	1170
NEWMAN William	One mile below Oliver Green beginning by a swamp that runs by Mr. Cooks land. Renewed in Mr. Peter Knights name 1662. HR: Robert Davis, Wm. Jenkins, Jno. Foster, Daniel ___, James Fisher, Tho.Jones, Adam Church, John Turbis.	G.	4	157	1657 April 20	400
NORMAN William	Adjoining Thomas Amies, "Rich[d] Credendines [Crittendin?] line now John Kellies line". Due by two several purchases & deeds from Roger Shacke[l]ford and Rich. Holloway.	G.	6	666	1678 Nov. 20	177½
NORMANSELL Richard	On the W side of Eastermost R. in Mockjack Bay adjoining John White & Wm.Holder. 150 acs. by patent 1651, residue 300 acs.	M.	3	14	1652 Nov. 28	450
NORRINGTON..NORTHINGTON Samuel	PETSOE P. ".. in right of his wife Hannah" on E side of Poropotank Crk. 120 acs. granted Oliver Greene 1653 who assigned to Edward Corderoy who sold to Wm. Corderoy & by Wm. Corderoy given unto Jno. Corderoy son of s[d] Edward. 200 acs. called Tapses neck part of a grant to Samuel Sallis & Robert Taliaferoe 1652 who sold to Taps who sold Richard Crowshaw who sold to William & Edward Corderoy & by "oath of s[d] William fell to Edward as survivor & by oath of Edward	G.	8	142	1691 April 28	540

NAMES	DESCRIPTION	CO.	BK.	Pg.	DATE	ACRES
NORRINGTON etc. (Continued) Samuel	PETSOE P. descended to John Corderoy as son & heire of Edward & Jno. Corderoy upon contract of marriage with Hannah Jones did by deed...dated Oct. 20, 1682 convey the said lands unto her and her heires as relict of the said Corderoy". Residue 220 acs. HR: Samll. Nichols, Jon. Staples, Barbary Rewman, Jno. Cosby.	G.	8	142	1691 April 28	540
OBERT..	See Hobart.	G.?	1(2)	827	1642	650
OKEHAM..OAKHAM..OAKUM John	On N side of York R. and E side of Poropotank adjoining Mr. Jarnew and Wm. Ginseyes and Mr. Pate. Granted Jno. Pate 1662 and deserted. HR: Wm. Crone, Ant. Jones, Ralph Lenor, Timothy Flips.	G.	5	595	1666 March 22	200
PALIN Henry & John Swingleton [Singleton?]	Lying on the E side of a run at the head of Ware R. adjoining John Walker. HR: Rebecca Browne, Thomas Lee, Thomas Fry, Rich. Reynolls, James Willimott, Richard Buckcocke.	G.	3	137	1652 Dec. 6	300
PALLISSER..PALLISER..PALLISTER..PALISTER Thomas	KINGSTON P. On the S side of the Pyanketank R. beginning at the head of a divident formerly belonging to Gilbert Metcalf dece'd and adjoining George Curtis, Coll: Kemp, John Waters and Mr. William Elliott dece'd to a "great path upon the Ridge" and to Coll: John Armestead's land. HR: Nine persons of a certificate granted Mr. Palliser by Mr. Ed. Chilton dated 9br 1684 was made use of to this patent.	M.	7	623	1687 Oct. 21	421
PERROTT..PARROTT..PARRETT..PARROT Lawrence Perrott	KINGSTON P. Adjoining Coll: Rich. Dudley, Capt. Armestead and Wm. Beard. HR: Tho. Jones, Tho. Browne, Richd. Byronton.	M.	6	660	1678 Sept. 26	137
Lawrence Perrot	KINGSTON P. Adjoining Gwynns Ridge, to Coll: John Armestead, to Mr. Roberts "by the Pease patch" to Coll: Richard Dudley. 137 acs. granted 1678, residue 203 acs. HR: Jno. Acorne, Abraham Buckley, Edwd. Davies, James Bradick, Jno. Williams.	M.	8	98	1690 Oct. 23	340
Michael Parrott	KINGSTONE P. Adjoining Lawrence Parrott, Capt. Todd, Capt. Knowles, Capt. Wm. Armistead. HR: Robert Flecher, Gibeon Jones, Tho. Bayly.	M.	9	615	1704 Oct. 20	110
Richard Parrett	KINGSTONE P. Beginning at a corner gum of Capt. Ambrose Dudley at the S end of Chestnut ridge & adjoining Lawr. Parrett, George Burgis [Burgh] and Charles Jones. HR: Richard Williams.	M.	10	127	1714 June 16	43
PATE Richard & Wingfield Webb	On the N side of the York R. & the Eastermost head branch of the Poropotank River. HR: Richard Pate twice, John Kedate, Wm. Beate, Thomas Steevens, Wm. Harrison, Winnifred Webb 3 times, Wm. Bragg, Chris. Gallinson, Alice Jones, Andrew Sackhill, Joseph Amber, John Leviston, Isaac Richardson, Robert Myles, Sen'r, Robert Myles	G.	2	271	1650	1141

NAMES	DESCRIPTION	CO.	BK.	Pg.	DATE	ACRES
PATE (Continued) Richard	Jun'r, Barbery Myles, Kath. Myles, Jane Perkins, Edw. Madison, Tho. Perkins, Rose Allen, Wm. Lamb, land due for last name.	G.	2	271	1650 Dec. 12	1141
John	On N side of York R. and E side of Poropotank adjoining land formerly Mr. Jarnew's, W on Wm. Ginsies, S'ly and N'ly on his own land. Granted Michaell Grafton 1658 and deserted. HR: Jno. Mobbs, Geo. Ceely, Henry Chitwood, Fra. Michaell.	G.	5	377	1662 Dec. 31	200
John	Same description as above but with the following: Granted March 27, 1661. HR: Jno. King, Eliz. White, Mary Bates, George Steines.	G.	5	594	1662 Dec. 31	200
John	On a branch of Ware R. running W'ly to a branch by Robinhoods Well. Granted to Mordecay Cooke 1662 and deserted. HR: Walter Bradley, Wm. Farmer, Susan Tine, Mary Groome, Timothy Fine, Anthony West.	G.	5	594	1665/6 March 22	300
Thomas, Col°:	Same description as for 200 acs. 1662 Formerly granted John Pate 1662 & by him deserted then granted John Okeham 1665/6 & by him deserted.	G.	6	665	1678 Oct. 10	200
PEACH William	WARE P. In the branches at the head of Ware R. adjoining Regault Plantacon & a branch neare Thos. Purnells plantacon and neare Mr. Toliferoes quarter. 300 acs. granted Capt. Thomas Breman, 1653, who sold Mr. Tho: Peach father of William the "sonne and heire". Residue 270 acs. HR: Margarett Overdell, Sarah Baxter, Robt. Greenaway, Alice Bradshaw, Eliz. Banckes, Hen. Gibbs.	G.	6	277	1669 May 7	570
PEAD..PEADE..PEED John	At Wm. Beartines Crk. on S side of Winter Harbour to the Bay. HR: John Pead, Mary Pead, John Motley.	M.	3	127	1652 Sept. 21	150
George	Former grant to John Pead father of George:	M.	6	231	1671 Sept. 25	150
John, Orphant	KINGSTON P. On S side of Winter Harbour Crk. to the mouthn& along same to Bayside. 150 acs. granted to John Peade father of George 1652, renewed 1671, residue 220 acs. HR: Tho. Powel, Tho. Walker, Wm. Davis, John Beymon, John Corbin.	M.	7	215	1682 Dec. 22	370
PEASLEY..PEASELEY..PEASLY Henry Peaseley	On a swamp running down Cow Crk. in Ware R. beginning at Jos. Grigiries on E side of a branch to the N'most tree of Richd. Duning. HR: Richard Tilson, Richard Rash, John Coates, John Crismass, Wm. Bruneall, Michael Peasly, Henry Peasly, Peter Jemons, Susan Peaseley, Michael Peasley twice, Henry Shoute, James Wonell [?], Stephen Jones, Thomas Savidge.	G.	2	267	1650 Oct. 2	700
PELLOE..BELLOE Mary Pelloe	On N side of Charles R. in Poropotank Crk. NE & ESE adjoining Capt. Wormeley. Granted Capt. William Leigh 1642. Renewed in the "name of said Mary Belloe being daughter & heire of s[d] Leigh".	G.?	3	84	1653 Oct. 8	1000

NAMES	DESCRIPTION	CO.	BK.	Pg.	DATE	ACRES
PEPPETT Temperance, Mrs. & Thomas Purifye	On W'ward side of North R. on S side of a creek dividing ffom the land of Thomas Symons Dece'd, and adjoining Jos. Gregory & Dunning and along the river. HR: Humphrey Lee, John Lee, George Morey, James Andrews, Wm. Andrews, John Elsey, Wm. Chase, Robt. Lynsey, Elizabeth Thompson, Margt. Andrews, Susan Andrewes, Mary Woodmint, Anne Shaw, Wm. Price.	G.	3	108	1652 Sept. 15	760
PERINES..PERINS..PERRINE..PERINT..PERRINGE..PERIN- John Perines	In YORKE CO. On N side of Charles R. NW to Perins Crk. which divides from Ashwell Battin, adjoining NE & E land of Thos. Bell, SE on the river. "Assigned by Abraham Moone assignee of Capt. Nicholas Marteaw who marryed the Exix. of Capt. Robt. Felgate". HR: Capt. Robert Felgate, his son Erasmus, his wife Sibella twice, 3 negroes.	G.?	2	301	1651 April 3	400
PETERS Edmund	At the head of Timber Neck Crk. and adjoining his own land, Capt. Peryes, Wm. Alsopp and near Mr. Lewis Burwell,dec'd. 192 acs. granted Wm. Smoote [Smeete?] 1642.	G.	4	391	1659 March 22	442
PEYTON Robert	"Of the County of Glosester Gent'l:" KINGSTON P. Beginning at the "head of land formerly belonging to Mr. Edmund Welsh...lying on the North side of Blackwater Creek" adjoining NW to Mr. Tabb & N to Humphrey Tomkins dece'd. HR: Augustine Caudle, Thomas Roe, Jeffrey Hardle.	M.	7	233	1682/3 Feb. 28	150
Thomas, Gentleman	On Blackwater Crk. beginning at a corner of Elliott's land at a Persimmon Corner tree of Elliott's & Tomkins' and adjoining land granted to Mr. Robert Peyton for 150 acs., and along Dividing Crk. and a line of Nevetts patent. For the sum of 15 Shillings.	M.	17	524	1738 June 16	110
PICKERING John	KINGSTON P. Adjoining Mr. Marke Warkman dece'd, Joanna Careless lands now Charles Jones his lands, beginning at the Dam side, & adjoining Mr. Wm. William Marlow. 110 acs. purchased of Mr. John Carver. Residue 87½ acs. HR: Math. Woodnott, Charles ___.	M.	6	679	1679 May 1	197½
PLUMER..PLUMMER William Plumer	Two necks of land one on Ducking Pond Crk. and bounded by Mobjack Bay. The other neck NNE, and each containing 200 acs. Part of 4000 acs. granted Capt. Christopher Wormeley in 1639 by Governor & Council, and by Ralph Wormeley, Exec^{tr} assigned to Plummer.	M.	2	256	1650 Oct. 7	400
William Plummer	Escheat land. On the N side of Pepper Crk. formerly granted Nich. Beates [or Boates] who "dying without heirs...orwill".	M.	6	374	1671 Sept. 29	150
Thomas Plumer	KINGSTONE P. On the W branch of Ducking Pond Crk. adjoining the line of Isaac Plumer to the corner of John Davis & Thos. Plumer, to Ralph Armestead's corner to New Point Comfort Crk. now called Dyers Crk. to corner of Bannister & Gundry to Mobjack Bay side N 270 poles to the	M.	10	324	1717 July 15	395

NAMES	DESCRIPTION	CO.	BK.	Pg.	DATE	ACRES
PLUMER..PLUMMER (Continued) Thomas	beginning on Ducking Pond Crk. 200 acs. granted to Wm. Houlder 1650. 100 acs. granted John Gundry 1650.	M.	10	324	1717	395
POOLE..POOL..POLE George &	For description see Richard Farthingale Farthingale, Barringham & Forsith.	G. G.	6 6	52 352	1671 1671	800 800
PORE..POORE..POOR Edmund	KINGSTON P. Adjoining Richard Long and Philip Hunley. HR: Elizabeth Scroope twice.	M.	6	448	1672 March 18	77
Edward [Edmund?]	KINGSTONE P. Adjoining Marke Foster. HR: Ann Gibbs, Jno. Rogers, Tho.Okeham.	M.	6	536	1674 Sept. 21	150
PORTEUS..PORTEOUS..PORTIES Robert	PETSOE P. Beginning on the E side of Tyndalls Point path being Mr. William Thornton's corner & adjoining Thomas Cooke to the head of Cookes mill dam, down the branch and across same and "by the path that leads between the houses of s[d] Cook & Porteus", SW to the corner of Cook & William Howard, to a branch of Cowpen Neck Crk., to land late belonging to Ralph Wormeley Esq[r], across Porteus Quarter branch & along land late of Ralph Green. 542 acs. granted to Robert Lee 1662 & by several conveyances now to Porteus. 150 acs. Waste land. HR: Tho. Mitchell, John Strange,Edw.Harris.	G.	9	603	1704 April 26	692
POTTER Cuthbert	On the N & S sides of the swamp that divides Lancaster and Gloucester two miles above the horse path "nigh Mattapony path that goeth from the plantation of John Curtis" & adjoining Charles Grymes. 400 acs. on S side of Swamp.	G.?	4	379	1659 June 20	5380
POYNDEXTER..POINDEXTER George & George Tompson	At the head of Eagle Nest Crk. in Milford Haven adjoining Richard Longe and Conglins land to the head of Greene branch. HR: Mary Joanes, Eliz. Depthford, Jno. ___, Alex. Duncombe, Christian Bensley, James Knuckly, 1 Negro.	M.	4	241	1657 March 15	350
PRATT John	Escheat land. Lately owned by William Smith, dece'd. Two lots in Gloucester Town, one N on Gloucester Street W on the great gully No. 79. One E on King Street and N of Gloucester St. No. 80. John Lewis Escheator. For the sum of 2 pounds of Tobacco.	G.	11	17	1719 March 5	1
PRESTON..PRESSON Thomas	"Son of Thomas Preston, Dece'd". On the W side of the Eastermost R. in Mockjack Bay. HR: Wm. Senter, Henry Barrow, Peter Farlin, James Land, John Groves, Richard Neale, Thomas Farnill, John Barber, Walter True, a negro child: by assignment from Thomas Conniers.	M.	3	204	1652 Aug. 2	500
Thomas, Jun'r	On the W'ward side of the Eastermost R. in Mockjack Bay at the head of Chestnutt Crk. to land of Thomas Todd, SW to the Bay & to Repulse Crk. Assigned by Conyer. HR: Henry Subtill, Sabina Davis, Richd. Davis, Thomas Conyer.	M.	3	128	1652 Sept. 28	200
Henry & Thomas	Same location. 500 acs. granted Thomas	M.	3	270	1654	650

NAMES	DESCRIPTION	CO.	BK.	Pg.	DATE	ACRES
PRESTON (Continued) Thomas & Henry	Preston, Aug. 2, 1652. Residue 150 acs. HR: Ed: Lucas, John Beard.	M.	3	270	1654 June 7	650
PRICE..PRISE Arthur	On S side of Peanckatancke R. and adjoining Wm. Hockaday, crossing the mouth of Tankes Cheskeyack.	M.?	1(2)	798	1642 July 10	1000
John, Mr.	WARE P. One quarter mile E of Indian Road. Granted John Benson 1667. Residue 184 acs.	G.	7	451	1685 April 20	550
PRIOR..PRYOR William, Gent.	On the N side of the Charles R. and E side of a great marsh at Hichmans Point. Bound on E with a creek dividing from Jno. Jones and from the small bay of the W branch of this creek it runs ENE 268 poles NNW 466 poles to a hill then SW to Priors Crk. to a marsh & parallel to same to the beginning. HR: Himself twice, his wife, John Perrin, Grace ___, 5 Negroes, Joane Eartes, Richard Errington, Gregory Bass, Michaell Sanders, Wm. Thorneton, Tho. Kingswell, Alex. Wike, Tho. Gumer [?], John Rutter, Wm. Johnson, Henry Goodgaine, Thomas Jervis, Robert Kingsbury, Wm. James, John Wood, Edward Braydon.	G.	1(2)	802	1642 Aug. 10	1300
Robert	WARE P. At the head of a branch of Craney Crk. adjoining Mr. Regault, X'pr Greenaway, Thomas Wisdome, 92 acs. granted Thos. Jefferson 1668, by him deserted & not seated since granted to Robert Collis 1688 who assigned to Robert Prior. Residue 217 acs. HR: Jno. Savory, Richd. Right, Phillip Macaskin [?], Mary Lowry, 3 negroes.	G.	8	16	1689 Oct. 20	309
Robert	Escheat land. On N side of Craney Crk. Swamp formerly granted Robert Jefferson. Mr. Wm. Todd D.E.	G.	8	248	1693 April 29	92
PRITCHARD..PRITCHETT..PRITCHET..PRETCHETT..PRICHETT Walter Pritchard	From Winter Harbour to the Bay adjoining Robert Grigg & Charles Sallace. HR: Rowland Ellis, Tho: Husman, Alice Watkins, Bridges Griffen, Tho. Russell.	M.	3	268	1654 June 6	250
John Pritchett	New Point Comfort Beach & Islands.	M.	83 C.G.	391-2-3-4/	1834	60 7 4½
PROUSE Henry	On the Eastermost R. beginning at a small creek dividing from Roger Leonard. HR: Roger Williams, George Hill, Tho: Hunter, Cownel Luglee.	M.	6	102	1667 Dec. 20	200
PURIFYE..PURFREY Thomas	& Mrs. Temperance Peppett See Peppett for description.	G.	3	108	1652	760
PURNELL..PURNALL Thomas	& John Benson See Benson for description.	G.	6	211	1668	950
PURSELL..PURCELL Morgan	Beginning at Buckners Mill pond at Wm. Jones corner to Henry Hughes corner & along Whites spring branch.	G.	55 C.G.	227	1805 April 19	132
PUTNAM..PUTTNAM..PUTTMAN Thomas	On branches of Milford Haven adjoining Richard Long, John Guyton, John Shapley. Resurvey of patent of 1662.	M.	6	494	1673 Oct. 23	333
RAMSEY Bartholomew	& Lambert Moore For description see Lambert Moore.	G.	6	429	1672 Oct. 8	350

NAMES	DESCRIPTION	CO.	BK.	Pg.	DATE	ACRES
RANSON..RANSONE..RANSOM..RANSOME Peter Ranson	On the Eastward side of North R. in Mockjack Bay, beginning on a small creek dividing from Richard Dudley to Isle of Wight Creek.	M.	3	108	1652 Sept. 2	1100
Peter Ranson	On North R. in Mockjack Bay at Isle of Wight Crk. & & to a creek dividing from Richard Dudley. Formerly granted Edmund Dawber. [Renewal and resurvey of above]	M.	3	22	1653 June 9	1100
James & George	"sonns of Peter Ranson dece'd" On North R. in Mockjack Bay at Isle of Wight Crk. & parallel to the river unto a creek dividing from land in the possession of Richard Dudley. Granted Peter Ranson June 9, 1653 and given by will to above named sonns.	M.	5	320	1663 Feb. 10	1100
James Ransome	On the E side of North R. at a small creek & running N to the land of Capt. Richard Dudley. HR: Wm. Sanders, Anne Dutton, Anne Gwyn, Tho. Bidell, Mary Lename, Theo. Pendesey.	M.	6	103	1667 Dec. 20	300
James Ransone, Coll^{o}:	KINGSTONE P. Adjoining Capt. Ambrose Dudley by Danl: Gwins plantation. Paid Mr. Auditor Byrd for one right.	M.	9	601	1704 April 26	40
RAWLINGS..RAWLINS Edward	On North R. & Mockjack Bay at a creek dividing from George Levitt to land of Thomas Todd. Part of 2400 acs. grant to Wm. Daines, who assigned to Rawlings.	G.	5	510	1665 Oct. 20	164
RAY Thomas	On the N branch of the Severne R. adjoining Roger Symmons and Thomas Williams & down the S branch of the Severne R. HR: Thomas Ray & his Wife, William Scott, John Barnes, Darby Ray, John May.	G.	1(2)	832	1642 Oct. 13	300
READ..READE..REED George Read, Gent.	On S side of Peanketanke R. & W side of Chiskyake Crk. at the mouth, running by creek and branch 650 poles SW, 520 poles NW, 480 poles NE to the river, down the river 780 poles SE. HR: Capt. Nich. Martin, Mrs. Jane Martin, Jane Bartlett, Eliza. Martin, Geo. Brookes, Eliza. Sharpless, Robt. Brown, Robt. Awly, John Felton, Wm. Galipin, John Broach, Ann Lockley, Charles Justion, Roger Leamin, John Fryer, Richd. Haward, Jno. Jenerles, John Corassue, Walter Pitchfork, Wm. Richard, John York, Peter Ford, Ann Hilton, John Shirt, Wassett Reyner & Jone his wife, Frances Compton, Mr. George Read, Sackford Brewster, one negro.	M.?G.?	-2	165	1648 Nov. 2	2000
John Read	WARE PARISH [First mention and second parish] By the main branch of Cow Creek adjoining land Read now lives on and to land of Anthony Gregorie & Francis Camfield. HR: Robt. Edge, Wm. Rand, Tho. West.	G.	5	280	1662 March 18	145
John Read	On W side of Cow Crk. adjoining Richard Cox, his own land and "Anthony Gregory sonne of Joseph Gregory" & Thomas Prices land purchased of John Benson & Thomas Purnell. Part of 800 acs.granted Richard Cox 1657 "who sould s^{d} Read".	G.	5	586	1666 March 26	300
John Reed	At the head of Cow Crk. [Same description	G.	6	331	1670	385

NAMES	DESCRIPTION	CO.	BK.	Pg.	DATE	ACRES
READ..READE..REED (Continued) John Reed	as above] 300 acs. purchased of Richard Cox. Residue 85 acs.	G.	6	331	1670 Oct. 19	385
Thomas Reade, Mr.	Escheat land formerly belonging to Edward Maise. Beginning near Edward Stubblefield's tobacco ground "from where his dwelling house Chimney funnel bears NE": distant from s^d dwelling house 26 poles to Whilocks' [Whitlock?] (now Stubblefields) spring & adjoining Wm. Debnam along Chismans line. Deeded to Edw. Maise by James Whitlock & Dorothy his wife dated June 5, 1691 "sayed to be granted to Thomas Russel [willed to Thomas Reade." Richard Johnson late Escheator. Price: 2 pounds of Tobacco per acre.	G.	10	173	1714 June 16	47
REGAULT..RIGAULT..REGALT Christopher Regault	On the E side of Craney Crk. of Ware R. on the head of Breemans Neck & adjoining Mr. Breeman. HR: Christopher Regault, William Frost, Symon Parrett, Joan Bugg, Wm. Woodars, John Brashere, Thomas Studdell, his wife and child, William Risbixt [Risby?] & his wife, William Todd.	G.	3	318	1654 March 6	600
Christopher Rigault	On NE side of Crane Neck Crk. adjoining Mr. Bew, Mr. Peach and his own land. 600 acs. by grant in 1654. Residue 170 acs. HR: Lambe & Maria negros, John Twyney, John Kelly.	G.	6	142	1668 April 10	770
RENN Nicholas	On the N side of York R. adjoining Mr. Fossaker. HR: Math. Fenney, Wm. Tolman.	G.	6	327	1664 Feb. 3	100
RENSHAW..WRENSHAW..WRENTSHAW Richard	On Bryre Branch of Ware R. adjoining unto Mrs. Cooks land. HR: Jon Pickering, Wm. Jones, Jno. Isbell, Jno. Darby, Alice Wellmay, Richd. Dirbishire.	G.	5	503	1664 March 23	300
REYNOLDS..REYNOLLS Cornehouse	Adjoining Mrs. Williams & X'topher Abbotts by the road path. HR: Saml. Franke, Mary Goden, Danl. How, Eliz. Vose.	G.	6	264	1669 Oct. 15	180
James	PETSOE P. Adjoining land of Walter Cant Sonn of David Cant Dece'd formerly called Knoxes land and also adjoining Tho. Dawkins, Saml. Partridge and along Dragon Swamp Runn. HR: Ja: Clarke, Robt. Dyer, Robt. Cannon.	G.	6	601	1675/6 March 11	140
RICE Thomas	KINGSTONE P. Adjoining land belonging to Mr. John Man, Edward Boram and Mark Thomas and by a path. HR: Edward Jenkins.	M.	8	261	1693 April 29	35
RICHARDS Richard, Mr.	CHARLES RIVER COUNTY. On the N side of the Charles R. NW by W upon Tymber Neck Crk., SW by S upon the said river. HR: Mr. Richard Richards, Eliz. Richards 3 times, Wm. Dorrell, Richard Harbott, Edw. Butcher, Tho. Butcher, Hen. Tompson, Jon. Mainson, Math. Isum, Jos. Winkeford, Ann Biker, Francis Moold, Tho. Hughes, Wm. Watkins, Tho. Dadson, Jane Evans, Henry Raye, Tho. Peeters.	G.	1(2)	883	1643 Aug. 2	1000
RICHERDSON	On N side of the Northermost Branch of	G.	1(2)	810	1642	200

NAMES	DESCRIPTION	CO.	BK.	Pg.	DATE	ACRES
RICHERDSON (Continued) John & James White	the Severne R. where Stillwells land ends & running NNW to the head of the Severne R.	G.	1(2)	810	1642 Aug. 15	200
RICHESON..RICHARDSON Peter Richeson & James Roe	GLOSTER COUNTY. [This is the earliest mention of the County of Gloucester that has been found] Upon the N side of York R. "lyeing between Rosewell Crk. SE and by S till it come to the land of Mr. Lewis Burwell" and adjoining another devident of Capt. Stephen Gill. 1150 acs. granted Stephen Gill April 30, 1649 and by him assigned to Roe, and the moiety thereof, by Roe, assigned to Richeson. Residue 350 acs.	G.	2	320	1651 May 21	1500
Peter Richardson	"& the heirs of James Roe". Beginning "in a plantation seated by Mr. Sawyer, dece'd" to the White Marsh, adjoining Mr. Burwell, Col°: Francis Willis, Wm. Debnam, to the high lands to "path from the mill to the Gleab land" to branch that runs to Mr. Chesemans Land. Formerly granted to Mr. Stephen Gill 1649.	G.	6	187	1672/3 March 17	1500
Isaac Richeson	LANCASTER COUNTY ALIAS GLOSTER. On the Poropotank adjoining Samuel Sallis, John Day on the head branches of Atapotomoyes. HR: Isaac Richeson, Elizabeth Parker, Eliz. Wells, Wm. Brown, John James, 1 negro, from Col. Gwynns Certificate.	G.	3	128	1652 Oct. 10	300
	Renewal		4	523	1661	
RIGBY..RIGBIE..RIGBEE..RUGBY..RUGGBYE Peter	In Milford Haven beginning at Rigby Point & running SSW parallell to Lilleys Crk. Due by assignment from John Story & Thomas Jolly of their rights. HR: John Harper, Tho. & Christopher Adkinson, Robert Hopkins, James Winders, John Pollard, Geo. Packman, John Batho, Eliz. Starr.	M.	1(2)	811	1642 Aug. 16	450
RIPLEY Richard	At the head of a branch in Winter Harhour neare New Point Comfort & running to the Bay. Rights assigned from Mr. John Walker. HR: Mr. John Walker twice, Josias Lackly, Katherine ___, Danll. Tacker, John Singleton, Elizabeth Elderwell, John Golding.	M.	2	357	1651 Jan. 29	400
ROANE..ROAN..RONE Charles	On Peancketank [Poropotank?] Swamp adjoining Col. Rich. Lee and the Rappahannock Road Path. HR: Edwd. Fox, Jno. Browne, Tho. Jordan, Eliza. Hayes.	G.	5	428	1664 Sept. 13	200
Charles	On the branches of Peanketanke R. adjoining Coll: Warner.	G.	5	597	1665	100
	Resurvey 1668		6	235	Dec. 6	150
Charles	At the head of the Peanketank R. on a swamp adjoining Gills land to road path across the swamp & adjoining Mr. Partridge.	G.	6	235	1668 Dec. 26	751
Charles	On branches of Dragon Swamp adjoining land "supposed to belong to Coll: Lees children" and adjoining Jno. Wittmores. HR: Jno. Jones, Wm. Kellam.	G.	6	470	1673 Oct. 20	100
Charles	On Dragon Swamp adjoining John Cant, Thos. Dawkins, James ___, Rich. Holloway Roger Shackelford, John Davies, & Mr. John Carver. Formerly lands of Saml.	G.	7	2	______	700

NAMES	DESCRIPTION	CO.	BK.	Pg.	DATE	ACRES
ROANE..ROAN (Continued) Charles	Patridges and James Reynolds. Resurvey due to misunderstanding of Dawkins.	G.	7	2	———	700
			7	83	1681	700
Charles	Part in New Kent. Resurvey of land. 500 acs formerly bought by Roane of Edward Row & Samuel Partridge, being part of a greater patent to Coll: Cuthbert Potter in 1659. 297 acs. now taken up. Beginning on a "branch called Hanks Folly in sight of Charles Roane & Hanks his old Plantacon" along Dragon Swamp Run adjoining George Mortin & John Kelley. HR: Wm. Walton, Howell Davis, David Williams, Phillip Aldman, Jane Whitehaire, James Squires.	G.	7	684	1688 Oct. 20	797
Charles	PETTSOE P. Adjoining his own land and W. Brooking. HR: Robt. Croper, Jno. Cramp, Wm. Oakley, Mary Willoe.	G.	8	192	1691 Oct. 20	164
Charles	PETTSOE P. On the N side and near the head of Coles Branch of the Poropotank Crk. at Coll: Richard Lees corner NE to the Maine Road that leads to Dragon bridge & along the road to Wm. Brookins Land. HR: Wm. Shaw, Judeth Butler, Mary Grant, John Hanks, 2 Negroes.	G.	8	192	1691 Oct. 20	278
ROBERTS William	On the N side of York R. at the mouth of Jones Crk. & NW side, adjoining Edw. West and E upon a White Marsh.	G.	3	160	1652 Nov. 29	200
William	On W side of a swamp at the head of Crany Crk. adjoining Jeffrey Bew. Granted Wm. Corderoy 1657 who assigned to Roberts.	G.	4	533	1661 Nov. 20	150
	Renewal		4	533	1661 Nov. 27	200
William	On North R. in Mobjack Bay adjoining Richard Bayly & Mr. Debnam. HR: John Boteley, Edward Williams, Anthony Sharpeley.	G.	6	102	1667 Dec. 20	170
ROBINS..ROBBINS John	In Mockjack Baye beginning at the mouth of Sedgy Crk. extending to the mouth of Ware R. & up the Severne to Lucas his creek. 1000 by assignment from Capt. Wm. Brocas to whom Argoll Yeardly assigned & 1000 acs. for transfer of 20 persons. HR: Wm. Jones, David Raddish, Tho. Horner, Jno. Ondale, James Kenney, Francis Huett, Peter Roberts, Richard Love, Henry Gillingham, Jane Harris, Dyan Holleney, Lionel Holley, Willi. Loftis, Robert Davis, Samll. Creame, Tho. Jenkins, Abraham Harmata, Thomas Pinhill, Robert Baskerville, George Brocas.	G.	1(2)	833	1642 Oct. 12	2000.
	Renewal:		2	43	1645	2000
John & Capt. Augustine Warner	On N side of Severne R. in Mockjack Bay beginning at the mouth of Lutus Crk. along Warner's and his own line and down Severn R. HR: Wm. Thomas, John Williams, Richard Williams, Mary Smith, John Mockay, Daniel Frissell Sen'r, Dan Frissell Jun'r.	G.	3	317	1654 March 14	594
ROE..ROWE..ROW James Roe & Peter Richeson	GLOUCESTER COUNTY [Earliest mention] For description see Richeson.	G.	2	320	1651 May 21	1500

NAMES	DESCRIPTION	CO.	BK.	Pg.	DATE	ACRES
ROE..ROWE..ROW (Continued) James	"heirs of James Roe" & Peter Richeson. See Richeson for description.	G.	6	187	1672/3 March 17	1500
Edward	Adjoining Lee & Roe lands near a corner supposed to be formerly Coll: Lees' and adjoining Divident s[d] Roe lives upon. HR: Jno. Smart [?], Wm. Stamp, Mary Curtis, Francis Black, Edward Mason, Symon Ash, Elizabeth Hubberd, Thomas Jenkins.	G.	5	47	1664 May 27	375
ROSS John	Adjoining the orphants of Wm. Cooke and lands of Joseph Coleman and Wm.Fleming.	G.	9	146	1698 April 26	35
ROYSTON..ROYSTONE..ROYSTOANE Thomas, Mr.	Adjoining Lt. Col. Warner by Chesecake path & branch. HR: Edward Young, John Ferby, Tho. Fowler, Wm. Johnson, Tho. Carew, Fra.Fleet.	G.	5	84	1662 March 18	270
Thomas	PETSOE P. At a corner of David Monorgan & adjoining s[d] Roystons plantacon, on Bryory Branch of Ware R. swamp to Rappa. Road path. HR: Anthony Ashley, Robt. Frey, Jno. Franklyn, Jno. Fryer, Peter Craven, Francis Cole, Nich. Thompson, Francis George, Steph. Tifle, Humphrey Goodman, Tho. Stephens, Edward Greene.	G.	6	145	1667 Feb. 6	608
Thomas & John Buckner.	See Buckner for description	G.	6	240	1669	1000
Thomas Roystone	PETTSOE P. Adjoining Coll: Augustine Warner dece'd, Wm. Collaine, along Rappahannock Path & Road, adjoining John Wheystoane, Coll: John Pate, dece'd, Lorraine, Jeremy Darvell by a path to Mr. Roystoanes. 270 acs. granted 1662; 608 acs. granted 1667; 500 acs. by patent to Roystoane & Buckner. Residue 238 acs. HR: 5 negroes.	G.	8	272	1693 April 29	1616
RYLAND Thomas	KINGSTONE P. Adjoining Caleb Holder, Major Robert Bristowe & his own land. HR: Alice Ryland, Tho. Rush,Rich.Lake.	M.	6	453	1673 May 23	120
Thomas	KINGSTONE P. Adjoining his own land and Caleb Holder & Major Bristow. HR: Mary Higgins, Wm. Burdon, Geo. Thacker, Jno. Wood, Eliza. Holder	M.	6	679	1679 May 1	240
SAIES	WARE P. Alice & Sarah Butler. See Butler.	G.	10	452	1719	220
SALLATE..SALLACE..SALLIS..SALLET..SALLY..SOLLACE..SOLLIS Samuel Sallate & Robert Troliver	GLOSTER COUNTY. 200 acs. on the SE side of Poropotank adjoining land of Oliver Green. 600 acs. adjoining Isaac Richeson.	G.	2	359	1651 Feb. 12	800
Samuel Sollace & Robert Troliver	On Poropotank. [Same description as above] 800 acs. granted in 1651, residue 100 acs. HR: John Mattro, William Lewis.	G.	3	341	1655 March 26	900
Samuel Sollace	On SE side of Poropotank on a swamp adjoining Isaac Richeson & John Day.302 acs. granted Wm. Ginsey in 1652. Residue 50 acs. HR: Mary Land.	G.	3	342	1655 March 26	352
Samuel Sollis & Robert Tolliver	Renewal of patent of March 26, 1655	G.	4	534	1661 Nov. 27	900
Samuel Sollis	"Son of Samuel Sollis dece'd" [Same description as patent of March 26, 1655] "Now due the above named as	G.	4	536	1661 Nov. 27	352

NAMES	DESCRIPTION	CO.	BK.	Pg.	DATE	ACRES
SALLATE..SOLLIS etc. Samuel Sollis	(Continued) as son & heir". [Patent for 900 acs. March 26, 1655, renewed in Tolliver's name Dec. 1, 1662]	G.	4	536	1661 Nov. 27	352
SANDERSON John	On a branch of Ware R. adjoining Mrs. Cooke. HR: Rowland Prince, Wm. Free, Alexander Smith, Richard Badger, Jno. Smith, Joane Sandwicke.	G.	6	104	1667 Dec. 20	300
SAWYER William	Escheat land. Late in the possession of Thomas Hughes, dece'd. Richard Johnson, Esq., Escheator, Peter Beverley, Deputy.	G.	9	422	1701 Oct. 24	400
SAY..SAYES..SAIES Thomas Say	On Mockjack Bay at a point called Sayes Point that faces easterly down the bay, to Wrights Crk. N to the head of Curtis Branch, down the creek branch & down Blackwater Crk. Bounded on the S side with the river. 100 acs. assigned from Rendall. HR: Thomas Say, Henry Norman, Mathew Burras, Jon. Bullard, Charles Bater.	M.	1(2)	808	1642 Aug. 20	350
SEATONNE..SEATON..SETON George Seatonne	"...lying on the head of 1000 acs. formerly known by the name of Coll: Hugh Gwynns Devid't of Land in the maine upon the Southside of peanketank River" and adjoining a tract Surveyed for Coll: Humphrey Higgenson. 200 acs. formerly granted to Geo. Thompson 1653; assigned by Thompson to Edward Jelfee [?] who assigned to Seatonne May 2, 1659. 100 acs. sold by Oliver Rolfe to said Jelfee 1653 & assigned to Seatonne. Beginning at the first branch of old mans creek at Peanketank adjoining Wm. Lewis.	M.	6	139	1668 Aug. 16	300
SEWELL..SEAWELL Thomas Sewell	ABBINGTON P. Adjoining Danll. Langham, Robt. Coleman, Tho: and Jeffry Graves & Capt. Lawrence Smith, "along the edge of the high lands & the Roade".	G.	6	560	1675 June 15	150
SHACKELFORD..SHACKLEFORD Roger Shackelford	At a Chestnut on Mattapony old path in Spring Branch, up Spring Valley to Edward Parkers path side to Mr. Partridges line, to back line of Roger Shackelfords now plantation & adjoining Wm. Norman, & Thomas Amies. Due by "two severall purchases and...deed of sale from Mr. Samuel Patridge & Thomas Hancks now both deceased".	G.	6	665	1678 Nov. 20	313
SHAPLEY..SHIPLEY..SHAPLE John Shapley	In the narrows of Milford Haven at a small creek dividing from Mr. English. 200 acs. formerly granted to George Cabell who assigned to Mr. Abraham English who assigned to Shapley. Residue 150 acs. HR: John Pratt, Wm. Thomas, Antho. Perin.	M.	6	191	1668 Oct. 1	350
Mary Shipley & Sara Long	"Daughters of Abraham English dece'd" According to the ancient bounds of a grant to Abraham English lately found to be escheat. Capt. Phill. Ludwell D. E.	M.	6	250	1669 July 4	350
Richard Shapley	"...son of John & Mary Shapley" In Milford Haven adjoining Richard Long, Guy Knight. Part of a grant to Abraham English "and by his last will...bequeathed to his daughter Mary Shapley...now due to the said Richd. Shapley her sonne by	M.	6	475	1673 Oct. 23	130

NAMES	DESCRIPTION	CO.	BK.	Pg.	DATE	ACRES
SHAPLEY..SHIPLEY (Continued) Richard Shapley	guift...Ratified...surveyed by Robert Beverley...by consent...and in the presence of Rich. Long and Mary Shapley...and divers witnesses".	M.	6	475	1673 Oct. 23	130
John Shapley	In the narrows of Milford Haven at Hollowing Point & Third Neck Creek along the waterside of the Thoroughfare from Mobjack [?] Bay to Pianketank R., on a creek dividing from Peter Arrundell adjoining John Griton [Guyton?], Tho.Putnam, Guy Knight, Mr. English's creek side (alias Third Neck Creek). 350 acs. formerly granted in 1668. Residue 80 acs. HR: James Forland, Roger Pierce.	M.	6	476	1673 Oct. 23	430
SIMPSON Edward	300 acs. adjoining his own land, Ashwell Batten and Leo. Chamberlaine on Pepetico Creek. HR: George Atkins, Robert Weekes, Wm. Wragg, John Powell, Ja: Muskatine, Robert Ward, James Wilson, Robert Foster, Fra. Wright, William Short, James Davis, Robert Lamb.	G.?	3	320	1654 Dec. 4	600
SINGLETON..SWINGLETON Henry Singleton	On the E side of Eastermost R. in Mockjack Bay beginning at Mr. Hamptons land. HR: John Hilliard, Mark Nethrock, Thomas Newman, Susanna his wife, Anne Newman, Susan Newman.	M.	2	312	1651 [?]	320
Henry	On the E side of the Eastermost R. at Ripleys corner to river and up same N'ward 200 poles. Grant to Wm. Leathermore & John Thomas in 1652.	M.	4	532	1661 Nov. 20	400
Henry	Near the mouth of the Eastermost R. adjoining his other dividend of land. granted Thomas Morgan who sold to Singleton Oct. 25, 1660.	M.	6	103	1667 Dec. 20	300
Henry	Lying between "the pattent of his Brother Samuell Singleton" and his own land. Beginning on the side of Mobjack Bay & running E & S adjoining Robert Gallis [Callis? Cully?] Plantacon, Wm. Morgan, John Martin, Walter Morgan. HR: Edward Davis, Tho. Lewis, Mathew Brown, Anne Mathews.	M.	7	588	1687 Oct. 21	155
John Swingleton	& Henry Palin. See Palin for description.	G.	3	137	1652	300
SKELTON William	Beginning at Tho: Dawkins near John Whittamores plantation adjoining Richard Holloway, Tho: Dawkins line "formerly called Knoxes Land now Walter Kants [Cant?]". Surveyed for Coll: Augustine Warner, dece'd, running to the great road, to James Reynalds and Edward Roes old Line. Being part of a great divident, & deeded to Skelton by "Thomas Dawkins & Anne his wife bearing date the 15th day of October 1673." Surveyed by Robert Beverley in the presence of Tho. Dawkins, Charles Roane, Edwd. Waller & other neighbors.	G.	7	82	1681 April 23	150
SMART William	In Winter Harbour adjoining John Smith. Granted Thomas Todd 1652, assigned to	M.	4	532	1661 Nov. 20	450

NAMES	DESCRIPTION	CO.	BK.	Pg.	DATE	ACRES
SMART (Continued) William	Smart by Todd. Renewal	M.	4 4	532 641	1661 1661	450
SMEETE..SMOOT..[SWEETE?] William	YORK COUNTY. Near the head of Tymber Neck Crk. on N side of Charles R. near land of Mr. Minifee.	G.	1(2)	874	1642 Feb. 4	400
SMITH..SMYTH..[SMITHER?] John	Lying within Horn Harbour Crk. butting SE on the creek and adjoining Wm. Holder. HR: Thomas Purner Senr., Dorothy his wife, Tho. Purner Junr., Wm. Larkin, Arthur Cannanna, Margaret Morton.	M.	2	227	1650 Aug. 13	300
John	On Horne Harbour adjoining S side of his former divident. HR: Christopher Wallis, John Nicholls, William Bandes.	M.	3	117	1652 Dec. 8	150
John, Capt.	Upon the branches of Milford Haven, adjoining Richard Long. Granted Thomas Morris 1655 who assigned to James Foster who assigned to Smith.	M.	4	82	1656 Oct. 8	400
John, Capt.	On a small creek running W'ly down the Poropotank to the river, SE to little Poropotank Crk. E E up same to the NE side of marsh and NNW by marsh. HR: Thomas Lacy, George Lacy, Jno. Drewe, Tho. Berry, Richard Langly, Wm. Pritchett, Katherine Rock, Margarett Watten, Jane Hutchison, John Readman, Henry Watton.	G.	4	184	1657 Oct. 14	500
John, Major	Marsh and land NW to the little Poropotank at a point SE to Purton Bay adjoining land on which he lives & down the creek to the river. HR: Peter Goffe, Martha Stanford, Wm. Steward, Susan Hart, An Jones, Mary Filmore, Thomas Norton, Jno. Toms, Arthur Upshott, Wm. Stevens.	G.	5	575	1665/6 Feb. 8	500
John, Major	Nigh the head of Poropotank parallel and adjoining Purton Devid't over Goodluck Branch to Totopotomoyes swamp and adjoining Mr. Peter Knight. 300 acs. formerly granted Mrs. Anna Bernard, July 2, 1652. Residue 200 acs. HR: Francis Bernard, Mary Mynns, John Reeves, Ehas a Frenchman.	G.	6	151	1665 April 1	500
John, Hon[ble], Esq[r]	ABINGTON P. Adjoining land of Robert Barlow S along York Rode to Mr. Boswells line & adjoining Mr. Banister and Smiths own land. For & in consideration of the sum of five shillings.	G.	10	6	1711 April 26	51
John, Esq[r] of Purton & John Lewis & John Washington	See Lewis for description.	G.	10	13	1711	46½
Joseph	At Poropotank adjoining John King and Bennett & Leechman. Granted Thomas Bell 1656 who sold to Robert Jones who sold to Smith.	G.?	5	437	1664 June 9	134
Lawrence	At the head of a branch to Ware R. & adjoining Lt. Col. John Walker. HR: Geo. Musick, Rob. Cooper, Roger Greene.	G.	4	253	1657 Feb. 11	119
Lawrence	On N branch of the Severne which divides this and the land of Col. Augustine	G.	6	41	1666/7 March 18	807

NAMES	DESCRIPTION	CO.	BK.	Pg.	DATE	ACRES
SMITH (Continued) Lawrence	Warner and adjoining Thomas Graves to Tymber Neck Crk. to Mr. Burwells land and Wm. Rawlings. 80 acs. granted Augustine Warner 1653. 148 acs. granted Warner 1657 who sold to Smith. Residue 579 acs. HR: Tho: Cooke, Geo. Ballentine, Jno. Casmida, Rich. West, Elizabeth Lettsom, Elizab: Pain, Wm. Prickett, Mary Cooke, Rich. Tawber, Fran. Brian, Ann Brown.	G.	6	41	1666/7 March 18	807
Lawrence	Marsh land adjoining land of X'topher Robins on N side of Turtle Poynt to Mockjack Bay side. HR: Wm. Davis, Timothy Sisse, Edward Brookman, Ed. Prease.	G.	6	144	1668 April 20	170
Lawrence	ABINGTON P. Adjoining Wm. Alsop dece'd, Mr. Thomas Graves Sen'r, & his own land to Timber Neck Crk. HR: John Fletcher, Jno. Wintersbottome.	G.	6	240	1668/9 March 15	75
Lawrence	On the branches of Ware R. on "Beech Swamp that issueth into the head of Ware R...near Mr. Cooke's quart'rs...alongst branch known by the name of Robin Hoods Spring." 119 acs. granted Smith in 1657. Residue 600 acs. HR: Edw. Bearitt, Jno. Goss, Nath. Mott, Susanna James, Mary Thwait, Jno. Lee, Jno. Pratt, Wm. Derrick, Peter Spray, Hannah Gold, Jo: Harbinger, Antho. Yates.	G.	6	357	1662 July 22	719
Lawrence, Capt.	ABBINGTON P. Adjoining Colo: Ludlow dece'd, Jno. Banister, Abbott,Coleman & Edw. Foster.	G.	6	550	1674/5 March 6	330
Lawrence, Major	ABBINGTON P. Resurvey: Beginning at a "poynt on the South side of the Severne R. near the head adjoining Coll: Augustine Warner dece'd" and adjoining Mr. Robert Bryan, Vallentyne Layne, Thomas Graves, Abraham Broadley to the dwelling house of Wm. Graves, to Mr. Thomas Graves dece'd, Gillion White, the house of Robert Earbrough, Jerimie Hoult, down Timberneck Crk. swamp to line of Mr. Peters dece'd, to the head of Mr. Richard Bookers land, along Mr. John Moggson line and land of Major Lewis Burwell, on two sides and crossing the Church path & to the Severne Swamp. Renewal of patent for 807 in 1666 & patent for 75 acs 1668. Residue 318 acs. HR: Eliza Long, Robt. Colles, Eliza Day, Tho: Fanch, Rich. Hust [?], Tho: Phypps, Hen: Cluthero.	G.	8	212	1691 Oct. 20	1200
Thomas	On the branches of Milford Haven beginning at Peach Point upon the creek s'ly to Richard Long and NW to another creek. Granted to George Billips in 1653 and assigned to Roger Lennalls who assigned to Smith.	M.	5	647	1666 Aug. 27	100
William	Upon the N side of Horne Harbour Creek. Formerly granted to John Teage & Edward Morgan in 1657, purchased of them by Lieut. William Worleich not seated and now granted Smith. HR: Thomas Graves Howell, John Thomas, John Williams.	M.	10	49	1711 Dec. 19	150

NAMES	DEACRIPTION	CO.	BK.	Pg.	DATE	ACRES
SMITHY..SMITHEY..SMITHER John Smithy	On a branch of Milford Haven beginning at Geo. Billips. [See Thomas Smith, 1666] HR: Elizabeth a maid servant & another maid servant.	M.	3	168	1652 Dec. 6	100
John Smithey	On the S side of Garden Creek. Rights assigned by Lt. Coll. John Walker. HR: Daniel Beaw, Morris White, Cormack Mallry, Teague Flanny, John Mathew,	M.	3	353	1655 July 14	300
	John O Grangenes. Renewal:		4	524	1661	300
John Smither [Smithey?]	Woodland and marsh on the Bayside betwixt the mouth of Garden Creek & the mouth of Winter Harbour, adjoining his own land. HR: Mary Squire, Tom & Betty negroes, Ma: Clinker, Ursula Paine, Hum: Eldridge, Mary Stiles, Geo: Ridley, 3 negroes, Wm. Blenkister, Hen: Williams, Eliz. Tindall, Tho: Combs, Richard Leighton.	M.	7	278	1683 April 16	890
John Smither & Mottrom Wright	On the N side of Winter Harbour along John Degge's line and adjoining Wrights plantacon, James Foster, Wm. Smith to the head of Winter Harbour by the path "that leads to little John Andrews plantacon als. Wrights...to Muddy Run Branch".	M.	7	587	1687 Oct. 21	395
SNAPES William	In Daunceing Valley adjoining Major Richard Lee, Spences lands, Capt. Richard Dudley, by courses to Beach Spring. HR: Thomas Hollins, Arnall Mouse, Anthony Little.	G.	6	514	1674 April 9	110
William	PETSOE P. Bounded round with Coll: John Lewis land, Samuel Clarke and James Dudley. HR: Tho. Wright, John Carpenter.	G.	7	36	1680 April 26	75
William	PETSOE P. Adjoining Mr. Nicholas Smith to the S side and along Spring Branch to the head spring. HR: Simon Brock.	G.	9	57	1696 Oct. 29	29
SNELLING..SNELLINGE John Snellinge	& Major Edward Bromfield [See Brumfield for description]	M.?	4	159	1657	1100
Alexander Snelling	"...sonn of Wm. Snelling dece'd" One and one half miles from North R. adjoining land of Thos. Chapman dece'd, Abraham Iveson. Granted to Wm. Snelling his father Oct. 11, 1659.	M.	6	515	1674 April 8	43
SOUTHGATE John	Treasury Warrant No. 454 exchanged. Land adjoining Benjamin Marrable, William Johnson, John Johnson, Francis Whiting.	G.?	42 (C.G.)	224	1799 March 7	110
SPINKS John	WARE P. Adjoining land of Mr. Cheasman, James Burton, Mr. Hansford and along the road. HR: Peter Gibeons, Ann Cock, Robt. Mc a Cleming, Henry Bayley, Geo. Querrell, Richard Pindar.	G.	10	15	1711 April 28	464
SPRATT Robert	On the head of the Pianketank R. & Kinninhams Crk. Adjoining Philip Grymes, Esq. For the sum of five shillings.	G.?	42	536	1774 July 5	50

NAMES	DESCRIPTION	CO.	BK.	Pg.	DATE	ACRES
STEPHENS Thomas	Escheat land. Formerly granted to Elias Wigmore. Part of a grant of 1050 acs. lying at the head of Clay Bank Crk. adjoining Capt. Gill. Peter Jennings, D. E.	G.	6	426	1672 Oct. 24	175
STARLING..STERLING Peter Starling	On Horne Harbour Crk. towards the head. 150 acs. additional to land formerly taken up. HR: John Munnypenny, Patrick Nash, Toby Butler.	M.	7	288	1683 April 16	300
Anne & Mary Sterling	KINGSTON P. Upon Horne Harbour bounding upon land which formerly belonged to Lt. Col^{o}: Wm. Worlich. Formerly granted to John Man of Gloster in 1662 and not seated. HR: Anne Latemore, Dorothy Love, Mary Gouge, Jane Payle, Eliza. Wand, Mary Harrison, Margt. Swan, Ringing Gardner.	M.	10	56	1711 Dec. 19	400
STILLWELL Nicholas	CHARLES RIVER COUNTY. On the Northermost branch of the Severne R. at Frosbury Crk. near Richard Burtes land, 2 acs. of which is allowed for a path.	G.	1(2)	826	1642 Oct. 8	202
SWEETE..SMEETE..SMOOT	See Smeete.	G.	1(2)	874	1642	400
STUBBINS [STUBBS?] James	At Poropotank in Danseing Valley adjoining Capt. Dudley, George Haynes, & Spencys Land "by Curles path & branch... & Rich Land Swamp...to Mr. Richd. Lee his line". HR: John Nicholas, Tho. Cooper, Jno. Westone, Tho. Goose, Jonas Rice, Wm. Bryan, Tho. Glover, Richd. Davis, Cha. Parson.	G.	6	537	1674 Sept. 21	450
STUBBS..STUBS John	Escheat land. Late in the possession of Christopher Webster. Recorded by Wm. Jones Deputy for Matthew Page,Esq.Escheat^{r}	G.	9	457	1702 April 25	100
John	ABBINGTON P. Adjoining Coll: Augustine Warner dece'd, Mr. Wells & Mr. Wm. Bowling dece'd. HR: John Matey	G.	9	535	1703 April 24	50
John	PETSOE P. Escheat land formerly in possession of Wm. Roberts dece'd, and for which Justophineca Bennitt, Wm. Sawer, John Absalom & Mary his wife obtained Certificate Oct. 1707. Since sold to Stubbs by Certificate 21st of October, 1708. Beginning at the mouth of Jones Crk. up said creek to a white Marsh, crossing Flemings little creek to said Stubbs spring, to York R. and down same S 110 poles to the beginning. 200 acs. granted Wm. Roberts 1661. John Lewis, Esq., Escheator, Thomas Cook, Surveyor.	G.	10	214	1714 June 16	300
STUBBLEFIELD Symon, Jun'r	WARE P. Beginning "by the Road side that leads to the Court house at the head of Wm. Roes Land dece'd...along the Gleabe Land northwest...adjoining Mr. Richard Whitehead", Mr. Thomas Cheeseman E, along land formerly belonging to James Whitlock E & SE. HR: John White, William Brewton, Tho.Brush.	G.	7	637	1688 April 23	188
SWINGLETON..SINGLETON?	John & Henry Palin. See Palin.	G.	3	137	1652	300
SYMONDS..SYMONS..SYMMONS..[SIMMONS?..SYNONS?] Thomas Symonds	By right of a patent formerly patent granted in: At the head of John Terryes & William Larkes land above the head of St.Michaells	G.	1(2)	949	1643 1639	800

NAMES	DESCRIPTION	CO.	BK.	Pg.	DATE	ACRES
SYMONDS etc. (Continued) Thomas Symonds	Crk., bounded on the SW by lands of [Dictoris] Christmas, NW & N to George Worldridge before Graves Crk. to Snare Crk. HR: Dorothy Castle, James Craven, Wm. Meadwell, Richard Hughes, Geo. Smith, Wm. Batts, Robt. Coleman, Tho. Warne, Henry Batts, Robert Auley, Richard Drue, Tho. Andrews, Wm. Blettsoe, Walter Warship, Elinor Deane, Anth. Haynes.	G.	1(2)	949	1643 Oct. 18	800
Thomas Symmons	At the mouth of a small creek of North R.- adjoining Geo. Levett. Assigned from Thomas Kerbye & Joseph Moore. HR: John Edden, Peter Baytes, Ellin Audrey Gilbert Reynolds, William Richards, Joseph Moore, Barbary Chapman.	M.	1(2)	830	1642 Oct. 10	350
Roger Symmons	In the first river of Mockjack Bay called the Severne where the said river divides; this neck of land called the Eagles Nest, and to the Southern branch. HR: Thomas Todd, Richard Cooper, James Sherborne, Robert George, Thomas Sadler.	G.	1(2)	831	1642 Oct. 19	250
TABB Humphrey Toy	Escheat land. Lately owned by Sarah Allaman deceased. Adjoining Mr. Burgess to Baylors line.	M.	24	348	1746 July 25	190
Humphrey Toy	Escheat land. Supposed to contain 713 acs., survey shows residue of 215 acs. Beginning on Queens Crk. NNE 160 poles along Mr. Armisteads line, W & N 200 poles to Allamans corner, NE 146 poles to Cartwheel Branch which parts from Armisteads, NE & NW 603 poles to Burtons Point, SE & SW 422 poles to mouth of Queens Creek, SW &WNW 604 poles. John Robinson, Esq., Escheator, John French, Surveyor. 2 pounds of Tob. for every acre.	M.	24	350	1746 July 25	928
Philip	Land lately owned by Robert Bristow British Subject. In consideration of the sum of 5525 pounds of current money. Lying on Ware R. near Griffins house near the road, to the supposed corner of Thomas Booth and adjoining George Booth, and along the river. Francis Willis, Escheator.	G.	B.H. (C.G.)	315	1783 July 7	276
TALIAFEROE..TALIAFERO..TALLIFEROE..TOLIFEROE..TOLLIVER..TROLIVER		G.	2	359	1651	800
Robert	See Sallate & Troliver.	G.	3	341	1655	900
Robert	See Sollis & Tolliver	G.	4	534	1661	900
TANKERSLY George	KINGSTONE P. Beginning on the W'ward side of Gwyns Ponds, on the S side of the Peankatank R., SSW 340 poles to Queens Crk., down the creek several courses, NW 530 poles to the beginning place. 500 acs. granted Coll°: John Armistead Sept. 25, 1679. 100 acs. "purchased by Armistead of severall men... the whole 600 acres...purchased of Armistead 14th Feb. 1689". Residue 113 acs.	M.	8	270	1693 April 29	713
TAYLOR John	On N side of the Charles R. Granted to John Joanes 1642 & by Edward Williamson assigned to James Johnson, who assigned to Wm. Tymon & due Taylor by intermarriage with Relict of Tymon.	G.	2	266	1650 Oct. 7	150

NAMES	DESCRIPTION	CO.	BK.	Pg.	DATE	ACRES
TEAGE..TEAGUE John & Edward Morgan	On the N side of Horne Harbour Creek adjoining land purchased of Lt. William Worlich, to the head of creek and down same Easterly. HR: Jno. Peade, Richard Cherry, Wm. South.	M.	4	211	1657 March 16	150
TEALE Edward	On the S side of Ware R. Swamp adjoining Oliver Greene & on Indian Branch. HR: Tho: Brassett, Stephen Johnson, Doro. Goswell, Tho. Henly.	G.	5	252	1663 Jan. 27	180
TERRY..TERRYE..TRACYE John	In Ware R. at the mouth of a creek dividing this from the land of Wm. Clarke, [William Larke? See Thomas Symonds] into the woods & S & E unto Ware R. & down the river to the beginning. HR: William Oliver, Mary Oliver, Thomas Hobbs, Andrew Huntington, Lydia Huntington, Phillipp Heanes.	G.	1(2)	808	1642 Aug. 20	300
THOMAS John	GLOSTER COUNTY. WNW on the Poropotank three miles up and along a creek dividing from Nicholas Jarnew. HR: Edmond Hide, Kath. Thomas, James Thomas, John Richards, Geo. Locke, Wm. Peale, Abigale Longdale, Grace Musgrove, John Brocas.	G.?	2	343	1651 Nov. 6	450
ap THOMAS William	On the NE side of Mockjack Bay, begining at Peter Ransons & to the land of Thomas Preston dece'd. HR: Christopher Dorgle, John Rawlins, John Barlow, Thomas Bayley, John Nash, Wm. Chichester, Joane Middleton. Renewal:	M.	3 4	146 416	1652 Nov. 16 1662	700
John Thomas & William Leithermore/	Mockjack Bay adjoining Richard Ripleys on the river & running E. Assigned by J. Walker. HR: Fra. Carr, Jno. Steward, Aug. Hart, Thomas a boy, Chris. Hurd, Robert Fletcher, 1 negro, Thomas a Scot.	M.	3	138	1652 Dec. 6	400
Marke Thomas	On S side of Horne Harbour adjoining Mrs. Morrison, Mr. Armistead, Mr. Hull, Henry Singleton, John Teague, Edw. Morgan. Assigned by Bannister, Foote & Borham wholly to Foote who sold to John Thomas & due Marke as son and heir.	M.	4	528	1661 Nov. 24	350
THOMPSON..TOMPSON..THOMSON George	Lying below the mouth of the Piankketank R. adjoining on the NW a tract of Richard Burton, NE on Pianketank als Stingrye Bay SE upon Queens Crk. HR: Jno. Richards, Wm. Bracon, James Lacy, James Leigh, David Donart, Richard Brent, Jno. Leech, Danll. Nash.	M.	3	44	1653 Feb. 26	400
George	Upon the head of 1000 acs. "formerly known as Col. Hugh Gwyns dividend in the main" upon the S side of the Peianketank R. & adjoining Col. Higgenson. HR: Jno. Bence, Patrick Manough, Mary Lewis, Wm. Foard.	M.	3	44	1653 Feb. 26	200
George &	George Poindexter. See Poindexter.	M.	4	241	1657	350
William Thomson	PETSOE P. Adjoining Mr. Fawcett, Mr. Wm. Howard, along the Rappa Path to Mr. Robert Lee, and adjoining Mr. Thornton, Mr. Jno. Viccars, Mr. Rich. Farthingalls &	G.	6	592	1675/6 Feb. 24	150

Note: the William Leithermore entry's description begins "On the E side of the Eastermost R. in" before "Mockjack Bay".

NAMES	DESCRIPTION	CO.	BK.	Pg.	DATE	ACRES
THOMPSON..etc., (Continued) William Thomson	Mr. Ja: Forsyth. Assigned by Mr. Jno. Buckner & Mr. Thos. Viccars, to Thomson. HR: Edward Best, Tho. Jones, Tho. Browne.	G.	6	592	1675/6 Feb. 24	150
THORNTON..THORNETON William, Mr.	PETSOE P.[First mention of this parish] Joining land he now lives on & adjoining Mr. Richard Barnards old line & SE to Rappahanock path & to Robert Lees land. HR: Wm. West, Mary Shepard, Rowland Cornelius, Nich. Corker.	G.	5	573	1665/6 Feb. 16	164
William, the younger.	PETSOE P. Beginning on the "great road that leads to Tyndalls point being Mr. Robert Porteus corner" adjoining Porteus to SW 260 poles to branch dividing from Greens Neck adjoining Mr. Wm. Thornton the elder along Tyndalls Point maine road 140 poles. Paid Wm. Byrd Esqr. Auditor for rights.	G.	9	589	1704 April 26	110
THRIFT Jeremiah	Beginning at a corner of Elizabeth Wagner & Thrift's land to a point in Robbins Road being a corner to said Thrift and Philip Lee's Paradise Tract, along Paradise line to John Hillingstine.	G.	60 (C.G.)'	87	1809 Sept. 18	33
THROGMORTON.. THROCKMORTON Robert	CHARLES RIVER COUNTY. Adjoining S upon Adjoining S upon the land of William Clarke & N to the woods and a white marsh being in the middle of same. Due for his own personal adventure. HR: Jno. Bristoe, Robert Turner, Henry Warren, Thos. Clarke, Richard Bilcliffe. [It cannot be proven by an exhaustive search of the Land Office records that the above patent is for land in the area of Colonial Gloucester. No reference is to be found of other Gloucester lands adjoining this land as is usual for one so early. However, there are several references to Throckmorton's land adjoining other patents in the area of the present York County, where it is most likely the above land was located. As several writers of early Gloucester history give this as the first grant of land in Gloucester, it is included here for that reason.]	G.?	1(2)	508	1637 Aug. 24	300
TILLITT..TILLETT..TILLID John & Gyles Vandecasteel	KINGSTON P. On the maine bay side & Horne Harbour before the land of Archibald Bromley. HR: Hum: Gwynn.	M.	6	658	1678 Sept. 26	25
TIMBERLAKE Richard	WARE P. Escheat land of Thomas Twining dece'd. Beginning on the road to Robert Radfords house, to Purnalls old field, to land formerly Bryants, to Ware R. swamp near old Beaver dams, along Radfords & Anne Belames line [Bellamy?]. John Lewis Esq[r] Escheator. Thomas Cook Surveyor. Price 2 pounds of Tobacco per acre.	G.	10	286	1715 March 23	290
TITTERTON Mary	Escheat land formerly in possession of Edward Titterton. Coll: Phillip Ludwell Escheator.	G.	6	623	1678 April 4	930
TODD..TOD Thomas	On Winter Harbour beginning at John Smiths land. HR: John Radford, John Rowlinson, Hen: Alwood, Edmd. Morenhana, Thomas Hughes, Giles Webb, Richard Roote, Thomas Smith.	M.	3	182	1652 Oct. 27	450

NAMES	DESCRIPTION	CO.	BK.	Pg.	DATE	ACRES
TODD..TOD (Continued) Thomas	On the E side of the Eastermost R. between Mr. Hampton and Philip Hunley. HR: Geo. Boone [?], Hewett Gepperson	M.	3	183	1652 Oct. 27	150
Thomas	On the W'ward side of the Eastermost R. in Mockjack Bay beginning at a Chestnut Creek adjoining Wm. Holder. HR: Thomas Uggins [Huggins? Hudgins?], John Torme [?], Mary Maddox, John Martin, Sanders Mandrose, James Mackay, John Blake, John Neale.	M.	3	70	1653 Oct. 15	600
Thomas	400 acs. thereof bounding on North R. in Mockjack Baybeginning at a small creek and running along said creek NW thence WNW thence NNE thence ESE thence SSW and along the river to the beginning. The residue of 300 acs. lying one mile from the river beginning on the head of Edward Rawlins land at a tree in the glade below Jos. Gregories plantation, WSW thence SSW thence ESE & NNE to the beginning. 400 acs. thereof being part of a patent for 2400 acs. granted Mr. Wm. Davies [Daines-Deynes-Deines?] who assigned and sold to said Todd. 300 acs. also assigned by Davies to Todd.	G.	5	473	1665 Oct. 9	700
Thomas	On the NE side of a creek near Horn Harbour along Mrs. Morrisons line. Granted John Needles 1652 and deserted.	M.	8	18	1689 Oct. 20	300
William	"...On the N side of Charles R. commonly called Tindalls Neck". Part of 4000 acs. granted Col: Argold Yardly, Esq[r], who sold to George Ludlow & Mr. Wm. Whitby who sold Thomas Beale, Esq[r]: who sold Robt. Todd, dece'd, "now due William as sonn & Heire of Robert".	G.	5	615	1666 May 7	500
Robert	At Tindalls Point on a cove dividing from John Leeke along York R. to Edwd. Mumfords line to John Bells path, down Tindalls Crk. courses to Chestnut Branch to "North side of the Greate Roade". 250 acs. granted to his father "Now deceased" in 1666. Residue 130 acs. HR: Edw. Cornish, Robert Yellow Sen'r, Robert Yellow Jun'r.	G.	6	534	1674 Sept. 21	380
TOLLIVER..TROLIVER	See Sallate & Troliver	G.	4	534	1662	900
TOMKINS..TOMKIN..TOMPKINS..[TOMPKIES?] Hannah	Escheat land formerly granted to Abraham Turner, dece'd. John Baskerville, Deputy Escheator for York County.	M.	6	562	1675 Oct. 4	200
William & Humphrey & John	"...sons of Humphrey Tomkins dece'd". On North R. adjoining Wm. Debnam, Thos. Tabb, along a creek betwixt this and Richard Creadles Land to the river & along same. 200 acs. due Abraham Turner in 1642. Residue $17\frac{1}{2}$ acs. HR: James.	M.	7	8	1679 Sept. 25 1642	$217\frac{1}{2}$
TOMPKIES..TOMKIES Charles, Gent.	WARE P. Adjoining land he now lives on and adjoining Corbell "in Roses Branch... to Jordens line...crossing Fools Branch". Price 5 Shillings.	G.	11	233	1723 Sept. 5	38
TOY Humphrey	KINGSTON P. On the Eastermost R. side ad-	M.	7	15	1679 Nov. 21	10

NAMES	DESCRIPTION	CO.	BK.	Pg.	DATE	ACRES
TOY (Continued Humphrey	joining his own divident of 540 acs. along Bennetts Creek.	M.	7	15	1679 Nov. 21	10
TRATE Edward	Adjoining land he lives on. Beginning at the mouth of a small branch dividing from Oliver Green. HR: Tho. Chambers, Jno. Settle, Henry Smith, Jno. Danies, Tho. Cox, John Cocke.	G.	6	25	1666 March 6	276
TROLIVER & SALLATE	See Sallate	G.	2	359	1651	200
TURNER Abraham	"In the river that lyeth in the NE side of Ware R. [North R.?] butting southerly upon the Northermost R. of Mockjack Bay." Adjoining William Debnam, Richard Creedle & Turners Creek. HR: Abraham Turner himself twice, Robert Carde, Thomas Harte.	M.	1(2)	828	1642 Oct. 20	200
TWYNING..TWINING John	Escheat land. On the E side of a run to Ware R. Formerly granted to Hy: Paline & John Swingleton in 1652. Adjoining the head of John Walkers dividend.	G.	6	287	1669 April 16	300
TYMAN William	CHARLES RIVER COUNTY. Near Richard Bennetts land & on the second creek from the mouth of Milford Haven. HR: William Tyman & Sarah his wife.	M.	1(2)	826	1642 Oct. 8	100
VANDECASTEEL & JOHN TILLITT	See Tillitt.	M.	6	658	1678	25
VANDERY..VANDRY Samuell	Escheat land late in the possession of George Osborne. William Jones Deputy of Hon'able Matthew Page Esqr Escheator.	G.? M.?	9	565	1703 Oct. 23	400
VAUS Robert	In Poropotank Creek alias Freshwater Crk. near Capt. Wormeleys land.	G.?	1(2)	806	1642 Aug. 10	1200
VICARS..VICARIS..VICCARS..VICARY..VICKERS..VICCARIS Thomas, Mr., Clerk	On the S side of a branch dividing from land of Mr. Richard Barnard and Mr. William Thornton & adjoining Wm. Roberts & X'top'r Regalt to Rappahannock Path. HR: Rich. Finch, David Thomas, Wm. Pilgrim, James Couchman, Richard Knott, Tho. Crane, John Conier, Thomas Fisher, Jno. Greene, Danll. James, Rich. White, Saml. Stubb.	G.	5	574	1665/6 Feb. 16	650
Thomas & John Buckner	PETSOE P. Adjoining John Day & Isaac Richardson, Oliver Green, Edward Teale, X'tppher Greenaway, Thos. Wisdome, Tho. Miller to Rappa. path. HR: Wm. Thompson, Math. Jackson, Anne Gusey, Eliz. Sucbery, Guss Andrew, C. Phillips, Jno. Buckner, Rich. Node, Debory Shibe, Jno. Cotgrave, John Clarke.	G.	6	144	1667 Feb. 19	517
Thomas &	John Buckner. See Buckner	G.	6	154	1668	122
Thomas	On Tottopottomoys Swamp adjoining Mr. Wm. Corderoys plantation. HR: Neale Cobley.	G.	6	154	1668 June 16	20
Thomas Viccars & Robert Littlefield	Betwixt the branches of Chiscake & Ware R. branches adjoining David Monorgan, Rich. Renshaw, to the head of Bryery Branch, and adjoining John Saunders & Tho. Chenyes [?] by the Indian Path to the corner of Lawrence Smith, and along Coll: Warners line to a branch of the Peanketank R. and by land of said Robert Littlefield.	G.	6	284	1669 Aug. 16	550

NAMES	DESCRIPTION	CO.	BK.	Pg.	DATE	ACRES
VICARS, etc. (Continued) Thomas Viccaris	WARE P. Adjoining Maj^{r} Lawrence Smith, Mr. Mordecay Cooke, Rich. Wrentshaw, dece'd, Robert Littlefield, Coll: Aug^{n} Warner near the head of Bryery Branch. HR: Ed. Best, Tho. Jones, Tho. Browne, Richard Bironton.	G.	6	649	1678 June 5	190
Thomas Vicaris, Clerk.	Adjoining Mr. Fawcetts to Rappa path, to Mr. Lee & Mr. Wm. Thornton, crossing Bull head swamp. HR: David Goosetree, Mary Grey, John Nitingall.	G.	8	195	1691 Oct. 20	150
Thomas Viccaris, Clerk.	PETSOE P. Adjoining Mr. Wm. Pretchett & William Cook, Dece'd. HR: John Camel, John Wornam.	G.	8	267	1693 April 29	81
WALKER John, Mr.	On the E side of a run to Ware R. adjoining Mr. Mordecay Cooke. Granted John Chew in 1641 who assigned to Walker.	G.	2	356	1651 Jan. 29	1000
John	On the E'ward side of Deep Crk. of Ware R. adjoining Geo. Beenes [?]. HR: Joseph Blaiton, Leonard Ambrose, Henry Clarke.	G.	2	357	1651 Jan. 29	150
John, Lt. Col.	Adjoining Zachary Cripps & Mordecay Cooke and his own land. 1000 acs. granted Walker 1651, residue 200 acs. HR: Edmund Orphew, Walter English, Thomas O Lyn, Mahan Carty. Renewal of above:	G.	3	346	1655 July 14	1200
			4	331	1658	1200
	Renewal of above:		5		1663	1200
John, Lt. Col.	On Milford Haven adjoining George Billipps. Granted John Smith 1652, relinquished. Assigned George Billips 1662. HR: Ellis Mackeneckhogah, Sander Mackonack.	M.	4	268	1658 June 11	100
John, Lt. Col: Esqr:	Renewal of patent of 1655	G.	6	151	1668	1200
WALLER John	WARE P. Adjoining his own land and Edward Teale. HR: Rich. Slater, Mary Humphreys, Sara Hopkins.	G.	6	159	1667 Febr. 20	126
John &	John Benson. See Benson.	G.	6	74	1667 April 10	423
WARE PARISH	The Trustees of: Philip Tabb, Thomas Baytop, Christopher Pryor, Matthew Anderson, Richard Baynham, Morgan Tomkies, Mordecai Cooke, George W. Booth, Peter B. Whiting, Philip Lansum, William Hall, and John Dixon, Trustees of Church property in the Parish of Ware, assignees of Elkanah Talley. Known as the Glebe of Ware Parish. Beginning on the E side of Parsons Bay on the N side of Ware R. north along the line formerly Bristows being a ditch, 320 poles to a spring on Back Crk. in Peter B. Whitings line, along the estate of Peter B. Whiting Deceased...to a cove on Ware R. and down Ware R. shore and bay 217 poles to the beginning.	G.	43 (C.G.)	611	1800 April 28	352
WAREING Henry, Mr.	KINGSTONE P. Near Gwins Ridge adjoining Edmond Roberts and Charles Joanes. HR: Katherine Singleton, Hope Taylor.	M.	8	159	1691 April 28	152
WARNER Augustine	Lying in the Severne R. the first river in Mockjack Bay beginning on the N side and called Austins Desire. Adjoining	G.	1(2)	873	1642	600

NAMES	DESCRIPTION	CO.	BK.	Pg.	DATE	ACRES
WARNER (Continued) Augustine	Humph. Hammore and John Robins. HR: Martin Barnes, William Reynolds "& others".	G.	1(2)	873	1642	600
Augustine	On S side of the Peanketank R. lying about the branches of old Cheescake town & adjoining Indians land to SE of old Chiscake. HR: 4 rights due as administrator of Thomas Chandiler York Court 1640. Wm. Streues [?], Robt. Torrington, John Robinson, Richard Floyd, Kath. Pettibones, Wm. Hutcheson, John Wilkinson, Mary Thrope, Sands Knowles, John Mullins, Nath. Holding, Richard Davis, John Bradford, John Poulson, John Scales, Charles Reeves, Thomas Barretts, Edward Canes [?], Henry Thacker, Samuel Pitts, Edmond Wallis, three negroes, Wm. Skinham, Thomas Thorninge, George White, Henry Ellis, Antho, a negro, Alex. Ray, Law. Smith, Wm. Bauldwin, Wm. Powell, Fra. Hurd, Peter Hopkins, Henry Naipes, Thomas Gray, Henry Burrage, Nicholas Hart, Robt. Cade, Mary Warner, John Jakes, Elizabeth Hull, Fra. Hathaway, Anne Downing.	M? G?	3	122	1652 Oct. 26	2500
Augustine	On the S side of a run falling into the head of the Severne R. adjoining his own land. HR: John Haward, Mary Gragg.	G.	3	2	1653 Oct. 6	80
Augustine & Capt. John Robins	On the N side of the Severne R. in Mockjack Bay beginning at the mouth of Lucas Creek. [See Robins]	G.	3	317	1654 March 14	594
Augustine	200 acs. on the branches of Pyanketank R. adjoining his own land. 148 acs. residue on the head of the Seavern R, adjoining his land and Col. Barnard & along the Indian path. Renewed 1662. HR: John Watson, James Marrow and 5 Irish.	G.	4	252	1657 Feb. 11	348
Augustine, Coll: Esq.	ABBINGTON P. Adjoining X'topher Robins to a creek dividing from Wm. Bowlin and down the riverside. 600 acs. due by former grant 1642, residue 624 acs.	G.	6	158	1666 Jan. 20	1224
WARREN William	On N side of Charles R. running to a marsh on the W side of Mock Jacks Bay. HR: Wm. Richards, Stephen Sandish, Tho. Paddison, Richard Powett, Wm. Hinde, ___ Locke, Michaell Ellis, Jno. Langley, Amos Warren, Eliz. Hutchins, Ellen Fetherston, Oliver Gibbons, Ann Grime	G.	1(2)	796	1642 Aug. 10	650
William	On the N side of Charles R. being a peninsula at the first piney point and running to the marshes on Mockjack Bay. Granted to Wm. Warren 1642 who assigned to X'pher Allen & Rice Maddox. Maddox assigned to Nath. Warren and becomes due to s[d] William as sonn & heire to Nath. Warren. The other half due unto s[d] William by intermarrying with Frances Allen only heir now living of X'pher Allen.	G.	3	281	1653 Jan. 23	650
WASHINGTON John, Jr.	& John Lewis & John Smith. See Lewis.	G.	10	13	1711	46½
WATERS..WATTERS John	KINGSTONE P. Beginning at a corner of	M.	6	660	1678	140

NAMES	DESCRIPTION	CO.	BK.	Pg.	DATE	ACRES
WATERS..WATTERS (Continued) John	Mr. William Elliott and adjoining Coll: Dudley & Richard Longest. HR: Edward Best, 2 Negroes.	M.	6	660	1678 Sept. 26	140
John	KINGSTONE P. Adjoining his former divident & Coll: Dudley, Law: Perrott, Charles Jones, Coll: Kemp, Mr. Wm. Elliott to Richard Longest. Former grant of 140 acs. residue 360 acs. HR: Jonas Vernay, John Morgan, Fra: Jarvis, Ann Jarvis, Math. Gale, Margt. Gale, Eliz. Gale.	M.	6	682	1679 May 1	500
WATTS John, Gent.	Being a neck of marsh and wood called Ducking Pond Creek out of Mockjack Bay on the W on the E by Wm. Holders land and creek on the W side of his mill. HR: Himself and Martha his wife, Bernard Bradshaw, Edward Hollowell.	M.	2	223	1650 Aug. 13	200
WEBB	Wingfield Webb & Richard Pate. See Pate.	G.	2	271	1650	1141
WELCH..WELSH Edmond	On the N side of North R. beginning at Saies Point & running W up the riverside to Wrights Creek N at the creek mouth to Curtis Branch & 100 poles down Blackwater Creek to s^{d} Point. HR: Fran. Carr, 1 negro, John Steward, Aug. Hart, John Pate, John Salvadge, Natha. Parker, Char. Riggan [?].	M.	2	325	1651 Oct. 12	400
Edmond	At the head of Queens Creek in Pyan. [katank]. Beginning at the corner of Richard Carye & to land of Richard Burton. HR: Nich Browne twice, his wife twice, Nich, Dean, John Bradshaw, Dan Tavenor, John Thickpenny, Anto. Mark, Edward Jelfe, Robert White, Eliz. Palmer, Dennis Mackernall, Joseph Preston, Ann Aurllott, Wm. Smith, Sarah Browne, Ann Browne.	M.	3	270	1654	900
WELLS..WILLS Susanna	WARE P. "Infant and only child and heire of John Wells Dece'd" & to her heire, "for default of such Issue...then to her mother Grizzell [Prizzell?]...wife and widdow of the said John Wells..." Surveyed by Mr. John Lewis for Edw. Wells father of John... but to this day never pattented. Adjoining Mr. Clarke, Humphrey Mead, Coll: Willis & other land of the said John Wells. [See patent of Edward Wills] HR: Edward Clarke, Joan Shoares.	G.	6	601	1675/6 March 11	57
WHITE James	James White & John Richerdson. See Richerdson.		1(2)	810	1642	200
John	On the head of the Upright Crk. of the Eastermost R. in Mockjack Bay. Beginning at Mr. Wm. Armisteads line.	M.	3	1	1653 Nov. 25	100
Peter	Adjoining Tho. Dawkins "near Rich. Holloways plantacon...near Walter Cant's Quarter". Formerly granted Lambert Moore & Bartho: Ramsey and deserted, since granted Robert Beverley who sold to White.	G.	7	15	1679 Nov. 26	350
William	Escheat land formerly owned by Henry Preston. Beginning on the W side of Hatters Crk. and adjoining John White & Richard White. Jno. Robinson, Esq., Escheator. For 2 pounds of Tob. per acre.	M.	33	366	1757 Jan. 7	125

NAMES	DESCRIPTION	CO.	BK.	Pg.	DATE	ACRES
WHITEHEAD Richard, Mr.	ABBINGDON & WARE P. Beginning at the head of Gills land, adjoining Mr. Thomas Cheesman.	G.	7	451	1685 April 20	180
WHITING..WHITEING..WHITEINGE James	On the N side of Charles R. bounded NW on James Besouth SW upon Timberneck Crk. SE on Thomas Hughes. HR: Ann his wife, Evan Davis, Mathew King, Nehemiah Causon, Richard Addams.	G.	1(2)	885	1643 Aug. 10	250
Henry, Maj^r^	& Mr. John Buckner (See Buckner)	G.	7	212	1682 Dec.22	2673
Henry, Maj^r^	& Mr. John Buckner (See Buckner)	G.	7	513	1686 Oct. 30	280
Henry, Maj^r^	& Mr. John Buckner (See Buckner)	G.	7	518	1686 Oct. 30	2400
Francis	"Sonn & heir of Francis Whiteinge, Gent. dece'd". Escheat land, lately owned by Ann Bellamy. Adjoining Timberlake, Henry Bray, dece'd, William Radford, and Swepston to the road. John Lewis Esqr, Escheator, Thomas Cook, Surveyor.	G.	11	200	1723 Aug. 31	98
Kemp	Beginning on the E side of Sluts Crk... by consent of Mr. Matthew Whiting jun'r who is owner to the land adjoining. Running to Morris's Crk. & down same to the mouth of Sluts Crk. and up same. For 15 Shillings.	M.	34	139	1756 Nov. 26	152
Peter Beverly	"heir at law of Peter Beverly Whiting, dece'd". Beginning on Back Crk. near the mouth & adjoining Peter Beverly Whiting to Cow Crk. swamp - to a corner of the Glebe Land, in the head of Back Crk. near the spring, along Back Crk. to the beginning. Late the property of Robert Bristow, Esq., a British subject. In consideration of the sum of 10,088 pounds of current money paid by Peter Beverly Whiting. Esqr dece'd unto Francis Willis, Esqr, Escheator.	G.	H (C.G.)	30	1783 May 20	388
WIAT..WIATT [See Wyat]						
WILCHIN Richard	On NE side of the Poropotank adjoining John Thomas, Mr. Canho, & Mr. Vaus. 200 acres by sale from Mrs. Eliz. Vaus Atty. of Robt. Vaus. Confirmed by Mr. Hump. Vaus & Mr. Joseph Croshaw. 100 acs. for Richard Wilchin & his wife Rachel.	G.?	3	289	1654 Sept. 30	300
WILLIAMS Edward	On the N side of the Charles R. beginning on the W bounds of John Jones & Parallel to Mr. Priors land. HR: Transfer of himself and 1 servant.	G.	1(2)	809	1642 July 20	100
Thomas	Near the land of Thomas Ray and running N into the southern branch of Severne R. HR: John Charnocke, Wm. Morris, Tho. Williams, Wm. Ediford, John Harsnett, Giles Foster, Christian Demacheto, John Compton, Grace Warkeham.	G.	1(2)	909	1643 Aug. 13	450
Rowland	On the S side of Garden Crk. 150 acs. part purchased by Charles Hill of Edw. Lucas & who assigned to Samuel Hattaway 1658. 150 acs. formerly granted John Hampton, by him & his heirs deserted. Granted Hill 1658 & assigned Geo. Mosely who assigned to Robt. Jones, to Williams.	M.	5	326	1662 March 18	300

NAMES	DESCRIPTION	CO.	BK.	Pg.	DATE	ACRES
WILLIAMS (Continued) John	of King & Queen. On the Poropotank adjoining Mr. Roger Shackleford, John Major and John Leviston at the head of Bennetts Creek just below the bridge, and NE "to the church road". 250 acs. granted Thomas Bell in 1659 who assigned to Andrew Cotton. Not recorded.	G.?	8	248	1693 April 29	410
George	Escheat land late in the possession of John Frame dece'd. Wm. Jones, Deputy Escheator.	G.?	9	425	1701 Oct. 24	100
WILLIS Francis	A point of land toward the head of the eastermost branch of the Severne R. where the branch divides & adjoining Richard Burt.	G.	2	199	1649 Jan. 29	450
Francis, Col.	On the SW side of the Ware R. beginning at Tho. Tracyes NW corner & by the said Terryes trees E by S to Ware R. & up the river to Snare Creek and to the head of said creek. HR: Jno. Bryant, Wm. Bush.	G.	5	654	1666 July 11	100
William	On Crane Neck Creek branch & adjoining his own land and Ralph Harwood and Col: John Cheesman. HR: Wm. Wilkinson, Danl. Miles, Walter Barefoot, Walter Croop, Wm. Hankins.	G.	6	146	1665 Oct. 20	250
WILLS..[WELLS? See Susanna Wells]..[WILLIS?] Edward	On Deep Creek of Ware R. in Mockjack Bay adjoining his own land. HR: Edward Wills, John Wills, Katherine Wills, Susana Wills.	G.	3	168	1652 Dec. 6	200
WISDOME..WISDOM Thomas	On the N side of Thomas Deacons Mill Swamp & adjoining Thomas Miller and Thomas Vicars. HR: John Reese, Judith Knight,Mary Godfry.	G.	6	72	1667 April 10	127
WOODWARD John	On the S side of the Pyanketank, bounded on the N & NE by the river and adjoining Abraham Moon. Relinquished rights to make good a patent for Col. Lee's children, viz: Wm. & Hancock Lee. Tho. Brereton, Clk.	G.	3	337	1655 May 17	500
WORLEIDGE..WORLEICH..WORLEIGH..WORLDRIDGE..WORLICH. William Worleidge, Lt.	Beginning at Chestnut Creek, SW to Repulse Creek, including marsh to the mouth of & on the NW NW side of the Eastermost R. to Mockjack Bay. HR: George Maior, Samll. James, Wm. Humphrey, Richard Gill, Francis Berry, Eliz. Curtis, Thomas Rimmington, John Tucker, Christ. Isaac, Robert Armeson, Christ Keath [?], Robert Large.	M.	1(2)	918	1643 Oct. 16	550
William Worleich, Lt.	Along Mockjack Bay beginning at Wm. Morgans line & running NE through Croynes quarter. HR: Francis Brown, John Thucker, Christopher Leake, Thomas Binniston, Margery Clements, William White.	M.	2	233	1650 Aug. 13	300
William Worleich, Lt.	Being a neck of land called New Point Comfort Neck & E on the Mockjack Bay W & S to John Gundrys land. HR: Nicholas Guilt, Jno. Worleich, Joane	M.	2	233	1650 Aug. 13	650

NAMES	DESCRIPTION	CO.	BK.	Pg.	DATE	ACRES
WORLEIDGE etc., (Continued) William Worleich	HR: Jones, Wm. Cadwell, Hump. Edwards, Wm. Humphreys, Henry Holt, John Evans, Elizabeth Curtis, Mary Blackford.	M.	2	233	1650 Aug. 13	650
William Worleich, Lt.	On Horne Harbour Creek & on the W side of Wm. Holders land. HR: Robert Armeson, James Foster.	M.	2	233	1650 Aug. 13	100
WORMELEY..WORMLEY..WORMELEYE Ralph, Esq[r]	Escheat land formerly purchased of Henry Thacker by deed dated 15th Sept. 1655 to Sarah Williams als Holdgate, & recorded in Glocester Court. Francis Page.DE	G.? M.?	7	707	1686	83
Ralph	PETSOE P. Escheat land late in the possession of Elizabeth Jennings. Richard Johnson, Escheator.	G.	9	134	1698 April 26	400
WRAY John	KINGSTONE P. Upon the head of Queens Creek adjoining Richard Cary & Edmond Welch. HR: Thomas Miles, Tho. Chambers, John Settle, Jno. Cox, Mary Sharpe.	M.	6	41	1666 March 15	240
WRIGHT Henry	"Sonne & heire of John Wright dece'd". Adjoining lands lately patented by Robert Beverley & Robert Elliott. HR: Jane Davis, Tho. Richards, John Boone.	M.	6	511	1674 April 8	140
Mottrom	Mottrom Wright & John Smither. See Smither.	M.	7	587	1687	395
Mottrom	KINGSTON P. Land and marsh on N side of Winter Harbour Creek, "which land belongs to the said Wright in the right of his wife Ruth daughter to Mr. Robert Greggs dece'd" who bequeathed it. Beginning at the N side of the northerly branch of Winter Harbour and adjoining another divident of said Gregg, and adjoining Jno. Degge, John Gardner, John Smither, by Horne Harbour Creek, "to the nead of the northerly branches thereof near the old dwelling house where the afores[d] Robt. Greggs formerly lived". 400 acs. patented by Richard Ripley 1652, who sold to Charles Sallet and by Symon Sallet heire sold to George Thompson Oct. 1657, who sold to Robert Greggs 1666. 370 acs. granted Robert Greggs & Edward Wyatt in 1662, moyety of Wyatt deeded to Gregg in 1663. Remainder 230 acs. granted Robert Gregg 1662.	M.	7	685	1688 Oct. 20	1000
WYATT..WIATT..WYAT..WIAT Richard Wyatt	Butting upon the narrow of Ware R. bounded on the W by Cow Creek, to the riverside 125 poles thence NNE into the woods thence 125 poles to Cow Creek. HR: Due for his own personal adventure thrice, Gertrude Bedell, Ralph Taylor.	G	1(2)	869	1642 Aug. 15	250
Richard Wyatt	On the Eastermost side of Ware R. and to Cow Creek, beginning at Oyster Shell Point, N 320 poles to land of Mr. Harris NW to his other devident, SW 296 poles to the river and down the river to the beginning. HR: John Bandwick, Silvanas Ricraft, Thomas Wilmot, Samuel Sures, Ann Griffen, Morcas Morgrave, Hen. Brightmon, Mary Wilkinson, Lydia Berry. "(The four last names are that due s[d] Wyatt which are assigned to Richard Diminge [Dunning?])".	G.	2	154	1645 Aug. 20	500

LAND GRANTED TO RICHARD YOUNG, SENIOR, IN 1665.

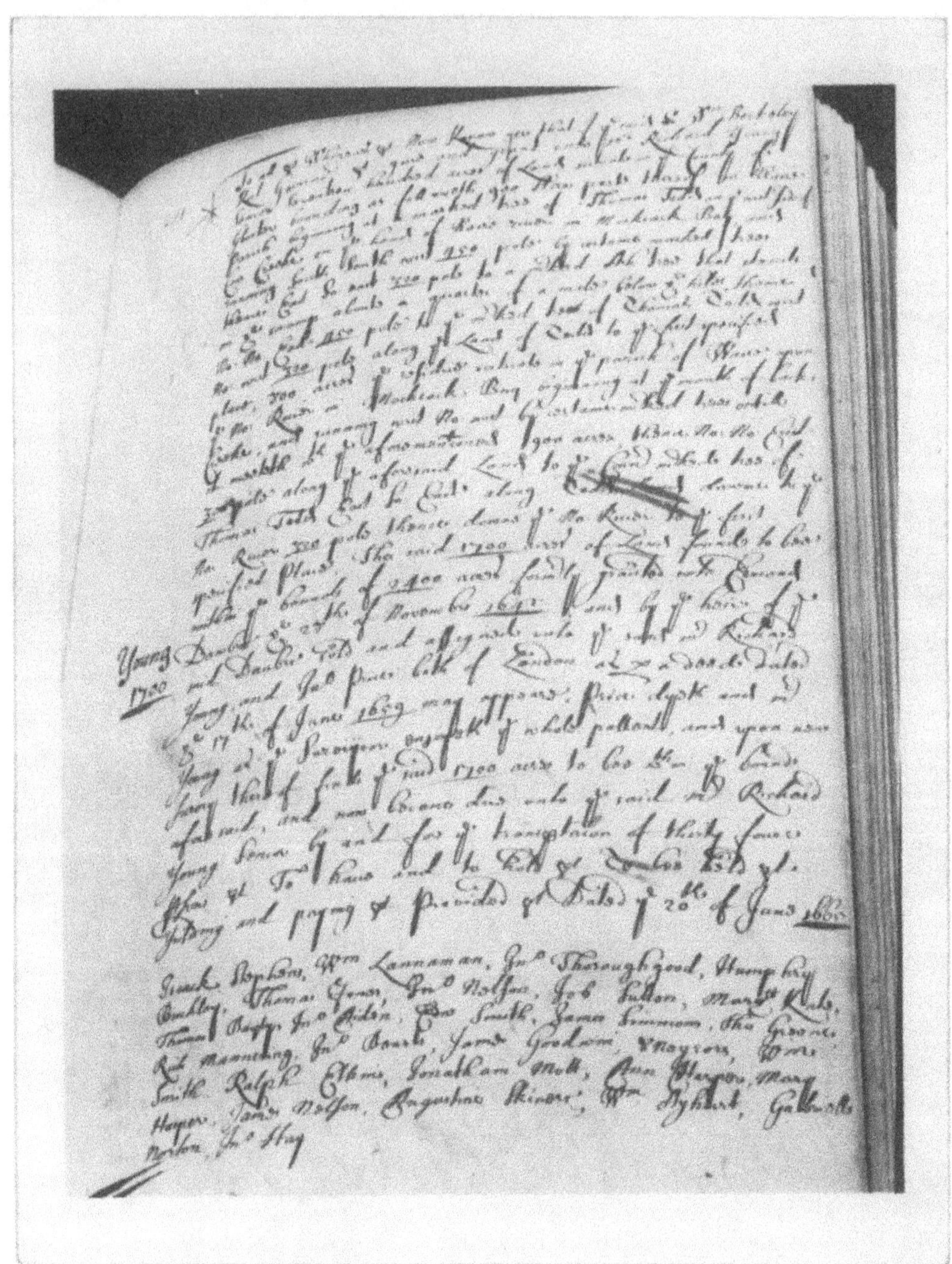

Patent Book 5, page 112, showing patent of Richard Young for 1700 acres on North River adjoining Thomas Todd's lands. Richard Young was the second owner of the present Elmington lands.

NAMES	DESCRIPTION	CO.	BK.	Pg.	DATE	ACRES
WYATT..WIATT etc., (Continued) Edward Wyatt	Upon the Peanketank R. along Wadeing Creek and adjoining Edward Kemp. HR: Wm. Jarvis, Tho. Jones, Mary Hart. [See frontispiece, Indian deed of gift]	M.	4	419	1662 July 20	1230
Edward Wyatt	& Robert Gregg. See Robert Gregg.	M.	4	439	1662	370
Thomas Wyatt	250 acs. on the E side of Ware R. in Mockjack Bay nere a little Oyster Shell Point. 250 acs. upon the narrow of Ware R. to Cow Creek. Granted to Richard Wyatt in 1645, father of Thomas, son & heire.	G.	5	608	1666 May 9	500
Conquest Wyatt	On the NW side of Hoccadayes Creek adjoining Wyatts old plantation and adjoining Robert Elliott, Mary Kibble, George Harper. 480 acs. due Edw. Wyatt dece'd by assignment from Lt. Coll: Anthony Elliot dece'd, who assigned to John Snelling dece'd who assigned to Erasmus Withers who assigned to Wyatt, "now due unto Conquest sonne and heire by last will & testament of Edward Wyatt dece'd." HR: John Bivers.	M.	6	437	1672 Oct. 10	530
YEARDLEY..YARDLEY..YARDLY Argoll Yeardley, Esq.	On the North side of the Charles River called Tindalls Neck. Beginning at Tindalls Creek upon the W side of the W branch of same & N'ly toward certain branches of Mockjack Bay. Due by order of Court in right of his father Sir George Yeardley, Kt. as parte of his divident in right of his adventure with the South Hampton Hundred.	G.	1(2)	759	1640 Oct. 12	4000
YOUNG Richard, Sen'r	WAIRE P. 900 acs. on North River beginning at Tho. Todd on the W side of Cow Creek on the head of Ware R. 800 acs. on North R. beginning at the mouth of Back Creek and running WNW till it adjoins the other 900 acs. to the corner of Thomas Todd, and along same to the river and down North River to Back Creek. Said 1700 acs. found within the bounds of 2400 acs. granted Edmond Dawber 28th November, 1642. HR: Isaack Stephens, Wm. Lannaman, Jno. Thoroughgood, Humphrey Buckley, Thomas Jones, Jno. Nelson, Job. Sutton, Margtt. Kale, Thomas Bayly, Jno.Bearts, James Goodwim, Wm. Smith, Ralph Elkins, Jonathan Mott, Ann Harper, Mary Harper, James Nelson, Augustine Skinerr, Wm. Ayhurt, Gabrielle Norton, Jno. Hay, 8 negroes, Jno. Hiden, Edw. Smith, James Simmons, Tho. Greene, Rich. Mannering.	G.	5	112	1665 June 20	1700

GLOCESTER RENT ROLL

From Virginia Quit Rent Roll of 1704

"Copy of the Rent Rolls of the Sev^{ll} Countys in Virg^{a} for the year 1704, referred to in Col. Nicholsons L^{re}. of the 25th July last.
Rec'd 8th October
Read } 1705 M. 61 Entered C: Fol. 365"

....

[The following Quit Rent Roll has been copied from a photostatic copy in the library archives of the Virginia Historical Society. The roll has been rearranged into alphabetical order for this compilation, otherwise it is given here as shown in photostat, with original spelling retained.]

....

A Rent Roll in Kingston Parish
1705

	Acres
Aldred Anne	350
Allaman Tho	842
Andrews John	50
Armistead Capt	3675
Armistead Wm	300
Bacon John	825
Bannister Jno	650
Beard Richard	380
Beard Wm	100
Bedford Thomas	50
Bell Andrew	128
Berry Patrick	250
Billups Geo	1200
Bohannah Dunkin [Bohannan?]	113½
Bohannah John... "	113½
Bohannah Joseph "	148
Bolton Henry	50
Borum Edw	360
Bristow Robt., Esqr	900
Brooks Joseph	500
Brooks Wm	720
Brumley Wm	750
Callis John	1000
Cray Tho	200
Credle Wm	50
Cully Robt	200
Curtis Rose	400
Davis Widd	300
Deggs John [Degge? Diggs?]	1200
Dixon Christopher	300
Dudley Ambrose (Recorder of the Roll)	
Dudley Rich	350
Dudley Capt	650
Edwards John	534
Elliott Robt	1247
Eliott Wm	1060
Fliping Tho	300
Floyd Jno	250
Forrest Anne	500
Foster James	225
Garnet Jno	250
Garwood Thomas	77
Gayle Capt	164
Gayle Math. junr	250
Glascock Rich	500
Gowing Edw	100
Green Widd^{o}	150
Green Sarah	200
Gundry Wm	200
Gwin Capt	1100
Hampton Wm	348
Hayes Thomas	140
Howlett Wm	300
Hundley Philip	660
Hundley Timothy	300
Hundley John	130
Hundley James	100
Hunley Richd	50
Hunter Daniel	200
Jarvis Francis	460
Jones Chas	225
Keble Walter	550
Kemp Coll	200
Kemp Thomas	200
Knight Hen	240
Knowles Capt	575
Lindseys Land	390
Linsey Caleb	140
Longest Rich	600
Lylley Jno	584
Marchant Richard	180
Martin John	200
Meachen Jno. junr	600
Miggs Tho. [Meggs?]	100
Miller John	100
Morgan Wm. Senr	50
Morgan Wm. Junr	200
Nevill John	100
Ofield Alexander	23
Parriott Mich	100
Parrott Lawrence	340
Perrott Rich	35
Peters Tho	30
Peyton Robt	680
Peyton Thomas	684
Plumer Isaac	200
Plumer Tho	400
Plumer Wm	510
Preston Henry	1500
Putnam Thomas	300
Ransom James, Coll:	1400
Ransom James, junr	310

GLOUCESTER RENT ROLL

Kingston Parish continued:

	Acres		Acres
Read Benj	550	Sinoh Widd	300
Rice Thomas	34	Smith Capt	550
Ripley Andrew	40	Sterling Capt	1100
Rispus Christopher	200	Taylor James	50
Roberts Geo	170	Thomas Mark	300
Ryland Tho	272	Todd Tho., Capt	775
Sadler Edw	20	Tompkins Humphrey	100
Sadler Robt	50	Tompkins Wm	100
Shipley Ralph	430	Toy Humphrey	1100
Singleton Henry	600	Turner George	50
Singleton Robt	650	Watters Chas	100
Singleton Sam	300	Williams John	50
[Total acres]	46,537		

....

A Rent Roll in Ware Parish 1704/5

	Acres		Acres
Ambrose Leonard	200	Hurst Wm	200
Anniers Elizabeth	250	Iveson Abraham, Senr	1000
Armistead Wm	100	Jeffes Widd	316
Bacop Tho. [Bacon? Batop?]	200	Jolley Dudley	100
Bailey Richard	800	Jones Wm	120
Bates Alice	200	Kemp Peter	650
Beverley Peter, Maj	800	Kertch Dorothy	220
Boswell Dorothy	1600	Kindrick Jno	100
Boswell Joseph	230	Lassells Mary	200
Bray Anne	100	Marinex Hugh	50
Bristow Robert, Esqr	2050	Marinex Jno	100
Buckner John	900	More Geo	40
Bullard John	100	More Sarah	67
Burton James	100	Morrin Robt	200
Burwell Nathan	600	Morris James	250
Cheesman Tho	650	Morris Wm	350
Clark James [Clack?]	250	Pamplin Nicholas	210
Collis Tho	100	Poole Thomas	600
Cook Capt	1500	Powell Thomas	460
Cook Giles	140	Price Jno	600
Cooper Philip	200	Pryor Robt	300
Couch Robt	100	Purnell Thomas	163
Cretendon Rich. [Crittenden?]	280	Radford Wm	200
Croxson Anne	300	Ransone Peter	220
Davison James	100	Ray John	100
Dawson John	780	Read Thos	400
Dawson Samuel	350	Robins John	900
Debnam Wm., Capt	1250	Shackelfield James [Shackelford?]	035
Dorrell Sampson	300	Simons Sam'l	120
Dudley Rich., Junr	300	Smith Philip	700
Easter Grace	200	Snelling Elizabeth	250
Easter John	350	Spinks Jno	300
Elliot Anthony	100	Stubelfield Simon	200
Foulcher Wm	100	Throgmorton Capt	500
Francis Robt	400	Tillids Lands [P.Maj. Peter Beverley]	150
Freeman Robt	135	Todd Thomas	884
Goodson Jno	150	Vadrey Samuel	400
Grady Philip	200	Valine Isaac	100
Greenaway Christopher	270	Waterfield John & Peter	143
Gregory Anthony	700	Waters Charles	200
Greswell Walter	50	Whiting Henry	800
Haywood Tho	70	Whiting Madm	950
Holland Wm	300	Willis Francis, Capt	3000
[[Total acres]	31,603		

GLOUCESTER RENT ROLL 1704/5

A Rent Roll in Petso Parish

	Acres
Acre John	100
Alexander David, Capt	1050
Amis James	250
Armistead Wm.	430
Bailey Richard	600
Baker Ralph	150
Barnard Wm.	810
Bernard Samuel	550
Booker Mary	100
Brooken Martha	600
Buckner Thomas	850
Camell Hannah	100
Carter Robt	1102
Clrake Jno. [Clarke?]	100
Clements Benj	400
Cobson Jno	100
Coleman Jno	200
Collone Wm.	400
Cook Thomas	350
Cooke Wm.	135
Crymes Wm.	400
Darnell Jerim	150
Darnell Jno	60
Day Jno	400
Dixon Thomas	300
Drument John	80
Dudley James	780
Dudley Richard	400
Dudley Thomas	200
Fleming Wm.	600
Fockner Wm.	180
Forginson Widd	150
Fowler Samuel	150
Glebe Land	127
Green Darcas	400
Grinley Susannah	200
Grout Jno	300
Grymes Jno	1400
Hall Robt	100
Hall Robt	250
Hanes Jno. [Haynes?]	150
Hansford Wm.	500
Harper Jno	100
Hawes Samuel	200
Hayes an orphen	60
Hill Richard	70
How Alexander	120
Howard Wm.	300
Hubard Richard	100
Hull Richard	250
Johnson Stephen	150
Jones Wm. for Northington	530
Kelly John, Orphen	150

	Acres
Kingson Jno	400
Lee Richard, Esqr	1140
Lewis Edward, Capt	1000
Lewis Nich°, Orphen	350
Mackwilliams Jno	50
Mastim Eliz	360
Milner Wm.	900
Miner Rich	250
Musgrove Edw	100
Nettles Robt	300
Norman Wm.	150
Northington, by Wm. Jones [above]	
Oliver Dorothy	130
Oliver Isaac	100
Page Madam	550
Parish Guy	100
Parsons Wm., Orphen	100
Pate Jno	1100
Porteus Madam	500
Porteus Robt	892
Price Richard	600
Pritchett Jno	850
Read Thomas	2000
Reynolls James [Reynolds?]	200
Richards Wm. in Pamunkey	150
Roane Wm.	500
Robinson George	300
Royston John	570
Shackelford Jno	280
Simpson Thomas [Swepson?]	280
Smith Augustin	200
Smith Augustin, junr	500
Smith Jno	1300
Smith Nich	280
Stanbridge Wm.	159
Stephens Edw	70
Stubs John	300
Symons Edward	500
Thornton Wm., senr	525
Thornton Wm., junr	800
Thurston Wm.	200
Upshaw Wm.	490
Waters Walter	200
West Thomas	112
Whiting Thomas	450
Whittmore Wm., Desarted	150
Wickins Seth	50
Williams George	100
Wisdom Francis	150
Wotham Jane [Wortham?]	60
Wyatt Conquest	2200
Yard Robt	450

[Total acres] 41,132 Tho. Neale [Recorder]

GLOUCESTER RENT ROLL 1704/5

A Rent Roll in Abbington Parish.

	Acres
Allen Hugh	1250
Austin Johanna	40
Babb Widd [by Jeremiah Holt]	150
Banister John	2750
Barlow Robt	62
Blackbourne Capt	550
Booker Capt	1000
Broadbent Joshua	200
Bryon Robt. [by John Smith, Esqr.]	400
Burwell Major	3300
Butler John	100
Camp Wm	175
Cary Edw	100
Cary James	50
Cleaver Tho. Sworne	200
Clements Benj	500
Coleman Joseph	200
Coleman Thomas	250
Dixon Richard	200
Dobson Edm	350
Dobson John	400
Dobson Wm	950
Foster Richard	150
Francis Robt	104
Grady Philip	150
Grathmee Owen [Gwathmey?]	250
Garves Jeffry [Graves?]	33
Graves Thomas	70
Grustam Clent [?]	100
Hall John	125
Hemingway Mary	150
Heywood Richd	100
Hilliard Wm	80
Holt Jeremiah, junr	150
Holt Jeremiah	350
Howard Hugh	200
Jackson George	117
Jones Widd	45
Kemp Wm	75
Kittson [by Wm. Smith]	50
Lane Benja	50
Lane Valentine	80
Lewis Jno., Esqr	2000
Mitchell Henry	50
Mixon Jno	400
More Joseph	150
Page Madam Mary	3000
Page Robt	175
Richardson Elizabeth	500
Richeson Peter	250
Roberts Rich. for wife	300
Row James	300
Russell Nathan[ll]	550
Sadler Jno	125
Sanders Tho	450
Satterwight John	50
Sawyer Wm	150
Seaton Henry	170
Seawell Thomas	200
Smith Guy, Mr	30
Smith John, Esqr	2000
Smith Wm. for Kittson	
Starkey Robt	100
Steavens James	100
Stevens Charles	75
Stevens Edw	80
Stevens Henry	60
Stoakes Jno	300
Stubbs Susannah	300
Teagle John	30
Thomas Mary	100
Turner Elizabeth	150
Walker Tho	300
Waters Jno	50
White Chillion	100
Woodfolk Richard	125
Yarbborrow Robt	100
[Total acres]	28,426

*GLOUCESTER RENT ROLL 1704/5.

These Rent Rolls of 1704/5 of the Gloucester parishes are arranged here in the sequence in which the parish names are first mentioned in the land patent records. No earlier records have yet been found of the formation of the parishes in Gloucester County than those discovered in the patents for land grants.

In the abstracts of land patents given herein, the earliest patent mentioning each of the four parishes is noted. These first appearances of the parish names, in the sequence in which they occur, are found in the following patents:

KINGSTON (Kingstone) : Patent of John Chapman, March 15, 1657.
WARE (Waire) : " " John Read, March 18, 1662.
PETSWORTH (Petsoe, Petso): " " William Thornton, February 16, 1665/6.
ABINGDON (Abington, Abbington): Patent of William Bowlin, April 14, 1668.

....

The Rent Rolls of the Gloucester parishes furnish us with interesting information on the relative status of settlement at this early stage of the county's development. A summary of this 1704/5 report gives us the following informative figures:

KINGSTON PARISH:

1. Total number of acres granted.. 46,537 acres
2. " " " land owners.. 116 persons
3. " " " large estates of 1000 acres or more.................... 11 estates
4. " " " acres in the above eleven large estates.................. 15,582 acres
5. Average acres per person for the 105 settlers remaining.................. 295 "
6. Largest estate in the name of Capt. Armistead, owning.................... 3,675 "

WARE PARISH:

1. Total number of acres granted.. 31,603 acres
2. " " " land owners.. 86 persons
3. " " " large estates of 1000 acres or more.................... 6 estates
4. " " " acres in above six large estates........................ 10,400 acres
5. Average acres per person for the 80 settlers remaining.................. 265+ "
6. Largest estate is in the name of Capt. Francis Willis, owning........... 3,000 "

PETSWORTH PARISH:

1. Total number of acres granted.. 41,132 acres
2. " " " land owners.. 104 persons
3. " " " large estates of 1000 acres or more.................... 9 estates
4. " " " acres in above nine large estates........................ 12,292 acres
5. Average acres per person for the 95 settlers remaining.................. 303+ "
6. Largest estate in the name of Conquest Wyatt, owning..................... 2,200 "

ABINGDON PARISH:

1. Total number of acres granted.. 28,426 acres
2. " " " land owners.. 77 persons
3. " " " large estates of 1000 acres or more.................... 7 estates
4. " " " acres in above seven large estates...................... 15,300 acres
5. Average acres per person for the 70 settlers remaining.................. 187+ "
6. Largest estate is in the name of Major Lewis Burwell, owning............ 3,300 "

....

It is found in the records of abstracted land grants given herein, and in the lists of the 1704/5 Rent Roll and the above summary, that KINGSTON PARISH (now Mathews County) stood first among all the Gloucester parishes in the following respects:

1. First grant of colonial Gloucester's land was to Hugh Gwin in 1635 in the area which became Kingston Parish.
2. First record of a parish formed in Gloucester was of Kingston Parish in 1657.
3. Kingston was first as to size and acreage, with 5,405 acres more than the next largest parish, Petsworth, as reported in 1705.
4. In 1704/5 Kingston stood first with the largest number of land owners.
5. Kingston was first with the greatest number of large estates of 1000 acres or more.
6. The largest single estate owned in any of the Gloucester parishes in 1704/5 was in Kingston Parish.

*Note: The summary of the 1704/5 Rent Roll on this page was made by the compiler, Polly C. Mason.

TAX LIST OF GLOUCESTER COUNTY, VIRGINIA.
1770 - 1782

The tax book of 1770 was formerly in the possession of Miss Sally Perrin of Gloucester County. Apparently, it is a list taken in the parishes of Abingdon, Petsworth and Ware, which were the parishes remaining in Gloucester after the division in 1791, when Kingston Parish of Gloucester formed the new County of Mathews. This 1770 tax book gives only a partial list of those names in the above three parishes, as a number of pages are missing and torn. Many of the names as copied are found only in the index, which is also incomplete, and for those no record can be given of land or property.

The first tax list of the Commonwealth of Virginia for Gloucester County was taken in the year 1782, agreeable to an Act of Assembly passed in the October Session, 1781. The following list is made up from the original books of 1770 and 1782, now in the Archives Division of the Virginia State Library.

The names for Kingston Parish as given in the original 1782 list are not included here, but are given in the first tax list of Mathews County which follows this list.

The material in both the Gloucester and Mathews lists has been rearranged into alphabetical order, combining in one list the records of land and personal property from both sources and giving the parish of each person wherever shown.

The names "White" and "Wright" are not found written as "Whyte" and "Right" in any other records.

* Denotes names appearing in both the 1770 and 1782 lists.
/ " " " only in the list of 1770.
M- " " " in both the 1782 list of Gloucester parishes and in the 1791 list for Mathews, after the division of the county.

---ooo000ooo---

Acres - 1770	Wheels-Chair	Name	1782 Acres	Males (Free)	Negroes	Horses	Cattle	Wheels	Parish
		Acra Thomas		1	2	3	4		Ware
		M-Adams Ambrose	35	1	1	1	2		Abingdon
		/Alexander Morgan							
		/Alger Dennis							
		*Allard William	50	1	4	4	5		Petsworth
		/Almund Edmund							
279	2	/Amory Thos. Chamberlin							
		M-Anderson Matthew	240½	1	11	8	25		Petsworth
		Anderson Samuel		1	4	1			Petsworth
		/Anderson William							
		Ash John	200	1	6	3	26		Petsworth
		*Austin Gabriel		1			10		Abingdon
		*Auston John		1		2	4		Abingdon
		/Bain John [Bayne?]							
		/Baker Ambrose							
		/Baker Benjamin							
		Baker Elizabeth	150			1	7		Petsworth
		/Baker James							
		/Baker William, Senr.							
		/Barbie George							
		*Bates Thomas	47	1	2	2	12		Ware
		/Bath Edward							
		*Bayne John [Bain?]		1		2			Ware
		Bayne Lewis		1		1			Ware
439	(Estate)	*Baytop James	332	1	11	3	11	2	Petsworth
220	2	/Baytop Sarah							
		Baytop Thomas	220⅓	1	10	2	13		Ware
		/Beckerton Ann							
		/Bell Adam							
		Bellamy Joseph	80		1	1			Ware
60	2	/Bellamy William							
		Belvin Aaron	47	1	2	3	8		Abingdon
		/Belvin Henry							
		/Belvin John							
		/Belvin Lewis							
		/Belvin William							

Acres - 1770	Wheels-Chair	Name	1782 Acres	Males (Free)	Negroes	Horses	Cattle	Wheels	Parish
		/Bennet Henry							
		*Bentley James	240	1	10	4	18		Petsworth
		Bentley William		1	6	3	10		Petsworth
450		*Berkley Edmund	450						
		*Beveridge John	103½	1	13	3	21		Petsworth
		/Bew William							
		M/Billups John, Junr.							
		Billups Sarah		1	8	1	6		Abingdon
		Blackburn Roger			4	2			Abingdon
375		/Blackley George							
		/Blackley John							
		/Blacknall George							
		Blake Benjamin		1	1	2	6		Ware
		/Bland Francis							
		/Blassingham James							
		*Blassingham John	150	1	4	3	15		Petsworth
		/Blassingham Sarah							
85	(Wife)	*Blassingham William		1			1		Petsworth
		*Blunt Bartholomew		1	2	1	7		Ware
		Bonafield Samuel	375						
500	2	*Booker Lewis	541	2	15	3	24		Petsworth
		/Booker Richard							
490	2 Ch.	/Booker Mary							
		Booker William		1		1	1		Petsworth
1150	4 (Jr.)	*Booth George - Estate	740	1	86	17	113		Ware
		Ditto	400						
501	Ch.	*Booth George	637	2	39	6	52	2	Petsworth
350		*Booth Thomas, Sen.	350	1	31	4	22		Ware
		Booth Thomas, Jr.	400						
	(Executrs)	/Booth Thomas							
		Boswell Abraham	220⅓						
73		/Boswell Elizabeth							
232		/Boswell George							
		/Boswell James							
		*Boswell John	308	1	3	6	21		Ware
	(Sn.M.)	*Boswell John, Jr.		1	2	1	4		Ware
		M-Boswell Machen		1	7	3	12		Ware
728	4	*Boswell Thomas, Maj.	263	1	15	3	16		Ware
	(Brunswick)	/Boswell William							
	(Estate)	/Bray George							
		/Breedlove Mary							
		/Bridges John							
	(Ware)	/Bridges Richard							
		Bridges Robinson		1	2	6	12		Ware
		/Briggs James							
		*Briggs William	2 Lots						
		Bristow John			1	3	2		Petsworth
2000	Ch.	M/Bristow Robert							
		*Brooking Samuel [1784]	140	1	8	3	20		Petsworth
		/Brown Ann							
		*Brown Charles		1	1	1	14		Abingdon
		/Brown Charles, Junr.							
	(Taylor)	/Brown John							
		/Brown Joseph							
		/Brown Thomas							
		Browning J[___]	450	1	1	2	20		Petsworth
		M-Brownley William		1		3	5		Abingdon
		/Buchannon John							
800	Ch.	*Buckner Baldwin	55	2	3	3	2		Petsworth
		Buckner Henry	87						
		*Buckner John	550	1	35	8	8		Ware
		*Buckner John, jr.			7	5	10		Ware
		Buckner Judith	70						
		Buckner Lemuel	148						
		Buckner Lucy			2	1	2		Petsworth
		/Buckner Mary							
		Buckner Robert	400	1	19	3	10		Ware
		Buckner Samuel	200	1	8	1	10		Ware
		Buckner Thomas	200		11	3	9		Ware
		Bunn Henry		1	1	8			Ware

Acres - 1770	Wheels	Chair	Names	1782 Acres	Males (Free)	Negroes	Horses	Cattle	Wheels	Parish
			Burk Arnold (Shoemkr)		1	4	1	7		Ware
			/Burk Jeremiah							
			*Burton Henry	830	2	9	4	24		Petsworth
			Burton John		1	2	1	6		Abingdon
7000	10		*Burwell Lewis - Estate	6800	2	140	14	205		Abingdon
			Ditto	1000	1	28	2	54		Petsworth
			/Busbie Adam							
			*Busby Edward	1 Lot	1	8	1	4		Abingdon
			/Busbie John							
(Taylor)			/Busbie John							
			*Busby William - Estate	95						
1280		Ch.	/Bushrod Mrs.							
			/Caffey [Cassey] Robert W.							
			*Cake Anthony		1		4	9		Abingdon
			Cake Jeremiah		1			5		Abingdon
			Cake Lewis		1			2		Abingdon
			/Call Richard							
			*Camp Jno., Capt.	400	1	9	5	29		Abingdon
			/Camp Thomas, Senr.							
132			/Camp Thomas, Junr.							
			Carr Andrew							
			/Carroll William							
1170			/Cary w. (Bought of Chas.							
170			/ Thuston)							
			/ Ditto (Bought of Tho.Kemp)							
3759			/Cary Wilson							
			/Chapman Henry							
			Chapman Joseph	487	1	14	6	24		Petsworth
			Clack [Clark?] William		1	1		7		Ware
			*Clark [Clack?] James	149	1	3	2	40		Ware
300	2	Ch M	*Clayton Jasper	400		9	2			Ware
(Salary 16000)			/Clayton Jasper, Jr.							
450	4		/Clayton John							
		Ch.	*Clayton Thomas	450	1	3	4			Ware
			/Cleaver James							
			/Cleaver John							
			Clemonds William	220	1	1	5	40		Ware
560	2		*Cluverius Benjamin	1292	1	47	4	14		Abingdon
			Cluverius Gibson		1	15	4	13	2	Abingdon
			Cluverius James		1	10	2	5		Abingdon
			Coleman Ann			3				Abingdon
			/Coleman Joseph							
200			/Coleman Johanna							
			Coleman Richard	136		4	2	8		Petsworth
			Coleman Richard [By Yates]	390		4				Petsworth
			/Coleman Thomas, Capt.							
566 (Estate)			/Coleman Thomas							
200 (Mother's Dower)			/Ditto							
			/Coleman William							
260			/Collawn John, Senr.							
			/Collawn John, Junr.							
260			*Collawn William	400	1	1	3	18		Petsworth
			/Colley Charles							
			Collier James	700						
			/Connelly Thomas							
			Conway & Fitzhugh	290						
			Cooke Dawson	14½						
			Cooke Elizabeth	477		15	2	34	2	Ware
		Ch.	*Cooke Francis W Estate			16	4	19	2	Ware
466½		Ch.	/Cooke Giles							
			Cooke Giles of Fairfax			3				Ware
			Cooke Giles, jun		1	1	4			Ware
1800	2	Ch.	*Cooke John	2132	3	53	14	81	2	Ware
800	2	Ch.	/Cooke John [Jr.]							
(Youngest)			/Cooke John							
(Senior)			*Cooke Mordecai	978½	1	22	13	41	2	Ware
			*Cooke Mordecai, jr.		1	2	2			Ware
			Cooke Miss Nancy			3				Ware
			Cooke Thomas		1	5	2			Ware

Acres - 1770	Wheels-Chair	Names	1782 Acres	Males (Free)	Negroes	Horses	Cattle	Wheels	Parish
		/Cooke William							
		/Cooper Abraham							
		/Cooper Jacob							
		/Cooper John							
		/Corker Johanna							
		/Cosby Overton							
		/Crabbins Hinson Charles							
		/Crew John							
		Crewdson Jno.	463						
140		/Crittenden Richd.							
		[See Kunningham-Keiningham]							
		/Cunningham Nathl.							
		Currey Hanry	50						
		Curry Ann	55		3		8		Petsworth
		Curry Richard		1		2	4		Petsworth
		/Curry William							
		/Curry William, Junr.							
		/Curtice Edward							
		Curtis Ann			12	3	12		Petsworth
77	Ch.	*Curtis *Christopher & James	365						
	Ch.	/Dalgleish Doctr Alexander							
		/Dalgleish Mr. John							
490		/Dalgleish Robert							
		Dame George	55	1	3	2	5		Petsworth
		/Dance Frances							
	2	*Dance William	70	1	5	2	20		Ware
		Daniels Beverley-Estate	800	1	6	1	30		Petsworth
		Ditto	430						
1180		/Daniel Robert							
1626 (1771)		/ Ditto							
34	and(	*Darnel Jeremy	50	1			5		Ware
	(	/Darnel Margaret							
290	Ch.	/Davenport Joseph							
595 (1771)		/ Ditto							
		*Davis Anthony	48	1	5		10		Petsworth
		/Davis Barbee							
54 (Estate)		/Davis Carter							
		/Davis Charles							
		Davis Dorothy	37						
(Overseer)		*Davis John		1		1	4		Ware
120		*Davis Mary	200		14	3	24		Ware
		Davis Reuben	100		2	3	5		Ware
		*Davis Richard		1		1	10		Abingdon
124		*Davis Richard		1	5	3	22		Petsworth
		*Davis Samuel	150	1	1	3	12		Petsworth
(Abingdon)		/Davis Thomas							
		/Davis Ursula							
		Dawson Ann	190	1	11	3	11		Ware
198		/Dawson Samuel							
200		/Day Mary							
		/Deagle Benjamin							
100	Ch.	*Debnam Thomas	279	1	16	7	20	2	Ware
227	2 Ch.	/Debnam William - Estate							
		Dennis James		1	1	2	10		Ware
		Dews Mildred	179						
128		*Dews William	2½						
		Dickerson David	425	1	8	3	21		Petsworth
		Dickerson William		1			3		Petsworth
325		*Dillard John	349	1	6	1	4		Petsworth
375		*Dixon James	372		8	2	38		Abingdon
		Dixon John	1566	1	80	37	126	4	Ware
		Ditto	883						
		/Dobson Edmund							
197		/Dobson Edward							
800		/Dobson John							
		Dobson Grace	65		3		10		Abingdon
		*Douglas Thomas [See Duglas]		1	4	4	18		Petsworth
120		*Douglas William	100	1	4	3	20		Ware

Acres- 1770	Wheels-Chair	Name	1782 Acres	Males (Free)	Negroes	Horses	Cattle	Wheels	Parish
		/Drewit Mary							
		/Dudley John							
150		*Dudley Thomas	249	1		1	6		Petsworth
		/Duglas Elinor							
		/Dugless John							
100		/Dunbar Gawen (& brother)							
		Dunford William	33						
		/Dunkin [Duncan] John							
		/Dunlop Ephraim							
		Dunlap Joanna	300						
		Dunsley James	1 Lot						
		Dunston Mary	25		2	1	10		Petsworth
		*Dutton James	42			4	15		Petsworth
		Duvall Francis	50	1	12	5	14	2	Petsworth
385	Ch.	*Duvall William	418	1	12	2	12		Petsworth
		Duvall William, Jun.	200	1	13	8	10	2/1	Petsworth
		Duval Samuel		1	2		3		Petsworth
		*Easter Richard		1		2	4		Petsworth
35		*Easter William	35						
		Edmonds Charles	3 Lotts						
		Enos John	150	1	5	5	13		Ware
		/Enos Mary							
		*Enos Lewis		1	1	4	11		Ware
		Evans Estate	2 Lotts						
		Evans John	65	1	3	2	2		Abingdon
		Fary Avey	50						
50		/Fary George							
50		/Fary Robert							
		Fary Sarah	50						
		/Figg James							
273		/Figg John, Senr.							
	Junr.	*Figg John	400	1	14	5	39		Ware
		/Figg Matthew							
		/Figg Matthew, Junr.							
		*Figg William		1	5	3	5		Abingdon
		*Filpots [Philpots] Benj.	71	1	2	3	21		Petsworth
435	Newbotl.	*Finney William	435						
		Fitzhugh & Conway [See Conway]							
		Fitzhugh George	1168						
		/Fleming Charles							
		*Fleming John for B.Tomkins							
		/Fleming Thomas							
250		*Fleming William	200	1	1	4	9		Abingdon
		/Fletcher Benjamin							
		/Fletcher Charles							
		/Fletcher Henry							
228		*Fletcher Nathan	228	1	9	2	14		Ware
	(Minister)	*Fontaine James M.	400	2	26	10	52	4	Ware
30		/Foster Jeremiah & Mary							
600	Ch.	/Foster Mary							
		Foster Rachel	175	1	23	4	16		Abingdon
		/Foster Thomas							
		/Fox John, Senr.							
3150-300	C.H.	*Fox John	640	2	53	19	52	6	Petsworth
	Ch.	Ditto	1350						
		Ditto	719						
		Ditto	805						
		Ditto	81						
		Ditto	50						
		Ditto in B. Town	3 Lotts	1	4				
		/Freeman Charles							
		*Freeman James		1		1	9		Petsworth
		/Freeman Richard							
		/Freeman Robert		1		1	6		Abingdon
		/Freeman Thomas, Junr.							
160		/Gardiner George							

Acres - 1770	Wheels-Chair	Name	1782 Acres	Males (Males)	Negroes	Horses	Cattle	Wheels	Parishes
		*Gardner Zach	188		6	8	16		Petsworth
		Garland Christopher	328	1	7	3	16		Petsworth
		Garland Elizabeth	223		10	5	7		Petsworth
		Garland George	234						
300 [Bought of		/Garland Robert							
123 [Guthry]		/ Ditto							
		/Gibson Henry							
		/Glass Mary							
		/Glass Thomas	100	1	8	3	11		Petsworth
	M-?	Glenn Capt. [Glyn?]	600						
		Ditto	48½						
		Goalder Tho. & B.Thompson	170	1	3	2	2		Petsworth
		/Going James							
		Gowen Mary	120						
		Granby William		1	20	1			Ware
		*Graves John		1	2	1	4		Petsworth
50		/Graves Thomas, Senr.							
		/Graves Thomas, Junr.							
		*Graves William	50	1		2	9		Abingdon
500	2 Ch.	*Green George	500	1	10	4	22		Petsworth
[Brot'r of G.]		/Green William							
		Gregory Mary	268		23	9	20		Ware
		Ditto	637						
		Ditto	30						
1398	2	M*Gregory Richard	287						
		/Gresset Frances							
75		*Gresset James	116						
85		*Gressit John	252	1	2	1	9		Petsworth
		Griffin Corban	500						
		/Griffin Edward							
		/Griffin Edward							
		/Griffin Henry							
		/Griffin Thomas							
70		/Grumley Francis							
[For Mother]		*Grumley Swan	75	1	8	1	14		Petsworth
1620-Estate		/Grymes Phill.							
		Grymes Philip L.	1000	1	8	1	14		Petsworth
		Ditto	620						
27		/Guthrey John							
		Guthrie Martha	180		9	5	12		Ware
		Guthrie Richard	58	1	1	1	4		Petsworth
		Guthrie Saml.	398½	1	7	6	19		Petsworth
[See Haynes]		/Haines Daniel							
		/Haines Morgan							
150		/Haines William							
		/Haley Maria							
		Hall Beverley	84	1	6	2	5		Abingdon
		Hall Francis	600	1	4	2	12	2	Ware
100		*Hall Henry	100	1	9	2	17		Ware
215 (Ware)		/Hall John							
385		/Hall John							
		/Hall John-Overseer,Capt.Whiting							
(Petsworth)		/Hall John							
		*Hall Joseph		1	1	2	22		Abingdon
		*Hall Lewis		1	4		2		Abingdon
		*Hall Richard		1	9	1	10		Abingdon
		*Hall Stephen	75						
60		/Hall Sarah							
160		/Hall Soloman-Chg. J.Dillard							
		Hall Susannah	375	1	12	6	30		Ware
		Hall Thomas		1		2	10		Petsworth
		*Hall Thomas	133	1	2	3	15		Abingdon
		Hall Thomas, Jr.		1	1	4	3		Abingdon
634		*Hall William, Sen.	395	2	12	2	9		Ware
		Ditto	230						
		Hall William, Jr.		1	3	4	14	2	Ware
		Hall William			4		23		Petsworth
325	Ch.	/Hamilton Arthur							

Acres - 1770	Acres-Chair	Names	1782 Acres	Males (Free)	Negroes	Horses	Cattle	Wheels	Parish
		/Hansford Thos.							
		/Harper Edward &							
		/ " Ann his wife							
		/Harris George (A negroe)							
		Harris Henry	30						
		/Harris John							
		Harris Mary	10						
	Ch.	/Harvey Elizabeth							
150	Ch.	/Harvey Wm. - Estate							
		Harwood Anne	200						
500	(W.Roan)	/Harwood John- King & Queen							
		*Harwood Thomas	340	1	11	4	13	4	Petsworth
		*Harwood William- Estate			9	4	23		Petsworth
	Estate	/Hayes Wm.							
	Junr.	*Haynes [Haines] George	200	1		1	5		
100	Junr.	*Haynes John	48	1		3	10		Petsworth
		/Haynes James							
		Haynes Mary	150	1			5		Petsworth
238		*Haywood [Heywood] Catherine	238						
		/Haywood Sarah							
		Haywood William	65						
		/Hearvy John							
		*Heaywood [Heywood]Richard	21	1		2	8		Abingdon
		*Henderson Francis		1	3	1	5		Abingdon
		*Heywood Abraham		1			11		Abingdon
		/Heywood Elizabeth							
		*Heywood Isaac		1	1	2	1		Abingdon
		/Heywood Jacob							
		/Heywood James							
60		/Heywood William							
40½		*Hibble George	201	1	5	3	24		
	Estate-	/Hibble Triplit							
	Estate-	/Hinds John							
400		/Hind Russell- Jno.Read Est.							
		Hipkinstall Alexander		1	1	2	3		Ware
		*Hobday Francis		1	8	2	9		Abingdon
		*Hobday Isaac	60						
600	Ch.	*Hobday John (Chr.Maker)	200	1	7	8	24	2	Abingdon
		/Hobday John (Pilot)							
		/Hobday Margary							
50		/Hobday Morgan							
		*Hobday Richard	143	1	11	5	11	2	Abingdon
		*Hogg Fielding		1		1	7		Abingdon
		*Hogg George		1	1	3	6		Abingdon
	Junr.	/Hogg George							
		/Hogg John							
	Senr. & Junr.	*Hogg Richard		1	1	2	10		Abingdon
		Holden George - Estate	813						
		/Hook Elizabeth							
		/Horseley Thomas							
		How Banister - Estate	60						
		Ditto	1 Lott						
		/How Edward							
		Howard John		1	3				Abingdon
		/Howard Thomas							
600		*Howlet Isaac - Estate	680	2	1	1			Ware
		Howlet Johanna	500		12	3	16	4	Petsworth
		Howlet John	325	1	8	1	19	4	Petsworth
		Howlet John	600	1	11	5	24	2	Ware
		Howley Betsy		1		2	5		Petsworth
1000	8	*Huberd James	2408	2	50	8	46	4	Petsworth
	Junr.	/Huberd James							
		/Huberd John							
	Capt.	/Huberd William							
		/Hugget Thos.							
		/Hugget Wm.							
701		/Huggins William							
892		*Hughes John	270	1	14		14		Ware
		Hughes John, Jun.	275						

Acres - 1770	Wheels-Chair	Names	1782 Acres	Males (Free)	Negroes	Horses	Cattle	Wheels	Parish
		Hughes Thomas	100	1	9	3	10		Petsworth
	[M-?]	Hunley Elizabeth	12						
		/Hunt Azariah							
100		/Hunt John							
150		*Hunter Mary			1	2	10		Petsworth
		Hurst Edward	20						
		Innis Robert	300						
		Ditto	100						
326		/Iveson Estate (By Jno.Whiting)							
326	Ch.	/Iveson Gregory - Estate							
		/Iveson John							
134	M-	/Iveson Richard							
		/Iveson Thomas							
		*Jackman William		1		1	4		Ware
		Jackman William, Jr.		1			8		Ware
		Jackman John		1			5		Ware
		/James John Elkin							
		/Jarvis Ben							
		*Jenkins Caleb		1			8		Abingdon
		Jenkins Caleb, Jr.		1					Abingdon
		*Jenkins James		1		3	8		Abingdon
		*Jenkins John		1	1	1	6		Abingdon
		Jenkins John, Jr.		1		1			Abingdon
		*Jenkins Obadiah		1			6		Abingdon
	M-	Johnson John - Estate	35						
		Johnson John	57	1	1	1	9		Ware
	M-	Johnson Jonathan				2			Ware
		/Johnson Samuel							
		/Johnson Thomas							
		/Johnston George, Doctr.							
		/Jones Ann							
		Jones Elizabeth	152						
		*Jones John	178½						
		Jones Mary	1170		35	6	36	2	Petsworth
		/Jones Nelson							
750	Ch.	*Jones Richard	750	1	36	5	21	4	Petsworth
450		/Ditto for Morgan Alexander							
		Jones Richard, Jr.				2			Petsworth
230		*Jones William	60	2	5	1	7		Ware
		*Jordan Thomas	82	1		5	13		Abingdon
		/Kammel John [Campbell?]							
		Keeling William		1	2	1	5		Petsworth
		/Keeton John							
		/Keiningham Banjamin							
100		/Keiningham Elizabeth							
		/Keiningham Jane							
		[See Kuningham-Cunningham]							
		Kemp Betty	300	1	12	3	16	2	Petsworth
		Kemp Dorothy			4				Ware
		Kemp Elizabeth	200		18	2	10		Petsworth
		Kemp Mary	230		3	2	22		Petsworth
831	Ch.	*Kemp Peter	401	1	9	4	9		Petsworth
		Kemp Peter		1	1		2		Petsworth
		/Kemp Robert							
300		/Kemp Thomas							
50 of Geo.Fary		/Ditto							
290	Ch.	/Kemp William, Jr.							
		*Kemp William	250	1	11	3	9	2	Ware
		/Kennon William, Colonel							
		*Keys John, Sen.	264	1	3		12		Ware
		Keys William	50	1		2	15		Petsworth
		Killigrew Sarah	100				5		Petsworth
		King Samuel		1		1			Petsworth
		/Knot William							
100		*Kuningham John - Estate	145½						
		Ditto	100						
[Keiningham]		Kuningham John	200	1	8	2	31		Petsworth

Acres - 1770 Wheels-Chair	Names	1782 Acres	Males (Free)	Negroes	Horses	Cattle	Wheels	Parish
[Keiningham]	Kuningham Mary			7	4	30		Ware
100 "	*Kuningham William		1	1	1			Petsworth
50	/Lamb Mary							
-150	*Lane Daniel	50						
	*Lankford Hiram		1	3	5	11		Ware
	Lankford John		1		3	8		Ware
	/Laughlin Francis							
	*Laughlin James	400	1	8	2	25		Petsworth
	Lawson Anthony		1	2	2			Petsworth
	Lawson Charles	38 3/4						
	*Lawson John		1	13	15		2	Ware
	Lawson Thomas	200		2	2	15		Petsworth
	Lawson William	100	1		2	2		Petsworth
	Leavet Catherine	140						
394	/Leavet Edmund							
	Leavet Elizabeth			4		10		Abingdon
	Leavet Ptolmy	221	1	6		6		Abingdon
50	/Leavet Susanna							
	/Leavet Thomas							
	/Leavit William							
	Lee's Land	1440						
1130 Estate -	/Lee Francis							
	Leigh Richard	56	1	9	1	6		Petsworth
	/Leith Sarah							
	/Lemmon Ambrose							
	*Lemmon James		1	1	3	15		Ware
	Lemmon John	125	2	1	1	7		Petsworth
	/Lemmon Joshua							
	Lemmon Mary				2	3		Ware
Junr.	*Lemmon Richard	76	1	1	1	10		Petsworth
	/Lemmon Robert							
Junr.	*Lemmon William		1	1	2	6		Petsworth
	/Levingston Cornel's							
	Levington Justice				2			Ware
	*Lewellyn Christopher	1						
	/Lewis Fielding & Compr.							
	*Lewis Henry		1		3	4		Petsworth
	*Lewis John		1	4	3	7		Petsworth
Junr.	/Lewis John							
	*Lewis Nicholas	94	1		1	5		Petsworth
	*Lewis Thomas		1	1	3	11		Petsworth
Senr.	*Lewis Warner, Esq.	3369	5	101	29	135	6	Abingdon
	Ditto	1457						
Junr. Ch.	*Lewis Warner, Jr.	705	1	58	22	86	6	Abingdon
	M-?Lilly Thomas	350	1	19	9	8		Ware
	Ditto	350						
	Ditto	498 1/3						
	/Livingston George							
	/Livingston Mary							
	M-?Longest Mildred							
	Louthun Robert		1					
	Lutwytch John		1		1			Ware
390	*Lyell Jonathan	350	1	9	5	18		Ware
(Miss.&c)	/Lyne John							
170	/Mackentree Johan[a]							
	/Mack Williams Thos.							
	/Mannys Henry							
	M-Marable Benjamin	438	1	44	7	62	2	Ware
	Ditto	249						
	/March John							
112	*March Richard	100	1	7	5	9		Abingdon
	March Richard, Jr.			13	2	2	2	Abingdon
	*March Thomas - Estate			9		2		
	*Marnix Isaac		1			2		Abingdon
	/Marnix John							
	/Marnix Thomas							
	/Mason Peleg							
	*Mason Thomas	10						

Acres - 1770	Wheels-Chair	Names	1782 Acres	Males (Free)	Negroes	Horses	Cattle	Wheels	Parish
		Mason William		1	1	2	10		Petsworth
		/Massenburgh Roger							
	Ch.	*Massey Robert		1	2	1			Ware
		/Matthews Moses							
		/McCosky Samuel							
		*Medlicott George		1		2	7		Ware
	M-?	Merchant Edward [Marchant]	50						
		/Meredith John							
		/Meredith Samuel							
		/Metcalf Thos.							
		Milbey Joseph		1	2		5		Petsworth
		/Mills Robert							
		Minor Benjamin		1	2	1	2		Petsworth
		Minor John		1		1			Petsworth
		Minor Mary	202		9	2	8		Petsworth
360		*Minor Thomas	250	1	11	3	21		Petsworth
		/Minor Thomas, Jr.							
		/Mitchel Isaac							
		/Mitchel John							
		/Mitchell Joseph							
		*Mitchell Richard	1						
		/Mitchel Thomas							
		/Moor William							
		Moore Edward		1	3	1	2		Abingdon
		Moore Dunford	1						
		Moore Isaac	22	1	8	3	7		Abingdon
		/Moore John							
185		/Moore Joseph							
		*Morris George		2			8		Petsworth
		*Morris James	100						
		Morris Thomas		1		3			Petsworth
		Morris William	55	1			2		Petsworth
75		*Morris William	99	1	5	3	26		Petsworth
25	Estate-	/Morris Wm.							
		/Mourning George							
		/Mourning John							
		/Mudie James							
700		/Murray James Foun[a] [?]							
133		*Naughton George - Estate				4			Ware
		Naughton William		1		2	11		Ware
		Neal Joseph		1		2	4		Ware
864		*Nelson Thomas G.	420						
75		*Nettles Robert	75						
		New Ann			2		4		Ware
127		*New Daniel - Estate	111½						
181	Mother's	/New Daniel							
110		/New James							
		*New John	39½	1	12	4	5	2	Ware
		Ditto [1784]	13						
		/Newcomb John							
		Newcomb [Will]iam		1	1	2	5		Petsworth
		/Nicholas Elisha							
		Noggins [ ]uel		1		1			Petsworth
163		*Nuttall George	600	2	20	14	32		Ware
		Ditto	363						
		/Nuttall Hazlum							
		Nuttall Iveson		1	6	1	8		Ware
180		*Nuttall James, Sen.	83	1	7	3	30		Ware
		*Nuttall James, Jr.	99	2	10	19	19		Ware
		Ditto B. Town	1 Lott						
	M-	*Nuttall John, Senr.	190	1	19	3	10		Ware
		/Nuttall Matthias							
		*Nuttall Thomas		1	8	2	17		Ware
		/Oliver James							
		*Oliver Thomas	266	1	16	2	7		Abingdon
		/Ozenbriggs Richd.							
2679	Ch.(Honbl)	*Page John	4000	3	162	31	188	6	Abingdon

Acres - 1770	Wheels-Chair	Names	1782 Acres	Males (Free) (Continued)	Negroes	Horses	Cattle	Wheels	Parish
1000 of Buckner		*Page John (Honbl.)	1000						
		Ditto	5000						
2000	2	*Page [Jo]hn at Paradise		2	13		21		Petsworth
		Ditto at Claybank		2	14		26		Petsworth
3515	Senr.	M-*Page Mann - Estate	2800	1	87	19	148	4	Ware
	4	/Page Mann, Junr.							
		Palmer Mary	1 Lott						
		*Palmer William - Estate			4	3	13		Ware
		Pate Jacob	14	1	1		7		Abingdon
		/Pate Obediah							
	[Peppin]	*Pepin Banister	1 Lott						
		*Pepin Richard - Estate	1 Lott						
2244	6 Ch.	*Perrin John	1300	1	64	9	33		Abingdon
		Ditto	100						
		Ditto Gloucester Town	2 Lotts						
	Ch.	/Perrin Mary							
	Estate-	/Perrin Thomas							
	Estate-	/Perkins Ann							
		/Perkins George							
		/Phillups Elizabeth							
		*[Philpots see Filpots]							
		/Phillpots Oakley							
		*Pitts Banjamin G.		1	6	4	33		Ware
		/Pitts Peter							
		/Pointer Elizabeth							
		Pointer Henry, Sen.	500	1	8	2	6		Petsworth
		Ditto	130						
384		*Pointer Henry		1	13	2	16		Ware
		/Pointer James							
		*Pointer Michael	260	1	7	3	17		Ware
		Pollard [Eliza]beth			4	1	2		Petsworth
		Pollard _____C		1	2	2	6		Petsworth
		Pollard Frances	512		5	2	11		Petsworth
		Pollard James		1	1	3	6		Petsworth
85		*Pollard William		1	4	2	5		Petsworth
		/Pomeroy Gilbert							
		/Pomeroy Robert							
	Senr.	*Powell Edmund		1			11		Abingdon
		*Powell Edmund, Jr.		1	2	2	3		Abingdon
		/Powell George, Junr.							
		/Powell Hudson,							
		/Powell James							
		M-Powell John		1			11		Abingdon
		Powell Seamour		1	1		3		Abingdon
		*Powell Thomas		1	6	2	6		Abingdon
		Powers Daniel		1					Ware
		Powers Wm.		1					Ware
		/Price John							
		/Price Thomas							
		/Prior Ann [See Pryor]							
		Proctor Griffin		1					Ware
		Proctor James		1		1	6		Petsworth
		*Proctor Richard		1		3	14		Ware
		Pryor Christopher	100	1	16	6	21	2	Ware
		Ditto	70						
		Puller Elizabeth	39½						
		/Puller James, Senr.							
		/Puller [Pullin] James, Junr.							
		/Puller Joseph							
		/Puller Ledford							
		Puller William		1		1	4		Petsworth
		Purcell George	100	1	3	1	3		Petsworth
185		*Purcell Henry (Harry)Estate			4	1	7		Petsworth
140 Buckner's land		/Ditto							
		Purcell [Jo]hn		1	5	2			Petsworth
		Purcell Peter	209	1	3	2			Petsworth
		/Purdie & Dixon							
394		/Pursell William							

Acres - 1770	Wheels-Chair	Names	1782 Acres	Males (Free)	Negroes	Horses	Cattle	Wheels	Parish
		/Quarrier William							
		/Ramsey William							
776	Ch.	*Randolph Agatha			8				Ware
		/Ransone Peter							
160		*Ransone Richard	140						
		/Ratchford William							
400	M-	/Read John - Estate							
		/Ditto-By Russell Hind							
		Reade Martha	140						
	M?-	Respess Elizabeth (for H. Hudgen)	28						
		Richardson John	152½	1		4	6		Ware
		/Rider Abraham							
		*Rider James		1					Abingdon
		/Rider William							
		Right [Wright] Ealy	34						
		Right Richard, jr.	294			2	9		Petsworth
		Rilee Thomas		1	6	1	1		Ware
		*Rilee [also Rylie] William	150	1	2	1	4		Petsworth
166		*Roan Alexander	406	1	7	3	27		Petsworth
500		/Roan William (By John Harwood, K.& Q.)							
		/Roberts William							
		*Robins John		1	10	7	30		Ware
1000	Ch.M	*Robins William, Sen.	513½	1	16	8	29		Ware
		*Robins William, Jr.	92	1	18	9	40		Ware
		Ditto for B. T.	695						
		*Robinson Benjamin	150	2	11	5	23		Petsworth
		/Robinson Charles							
		Robinson Christ.	2500						
95	M-	*Robinson John	311	1	10	3	22		Petsworth
		/Roe Mary							
1020	Ch.	*Rootes John	665						
		/Ross Francis							
200		*Row Banister	170	1			8		Abingdon
		*Row Hansford		1	9	3	12		Abingdon
		/Row Joseph							
500	Ch.	*Row Rebeckah	458						
700	Estate-	/Row Thomas							
		Row Thomas	300						
700	2	/Row William							
200		/Ditto (Cluverius land)							
200		/Ditto							
70	(Mother's)	*Row Zachariah	200	1	18	3	11		Abingdon
200		*Royston Conquest	200						
800	Ch.	*Royston Richard W.	424	1	7	2	8		Petsworth
		/Russell Lucy							
		Russey James	1 Lott						
		/Ryland Sarah							
150		/Rylie John							
260		/Saddler John							
300	2	/Scott John							
		Scott Mary	300		10	2	16		Abingdon
		Scott Mildred	70		10		8		Petsworth
		/Scott Thos., Colo:							
		/Scott Thos., Jr.							
	[M?]	Scrosby Mary	83						
172	Ch.	*Sears William	172	1	27	4	48		Petsworth
		/Seawell Benja.							
525	Ch.M	*Seawell John	520	2	27	10	34	4	Abingdon
525	Ch.	*Seawell Joseph	560	1	8	7	11	2	Abingdon
		/Shackelford Charles							
		/Shackelford Charles, Junr.							
75		/Shackelford James							
		/Shackelford John							
		Shackelford Mord.		1	1	2	7		Petsworth
		*Shackelford Warner		1		1	7		Abingdon
		/Shackelford Wm.							
		/Shackelford Wm., Capt.							

Acres - 1770	Wheels-Chair	Names	1782 Acres	Males (Free)	Negroes	Horses	Cattle	Wheels	Parish
		*Shackelford Zachr.,Sen.		1			3		Abingdon
		Shackelford Zachariah		2	4	3	6		Abingdon
		Shaw Elizabeth	42				7		Petsworth
		/Shaw Wm.							
		/Shepherd Edward							
		/Shepherd John							
		/Shin John							
		/Shurles Robert							
		*Singleton Isaac	92	2	10	8	27		Ware
		Ditto for B.T.	150						
		/Singleton Joshua							
		*Singleton Robert	100	1	9	5	15		Ware
		Smith Anthony		1	3	4	5		Abingdon
1200		/Smith Augustine							
		Smith James		1		3	10		Abingdon
		M-*Smith James		1		4	14		Ware
133 (Ware)		/Smith John							
(Abingdon)		/Smith John							
819		/Smith John (Northumberland)							
		/Smith Michael							
		*Smith Thomas	11	1		2	5		Abingdon
		Snow Cuthbert		1			3		Petsworth
75		/Soles John							
		Soles William		1			1		Ware
		/Span John							
		/Speed George							
		/Speed Phillip							
		/Spencer David							
		Spencer Francis		1		1	6		Abingdon
		Spencer John	1 Lot	1		1			Ware
		/Spotswood Eliz'th							
		Spratt Robert	875		13	3	29		Petsworth
		Stevens Benjamin	100	1	1	3	3		Petsworth
135		*Stevens Henry	60						
		/Stevenson Richd.							
		M-/Steward James (Tho.Booth's Over'sr)							
		[M-?]Steward Ann							
		/Stoakes Moses							
		/Stoakes Robert, Junr.							
		*Stoakes Robert		1			3		Abingdon
		Stoakes Sarah			4		3		Abingdon
305		*Stoakes Thomas			5	2	11		Abingdon
		/Stoakes William							
		Stubblefield Boots		1		1			Petsworth
350		*Stubblefield Simon	400	1	19	9	54		Ware
		Ditto	350						
		/Stubblefield Thomas							
536		/Stubbs - Estate (By John Whiting)							
		Stubbs Francis S. -Estate	536	1		1			Petsworth
		/Stubbs James							
686	2	*Stubbs John		1	7	5	25		Petsworth
		Stubbs John S.	462	1	10	4	11		Petsworth
		/Stubbs John, Junr.							
418		*Stubbs Lawrence	75	1	4	1	9		Petsworth
		Stubbs Mildred			2				Petsworth
163		*Stubbs Peter	71	1		1	11		Petsworth
		Stubbs Robert		1		1			Petsworth
100		*Stubbs Thomas		1			1		Petsworth
300		*Stubbs William - Estate	18	1	3	1	7		Petsworth
		/Stubbs William, Junr.							
		/Surters Antho., Capt.							
148		/Symmons Land (By Jno. Whiting)							
		/Tallaferro Philip							
415	Ch.	*Taliaferro Richard	415	1	41	5	35	2	Petsworth
		/Tandy Roger							
		/Taylor Mary							
		*Taylor Nathaniel		1			1		Petsworth
75		/Teagle Richard							
		*Teagle Teagle	150						

Acres - 1770	Wheels-Chair	Names	1782 Acres	Males (Free)	Negroes	Horses	Cattle	Wheels	Parish
		*Teagle Teagle (Continued)							
		Ditto Gloucester Tn.	1 Lott						
		M-Thomas Geo. - Estate	100						
		Thompson & Goalder	170	1	3	2	2		Petsworth
		*Thompson Charles		1			6		Abingdon
		M-Thompson John - Estate							
		Ditto Gloucestertown	2 Lotts						
230		/Thornton Esther							
		Thornton Francis	550	2	18	7	37	2	Abingdon
		Ditto	268						
		/Thornton John (Hanov'r)							
		Thornton Meaux	260	1	15	6	20		
		Thornton Presley	230						
230		*Thornton Sterling	230	1	43	14	36		Petsworth
232	Ch.	/Thornton William							
		Thrift Thomas	196½	1	3	2	7		Petsworth
		Thrift William	428	1	6	4	12		Petsworth
	(Senr.)	/Throckmorton John							
	(Junr.)	*Throckmorton John	1 Lott	1	15	6	13		Ware
		*Throckmorton Robert		1		1			Petsworth
		Throckmorton Warner	1920	2	55	11	76		Ware
1000		/Thruston Charles M. [See Thurston]							
		Thruston John - Estate	350		19	6	9		Abingdon
		Ditto Gloster Town	4 Lotts						
		*Thruston Sarah	1001	1	22	7	36	2	Abingdon
		Ditto Gloster Town	4 Lotts						
		Thurston Charles	1000						
		/Thurston Elizabeth							
		/Tillage James							
		*Tillage Thomas - Estate	97						
100		/Timberlake John							
		Tingle James		1					Abingdon
		/Todd Thomas							
		M-*Tomkies Chs:	462		6		11		Ware
		Ditto	455						
	(Capt.)	*Tomkies (Tompkies) Francis	900	1	14	8	21		Ware
		Tomkies Mary	640		10	6	6	2	Abingdon
		Tomkins B. [By A. Boswell]	695						
		Ditto [By J.Fleming]	50						
		Tomlinson Soloman	25						
		Tompkies _____		2	13	12	55		Petsworth
		/Tompkies Charles, Junr.							
1590		/Tompkies Ann							
131		/Tompkins Samuel							
		Tompson ___nard		1			2		Petsworth
		*Tool Richard	1 Lott						
		Tool Robert		1	5	2	2		Ware
		Travillion Mary				1	7		Petsworth
		Tureman William			2	5	7		Ware
		*Urey (Ury) John		1	1		10		Ware
700	2	*Vaughan David	300	1	3	1	12		Abingdon
		*Vaughan Edward		1	4	1	8		Abingdon
41		*Vaughan Jas. - Estate	50						
		Vaughan John	5 Lotts						
		*Vaughan William	160	1	14	7	42		Abingdon
		*Vincent John	8½						
		Waggoner Elizabeth			11	1	11		Ware
247		/Waldin Lewis (You live on)							
		/Walker Edward							
		/Walker George							
		/Walker Martin P.							
		/Walker Michael							
		/Walker Hancel							
160		/Walker Hugh							
		Walker John	141	1	2	1	9		Petsworth
		/Walker Robert							

Acres - 1770	Wheels-Chair	Names	1782 Acres	Males (Free)	Negroes	Horses	Cattle	Wheels	Parish
		Walker Susannah			2				Petsworth
400	2	/Walker Thomas							
		Waller Nelson	20						
		/Washer Richard							
		/Washer William							
1838		/Washington Warner							
		Watlington Elizabeth			1	2	2		Abingdon
		Watlington Nathaniel		1	11	6	20		Abingdon
		/Watlington Paul, Junr.							
		/Watlington Rowland							
		/Watlington William							
1838	8	/Watson Jonathan							
(Petsworth)		/West James							
(Abingdon)		/West John							
142		*West Mary	48		2		10		Petsworth
		West Mary	52				8		Petsworth
		*West Thomas - Estate	74						
		West Thomas	136½	2	7	3	18		Petsworth
		*West William		1			8		Abingdon
		/West William							
		/White Abram							
		/White Catherine							
(Petsworth)		/White John							
		/White Stephen [See Whyte]							
		Whiting Beverley		1	8	8	11	2	Ware
		Whiting Elizabeth			48	5.	30		Abingdon
		Whiting Frances			17	7	24	4	Abingdon
1200	6	/Whiting Francis							
446		/Whiting Henry							
383	2	*Whiting John	1966	1	53	15	42		Ware
1280	Ch.	/Ditto (Mrs. Bushrod)							
		/Whiting Kemp							
		/Whiting Mary							
1850	4	*Whiting Peter Beverley	900	1	70	20	97	4	Ware
		Ditto	40						
		Ditto	800						
1770	6	*Whiting Thomas - Estate	1410						
		Ditto-Gloster Town	2 Lotts						
		*Whyte Joseph		1	1		9		Ware
		Whyte Lawrence	150		1	3	1		Petsworth
		Whyte William	200	1	7	4	8		Petsworth
1038		/Wiatt Edward, Junr.							
332	Ch.	/Wiatt Peter [See Wyatt]							
700		/Widdeburn Alexander							
		Wiler Sarah	250						
		Wilkins Nathl.	131						
		Wilkins Thomas	80	1	1	3	6		Ware
		/Williams Joanna							
418		M-*Williams John - Estate	334						
		Williams Lewis		1	1	2	12		Ware
2800	Ch.	/Willis Francis, Senr.							
1500	4	(Jr.)*Willis Francis	1200	1	65	18	76	6	Ware
		/Willis Robert C.							
		M-/Willis Thos.							
		Wilson James		1	9	2	7	2	Ware
		/Wilson Thos.							
		*Wilson William		1	2		10		Ware
		M-Winder Ann	50						
		/Winston John							
		/Wise John							
		Witherspoon John		1		1	1		Abingdon
		Wood Lewis	500	1	17	11	29	2	Petsworth
		Wood Mary			6				Petsworth
700		/Wood Rachel							
(Estate)		*Wood William - Estate	300		4				Petsworth
60		/Wormley Ralph							
		/Wright Jane [See Right]							
		/Wright John							
253		/Wright Richard							

Acres - 1770 Wheels-Chair		Names	1782 Acres	Males (Free)	Negroes	Horses	Cattle	Wheels	Parish
253		*Wright Thomas		1	7	2	5		Ware
333	(Capt.)	*Wyatt (Wiatt) John	360	2	9	6	41		Petsworth
		M-*Wyatt " Richard	50						
		Wyatt Sarah	840	2	39	9	95	2	Petsworth
		Ditto	400						
		M-*Wyatt (Wiatt) William	1018	1	1	1	5		Petsworth
		Yateman John [Yeatman]	60						
		/Yates Beverley							
		/Yates Humphrey							
		/Yates James							
		/Yates John							
250		/Yates Mary							
		Yates Robert	230	1	9	2	15		Petsworth
		/Yates Simeon							
		/Yates William							
60		/Yeatman Thomas							

The first tax list for the NEW COUNTY OF MATHEWS was taken in 1791. The boundaries of Mathews follow - almost entirely - the boundaries of Kingston Parish of Gloucester, which was the earliest mentioned parish formed in colonial Gloucester.

The following tax list is made up from three sources: a photostatic copy of Kingston Parish Record of Titheables 1774/1775; the 1782 Tax List of Gloucester for Kingston Parish; the first Tax List for Mathews County taken in 1791. These are all found in the Archives of the Virginia State Library. The list as given here shows land and personal property as recorded in the originals, but these combined lists have been rearranged into alphabetical order.

* Denotes names appearing in both the 1774 and 1782-1791 lists of Kingston-Mathews.
/ " " " only in the 1774/1775 list.
G- " " " in the 1782 list of the three Gloucester parishes, given in the list for Gloucester, and also in the list of the new County of Mathews.

---ooo000ooo---

Gloucester Tax List - 1782 Kingston Parish						Name	Mathews Tax List - 1791				
Acrs.	Men	Neg.	Hors.	Catl.	Whl.		Acrs.	Men	Neg.	Hors.	Carriage
35	1	1	1	2		G-Adams Ambrose	35	1	1		
						/Adams Chris.					
42	1	2		9		*Adams Zachariah	67	1	3		
						Ditto	7				
100						*Allerman John	100	1	2	2	
66	1	4	4	8		*Anderson Edward	66	1	2		
						Anderson Edward, jr.	7	1	1		
						Anderson John	120	1	1		
						Anderson John (Island)		1			
240½	1	11	8	25		G-*Anderson Matthew					
85	1	2				Anderson Richard	35	1	1		
						Anderson Thomas		1			
						/Anderton Isaac					
						/Anderton John					
						Anderton Ralph		1			
						Anderton Thomas		1			
						*Anderton William-Estate	24	1	1	1	
						Angle Robert		1			
						Annadale Joseph		1		1	
856	1	16	5	17		Armistead Churchill	746	1	7	3	
						Ditto (Old Town)	342				
79						*Armistead Currell					
167						*Armistead Dorothy	167				
						Armistead Francis	79				
300	1	18	3	19		*Armistead George	300	1	7	3	
						/Armistead Isaac					
376	1	27	1	18	Estate	*Armistead John, Senr.	85	1	4	1	
						Armistead John, Jr.	188	1	2		
						Armistead Maria			17	8	
	1		3	8		*Armistead Richard	21	1	1	2	
113	1	5	1	20		*Armistead Robert	92	1	1		
						/Armistead Robert, Jr.					
3000	1	81	10	69	4	*Armistead William- Est.	3000				
						Armistead William	188	1	2	1	
50	1		1	5		Ashberry Joseph	50	1	1	2	
						Ditto	33				
						Atherton Ambrose		1		1	
	1	2	2	8		Atherton Charles					
						Atherton John		1		1	
	1	3	2	2		Ayres John					
						Ayres Richard		1			
						Ayres Ritchie		1	3	1	
						Bagniers Augustine	250				
						Bailey George		1	6	3	
150						Bailey Mary	150				
150						Bailey Matthew	150	1	6	3	
						/Bailey Thomas					
						Banks Mrs., Senr.	267				
						Banks Isaac		1	1	1	

Gloucester Tax List - 1782 Kingston Parish Acrs.	Men	Neg.	Hors.	Catl.	Whl.		Name	Mathews Tax List - 1791 Acrs.	Men	Neg.	Hors.	Carriage
600	1		2	5			Banks James- Estate	333	1		1	
							Basset John		1		1	
6[illegible]	1		2	7			Bassett Richard, Jr.	45	1	2	2	
							/Bassett Sarah					
	1		1	13			*Bassett William, Sen.	37½	1		1	
	1		1				*Bassett William, Jr.	68	1	1	2	
							/Baxter John					
	1		1	12			Bell Peter					
							Bell William	22	1		1	
230	1	12	3	3			*Bernard Peter					
							/Billups Ann					
							Billups Christopher	307	1	5	1	
40	1	6	2				Billups George	100	1	5	1	
100	1	5	2				*Billups Humphrey					
725	3	29	10	16		Capt.	*Billups John, Senr.	450	1	10	4	
							G-*Billups John, Jr.	100	1	1	2	
							/Billups Joseph- Estate					
174	1		3	6			Billups Joseph, Jr.	177½	1	6	3	
	1	9	5	17			Billups Richard	275	1	9	5	
							Ditto	190				
320	1	18	4	16		Jr.	*Billups Robert	108				
375	1	12	2	8			*Billups Thomas					
400	2	22	5	17			*Blacknall Mary					
							Blacknall Thomas	175	1	6	2	
							Blake James	1½	1		1	
83 1/3	1	7		8			*Blake Thomas					
40	1		1	11			Blake William	40	1			
74							*Bohannan William	160	2	3	1	
							/Bolton Mary					
385	1	9	1	6			Booker James - Estate	355		8	4	
75							*Booth Elizabeth, Est.(PC)	75				
400	1	17	1	17		(Senr.)	*Borum Edmund	400	1	8	1	
	1	7	1	11			Borum Edmund, Jr.		1			
	1	2	1	5			Borum John		1		1	
							Borum John, Jr.		1			
							/Borum William					
							/Boss John					
	1	7	3	12			G-Boswell Machen	314	1	13	4	
							Boush George	10	1			
							Bragg Benjamin	200	2	5	6	
							Brandham Richard		1			
							Bridge Joshua		1		1	
							Bridge Ransone	4	1	1	1	
							*Bridge William		1			
2000						G-Estate	*Bristow Robert					
							Brodie Alexander		1	4	2	
50		3	3	10		Brommil-	Bromwell Elizabeth	50		1		
161	1	11	2	11			*Brooks George	161	3	5		
							Ditto	100				
							Brooks John		1			
187½							G-Brookes Richard					
							Brooks Thomas	37	1	2		
100							Brown Christopher	100	1	8	3	
54½							Ditto	74				
							/Brown Francis					
248	1	4	2	9			*Brown George - Estate					
55	1	6	1	7			Brown Robert - Estate	233				
							Brown Susannah			3	1	
							*Brown William	57	1	1	1	
50							*Brownley Archibald	50	3		1	
							*Brownley Archibald		2			
	1			5			*Brownley Edward (Brounley)					
33							*Brounley Elizabeth	33		1		
							*Brounley Isaac	34	2		1	
60	1			2			*Brownley James (Jr)	60	2			
	1	1	1	7			Brownley John		1			
							Brownley Philip		1			
50							Brounley Sarah	50				
							Brownley Thomas		1			

Gloucester Tax List - 1782 Kingston Parish						Names	Mathews Tax List - 1791				
Acrs.	Men	Neg.	Hors.	Catl.	Whl.		Acrs.	Men	Neg.	Hors.	Carriage
	1		3	5	(Sr.)	G-*Brownley William		1		1	
177	1	9	2	7		*Buckner William	177	1	10	2	
88						Ditto					
						Burton Ann			1		
						/Burton Mildred					
						/Burton William					
						Callam Abel		1			
63						*Callis Ambrose	131	2	4	2	
						Ditto	125				
						Ditto	46				
						Callis George, Senr.	100	1	1		
						Callis James	107	1	2	3	
						Callis James, Jr.	41½				
319	1	5				*Callis John, Sen'r	86		9		
150						*Callis John, Jun.		1			
						Callis John (E.R.)	25	1			
	1		1	5		*Callis Richard	60	1			
40					(Sr.)	*Callis Robert		1			
						Callis Robert, jr.		1	3		
40					Estate-	*Callis William (Mac)		1			
						Callis William, Jr.		1	62	18	
						Carney William		1			
	1	9	2	4	(Pr.Edwd)	Carter James		1	2	3	
400		21	6	16		*Carter Jane, Estate	400		16	7	
						*Cary Ann			1		
						/Cary Dorothy					
330		25	10	26		*Cary Dudley	436	2	21	5	
						Cary John		1	6	2	
130	1	12	5	33		Cary Robert	50	1	9	5	
						Castins Joseph		1			
						Cellars William		1			
						/Chambers Mary					
						Charley Robert		1			
						Christian George		1		1	
						Christian John		1		1	
				5		*Christian Martha	15				
400		9	2			G-*Clayton Jasper	548	1	16	4	
						Clopton Thomas		1		1	
						Colton Job	62				
25						*Cooke Ignatious	60				
						Cooke Richard		1			
						Cotter Christopher		1	2	1	
	1			5		G-Cray John		1			
51					(Estate)	Cray Richard - Estate	51				
						Cray Thos.		1			
						Crudeson William		1	3	3	
					[Carithers]	Cruthers James		1			
					[Culley]	Cully Armistead		1	1		
167	1	10				*Cully Christopher	97	1	6	2	
214		4		4		Culley Judith			2		
87½	1	3	1	4		Cully Ralph	80½	1	4	1	
						/Cully Robert, Senr.					
						*Cully Robert	50	1			
						/Curtis Augustine					
						/Curtis Capt.					
						Curtis Charles		1			
	1	7	4	12		Curtis John - Estate			2	1	
						Davis Mrs. (P.C.)	50		1		
50	1	5		9		*Davis Edward	50	1	3		
						Ditto	100				
	1		2	3		Davis Edward					
						Davis Hillican		1	1		
117	1	9	3	8		*Davis Humphrey	99	1	4		
11½	1	4	2	10		*Davis Isaac - Estate	120	1	2	1	
	1	1		4		Davis Isaac, junr.	29½	1	3	1	
360						*Davis James (P.C.)	300	5	8	6	

Gloucester Tax List - 1782 Kingston Parish							Names	Mathews Tax List - 1791				Riding-
Acrs.	Men	Neg.	Hors.	Catl.	Whl.			Acrs.	Men	Neg.	Hors.	Carriage
200	1	2		1		(Senr.)	*Davis John					
							*Davis John (Son Isaac)		1	1	1	
							Davis John (Son James)		1	1		
							*Davis John (Shoemaker)		1			
250	1	5	1	8			*Davis Joseph, Sr.	248	2	3	1	
120	1	4	3	3			Davis Richard		1			
							Davis Richard H.		1	2	3	
15	1	2	1	6		(Junr.)	*Davis Thomas, Senr.	15	1	1	2	
							Ditto	60½				
	1	5		5			Davis Thomas (Son Isaac)		1	1	1	
140						(P.C.)	Davis William (Son John)		1			
							Dawson James	25	2		1	
39	1		2	4			*Dawson Leonard	14				
40	1		2	9			Dawson Thomas					
							Dawson William	7½	1	1	1	
	1			3			Deal James					
	1			2			Deal John					
							Dean Charles		1			
200	1	14	2	17			Deans Josias					
400							*Debnam Charles	172	1	4	3	
							Debnam Robert		1			
							/Degge Anthony [Diggs]					
75	1						Degge Augustine	30	1		1	
							Degge Bailey	75				
							Degge David		1		1	
							Degge Henry		1		1	
							Degge Jesse		1			
							Degge John	32	1	2	1	
							Degge Joicy			3	1	
400							*Degge Joseph	400	1	7	2	
							Degge Joseph, jr.		1			
							Degge Josiah		1		2	
175	1	2		10			*Degge Joshua	175	2	2	2	
		3	3	14			Degge Mary			3		
150	1	7		1			*Degge William, Senr.	150	2	4	1	
75	1			1			Degge William, Junr.	75	1	1		
	1			3			Degge William (Son Josh.)		1			
							Die John		1			
							Die William		1			
							/Dixon Finley					
1566	1	80	37	126	4	G-	*Dixon John - Estate	400				
							Ditto	106				
120	1		1				Dixon Michael					
							*Dixon Thomas	200	1	8	4	
							Ditto	119				
86							*Dixon William	159	1	1	2	
							Ditto	40				
							/Dodd Newcomb					
							Driscal William		1		1	
							Driver Emanuel		1			
							Driver John	45	1			
							Driver William		1			
270		5	1	9	2		Dudley Dorothy	60		1		
240	1	7	6	3		(Junr.)	*Dudley George - Estate	360				
400							*Dudley George A.	25½	4	3	1	
							/Dudley Judith					
	1		1	3			Dudley William		1	2	2	
							Dun John		1		1	
100							*Dunbar Gowan (Gawen)	76	1			
							Dunbar Sally			1		
							Dunlavy Ann			1		
	1	9		5		(Eddins)	*Eddens Dawson - Estate	263				
							*Eddens Elizabeth			5	1	
438	1	16	3	10			*Eddens John, Senr.					
	1	11	2	12			Eddin John					
							Eddens Letitia		1	3	1	
	1	8		3			*Eddens Samuel	175	1	7	1	
400	1	27	10	44		(Elliot)	*Elliott John, Sen.	350	1	11	7	
							Elliott John, Junr.	126				
							Ditto	110				

Gloucester Tax List - 1782, Kingston Parish | Names | Mathews Tax List - 1791

Acrs.	Men	Neg.	Hors.	Catl.	Whl.	Names	Acrs.	Men	Neg.	Hors.	Riding-Carriage
						Elliott John (Orphan)	405	1	3	3	
						Eliott Robert		1	2	2	
						*Elliott William		1			
	1	5	3	9		Enos Francis	25	1	1	3	
						/Evans Lewis					
						Evins James		1			
	1		1	8	(Evins)	*Evans William	30	2			
						/Fielde Thos.					
	1	11		7		*Fitchet Daniel	100	3	8		
						Fitchet Joshua	11	1	1		
	1	2		7		*Fitchet Thomas		1	2		
	1			2		Fitchet William	42½	1	1	2	
						/Flecher Ann					
						/Flipping Humphrey					
56						*Flippin John - Estate	56				
						Flippin John		1			
56						*Flippin Thomas - Estate	56				
						Ford John		1			
						*Forrest Abraham, Jr.		1			
	1	1		3		Forrest Edmond		1			
	1	7		10		*Forrest George	66	1	2		
	1	1	2	6		*Forrest George, Junr.	25	1		1	
						*Forrest George, Youngest	22	1		1	
	1			1	(Son Phil)	Forrest George					
41	1	11	2	12	(1784)	*Forrest Henry					
						Forrest James (Son Geo.)		1		1	
	1			4	(Sr.)	*Forrest John		1			
						Forrest Mary	22				
	1	1	1	7		*Forrest Philip	83	1	2	3	
						Ditto	28				
						Forrest Robert	66				
						Forrest Thomas		1	1	3	
	1			5		Foster Christopher		1	1		
		9		8		Foster Elizabeth	305		2	1	
	1	1		3		*Foster Francis	75	1	2	1	
	1		1	2		Foster George	32	2	2	1	
	2			7		*Foster Isaac	35	1	1		
						*Foster Jesse	35	1	1	1	
	1	10	1	16		*Foster Joel	445	2	6	2	
						Ditto	114				
						Ditto	53				
						Ditto	45				
		4		1		*Foster John - Estate	114				
	1		2	6		*Foster John, Jun.		1			
						*Foster Joshua, Sr.		1	1	1	
						Foster Joshua, jr.		1			
	1	16	2	13		*Foster Josiah, Sr.	214	1	9	1	
						Foster Josiah, Jr.		1			
	1	2	4	8		Foster Peter	100	1	2	4	
	2	6	4	16		*Foster Robert	270	1	3		
	1		1	1		*Foster Robert, Jr.		1			
						Foster Rose			3		
						/Foster William					
						Frary James		1		1	
1308½						Fulwell John - Doc'r	300		5	3	
270						*Gayle Catherine					
		5	2	8	Estate-	*Gayle Christopher					
86	1	4	2	3		Gayle Christopher					
400	1	4	3	–		*Gayle George	370	1	6	2	
						Gayle Hunley	4	1	3	1	
122	1	10	1	9		*Gayle John, Sen.					
						Gayle John (Son Mat.)		1			
108	1	6	3	14		Gayle Joseph - Estate	245				
84					(Hunley)	Gayle Jos. & Matthew	84	2	8	3	
						Gayle Leaven	124	2	9	2	
						/Gayle Matthias - Estate					
						Gayle Matthew, Sr.	25		1	1	
89	2	12	2	11		*Gayle Matthew	84	1	1		

Gloucester Tax List - 1782 Kingston Parish							Names	Mathews Tax List - 1791				Riding-
Acrs.	Men	Neg.	Hors.	Catl.	Whl.			Acrs.	Men	Neg.	Hors.	Carriage
							*Gayle Sally			2	1	
135							*Gayle Robert - Estate	135				
212	1	5	1	4			Gayle Thomas					
50	1		1	3			*Glasscock Abraham	50	1		1	
63	1		1	2			*Glasscock Isaac	63	2		2	
							Glasscock Milton		1	3	1	
648½						(Capt.)	G-Glyn Duncan [Glenn]	586½	1	4	3	
							Goulding John		1			
	1		1	4			G-Green Charles		1			
70							Green George - Estate	70				
50							*Green James - Estate	50				
	1			6			*Green John		1			
							Green Richard, Sr.		2			
							*Green Richard, Jr.					
250							Green Robert		3			
							*Green Simon, Sr.		1			
							G-/Green William					
							Gregory Mordecai	350	1	13	4	
287							Gregory Richard	287	1	7	3	
							Guthrie George		1	4	1	
	1	9	1	2			*Gwyn Harry					
209	1	9		12			*Gwyn Hugh - Estate	225		8		
	1	3	1				*Gwyn Humphrey, Senr.	311	2	10	6	
							Gwyn Humphrey, Jr.	25		1	1	
	1		1	8			Gwyn James		1		2	
180	1	6	1	12			Gwyn John	30		2	1	
	1		1	2			Gwyn John (Island)		1			
	1	4	1	4			Gwyn John					
160	1	4	2	4			Gwyn Robert	30	1	2	1	
	1	13	2	7			Gwyn Walter					
41½							Hall Ann	44½				
							*Hall Thomas		1	1	2	
400	1	15	5	20			*Harper James	400	1	6		
100							Ditto	120				
							Harper John		1			
23							*Harris James	23	1			
							*Harris Matthias	30	1			
							/Harris Thomas					
							Harrow Christopher	12	1	1		Chair
440	1	27	2	2	2		*Hayes Hugh					
297							Ditto P. Comfort					
200	1	22	4	12			*Hayes John	200	2	12	4	
370		19	1	12			*Hayes Mary	370		9		
700	1	26	2	24			*Hayes Thomas					
	1	1		7		(Haywood)	*Heywood Elkanah					
							Hillin William		1			
	1	2	2	4			Hobday Brookes					
	1	1		3			Hobday Richard					
							Hodges Ann	100				
							Hodges Benjamin - Estate			2	1	
							Hodges Charles	27				
	1	2	4	17			*Hodges Richard		1	2	3	
							Hodges William	20	1	2	1	
95							Holder Elizabeth	95				
						(Hudgen)	*Hudgin Albin		1			
	1			3			Hudgin Anthony		1	1	1	
							Hudgin Archibald		1			
							Hudgin Edward (Son Wm.)		1			
	1			6			*Hudgin Gabriel					
100	1			7		(Island)	*Hudgin George, Senr.	75	1		1	
25	1	4		7		"	*Hudgin George, Junr.	25	1			
							Hudgin George, Junr.	10	1			
							Hudgin George (Son Gabriel)		1			
28							Hudgin H. by Elizabeth Respess					
							Hudgin Hillican		1			
390	1	15	5	18			*Hudgin Holder (Houlder)	500	1	9	5	
							Ditto	63				
2	1	1		6			Hudgin Hugh	49 3/4		1	1	
							Ditto	2				

Gloucester Tax List - 1782 Kingston Parish						Names	Mathews Tax List - 1791				
Acrs.	Men	Neg.	Hors.	Catl.	Whl.		Acrs.	Men	Neg.	Hors.	Riding-Carriahe
300	3	5	2	11		*Hudgen Humphrey, Senr.	180	1	5	1	
						Ditto	25				
	1	3	4	8		Hudgin Humphrey, Jr.		1			
30	1	1		5		*Hudgen James		1			
170	1	5		12	Senr.	*Hudgen John	170	1	3		
	1			3		Hudgins John, Junr.	30	1			
						Hudgen John (Battery)	60	1	3	2	
						Hudgin John (Smith N.R.)	12	1			
						Hudgin John (Son Albin)		1			
						Hudgin John (P.C.)		3		1	
						Hudgin John (Son Hump.)		1		2	
						Hudgin Joshua		1			
						Hudgin Kemp		1		2	
60						*Hudgen Lewis	60				
						*Hudgin Lewis	30	1			
20						*Hudgin Mary					
30						*Hudgen Mary G.					
						*Hudgin Moses	11	1			
	1			3		Hudgin Perrin		1			
						*Hudgin Robert	30	2	2	2	
50						Hudgin Thomas	50	1	1		
50	1	7				Hudgin William (Smith)	50	1		1	
173	1		2	9		*Hudgen William (G.C.)	273	1	2	1	
						Ditto	25				
						Hudgin William (Son Wm.)		1		1	
						Hudgin William (B.S.)		1	1	2	
						Hudgin William (Son John)	50				
						*Hudgin William H.	420	1	3	2	
						Huggate James		1			
						Huggate John		1			
181	1	5		12		Huggins Estate-by James Wilson					
225	1	18	3	6		*Hughes Edward, Senr. Est.	225		7	1	
						Hughes Edward (Q.Creek)		1	1	1	
250	3	22	2	20		*Hughes Gabriel, Sr.Estate	180				
						Hughes Gabriel, Junr.	70	1			
	1	1	2			Hughes Henry					
270	1	14		14		G-Hughes John		1	4	1	
100	1	9	3	10		G-Hughes Thomas		1			
4	1	2	2	3		*Hunley Caleb	4	1	1	1	
240	1	5	2	10		*Hunley Henry for Tho.Lilly					
						*Hunley Henry, Senr.	60	1	1	3	
109	1	4	2	10		*Hunley James (E.R.)	107	2	5	3	
						*Hunley James (Shoemaker)		1			
						Hunley Jesse	40				
160	1	2	1	4	(Amc.)	*Hunley John, Senr.	80	1	1	1	
100	1	2	1	4		Hunley John, jr.		1	1		
200	1			4		*Hunley Matthew, Senr.					
						Hunley Nehemiah		1			
	1	2				Hunley Philip					
						Hunley Richard	46	1	1		
						/Hunley Robert					
12	1		1	7		Hunley Thomas (Island)	12	2		1	
	1		2	6		*Hunley William (N.R.)	43	1	1	2	
	1	6				Hunley William, Junr.	47				
						Hunley William,(Son Henry)		1		2	
20						*Hurst Edward - Estate	20				
						Hurst Jesse		1			
37	1	5	2	4		*Hurst John, Sr.	37	1	2	1	
						Hurst John, Jr.		1			
						Hurst John (Youngest)		1			
						Hurst John (Son Richard)		1			
						Hurst Mildred			4		
99	1	5	1	11		*Hurst Richard - Estate	99				
						*Hurst Richard, Sr.		1	1		
						Hurst Richard, Jr.		1			
						Hurst William		1			
500						Iveson Abraham		1	8	3	
134						G-*Iveson Richard		1			

Gloucester Tax List - 1782 Kingston Parish Acrs.	Men	Neg.	Hors.	Catl.	Whl.		Names	Mathews Tax List - 1791 Acrs.	Men	Neg.	Hors.	Riding-Carrisge
	1		1				*Iveson Robert					
							James Edward	78 2/3	1	4	3	
							James Elizabeth		1	4	1	
55							*James Matthias	84½				
						(Jr.)	*James Thomas		1	1	1	
60							*James Walter	60	1	2		
							James William		1			
						(Jarret)	Jarrot John		1			
25½	1		1	4		"	*Jarrat William	25			1	
12	1	2	1	5			*Jarvis Francis, Senior	12				
100	1	1		6			*Jarvis Francis, Junior	130	2	4	1	
101	1	2	1	5			*Jarvis Francis (P.Comf)	101	3	1	4	
							Jarvis James		1	1		
	1	4	1	2			*Jarvis John (H.Ft)		1			
	1						Jarvis John					
100	(L.by Wm. Respess)						Jarvis Lucy			1		
							Jarvis Machen		1			
25	1	1		1			*Jarvis William					
	1	2	1	2			Jarvis William, Jr.					
							Johnstone Ann			1		
35						(Johnson)	*Johnstone John - Estate	35				
			2				G-Johnstone Jonathan	600				
							Johnstone William	2	1	2	1	
							Joiner Edward		1			
							G*Jones Charles		1	3	2	Chair
	1	18	2	3			Jones Edward S.		1	1	1	
							/Jones Isaac					
							Jones James, Jr.		1	1	1	
							G*Jones James, Senr.	200	2	9	5	
							Jones Philip E.		1	1		
182½							*Jones Thomas					
							Keeble Elizabeth			1		
						[Kipple]	Keeble Stapleton	156	1	2	2	
500							G-Keeble Walter (Kibble)Est.	500				
							/Kennaday Capt.					
	1			4			Kennys Edward					
	1	8	2	17			*Kerr Andrew	105	1	8	1	
							*Keys Edward [Keyes]	52	1			
							/Keys Robert					
							/King Ann, Widow					
100							*King John					
50	1	5	4	13			*King Joseph	50		5	1	
							Ditto for H.H.	35				
							/King Thomas					
							King William		1	1	2	
							Knight Gabriel		1		1	
437	1	13	2	22			*Knight Henry	434	2	10	1	
							Ditto (Marsh)	100				
							Knight Joseph		1		1	
							Knight Joseph, Jr.		1			
							Knight Richard		1			
500	1	18	7	34			Lane Ezekiel	500	1	6	8	
51							Ditto	51				
							Ditto	277				
							Ditto	222				
							Lane William		1	4	1	
							G-*Laughlin Simon	254	1	6	1	
							/Layton Reuben					
		14					Leed Mrs. Elizabeth Lux					
						[?G]	Levington Sarah	73½				
40	1	2		7			*Lewis Christopher	40	1	2		
66 2/3	1	4	2	16			Lewis George	69 2/3	1	5	2	
							Ditto	35½				
90	1	4	2	2			Lewis John	100	1	5	1	
							Ditto	20				
							/Lewis Lucretia					

Gloucester Tax list - 1782 Kingston Parish | Mathews Tax List - 1791

Acrs.	Men	Neg.	Hors.	Catl.	Whl.		Names	Acrs.	Men	Neg.	Hors.	Riding-Carriage
25	1	1		7			*Lewis Robert	25	1	1		
50	1	2		4			Lewis Thomas	35	1	2		
35							G- Ditto					
160	1	4	2	7			Lilly John	160	1	4	2	
		7	2	8			Lilly Lucy					
240	1	5	2	10		[Hunley]	Lilly Thomas	216	1	12	1	
							Lilly Thomas, Junr.	240	1	2	1	
498 1/3	1	19	9	8			G-Lilly Thomas					
350							Ditto					
350							Ditto					
							/Lilly William					
							Litchfield Zadock	50	1		2	
							*Little John		1			
							/Longest Ann					
							G-/Longest Mildred					
							Longest Ross		1	1	4	
							/Longest Thomas					
							Longest William		1			
							/Lowery Mary					
	1						*Lucas William		1			
200							*Machen John - Estate	200				
							*Machen Judith					
		6					Machen Margaret					
		11					Machen Mary			5		
							Machen Richard		1			
							*Machen Robert		1			
	1						*Machen Samuel					
							Machen William		1			
438	1	44	7	62	2		G-Marable Benjamin	180				
249							Ditto	30				
184						[Merchant]	*Marchant Ambrose	130	2	8	3	
							Merchant Daniel	16				
							Merchant Edmund	50	1	1		
105	1	2		13			*Merchant Elisha	105	2	2		
							Marchant Frances			5		
							*Merchant Richard	8	1			
126							Merchant William	44	1	1		
							/Marchant William, Jr.					
249		8	1	9		[Mathews]	Matthews Dorothy (Mrs.)					
180							Ditto					
400	1	17	4	11			Matthews Edwards					
							*Matthews John		1			
							/Matthews Richard					
450	1	31	4	22	2		*Matthews Robert					
	1						Mathews Thomas					
							Mc Bride James		2	1	2	
							Micou James		2	1	2	
							Micou John	1000	2	13	7	
							Miller Anderson	187	1	3	2	
							Miller Averilla	150		1		
							/Miller Duncan					
100	1		2	4			*Miller Francis	100	1		1	
							Miller Francis, Jr.		1			
400	1	8	2	19			*Miller Gabriel	238	1	2	1	
	1	4	1	1			Miller James		2	4	2	
60	1	1	2	7			*Miller Joseph, Sr.	60	2	1	1	
							Miller Joseph		1			
	1			2			Minter Anthony		1			
	1	1					Minter Anthony, Jr.					
							/Minter James					
72	1	5		6			Minter John	72	1	2	1	
							/Minter Judith					
	1			4			Minter William					
50							Morgan James	50	1	1		
							Morgan John		1			
							*Morgan Mark		1			
							/Morgan Richard					
	1			4			Morgan Thomas					
							Morgan William		1			

Gloucester Tax List - 1782 Kingston Parish Acrs.	Men	Neg.	Hors.	Catl.	Whl.	Names	Mathews Tax List - 1791 Acrs.	Men	Neg.	Hors.	Riding-Carriage
	1			4		Morgan Thomas					
						Morgan William		1			
	1	1		4		*Morris John		1		1	
50	1	13	6	22	2	Sr.*Morris William (P.C.)	343½	1	10	3	
						Morris William		1		1	
						/Mullins Dorothy					
						Mullins George		1		1	
						/Mullins James					
						Nicholson John		1	8	5	Post Chaise
99	2	10	19	19		Junr. Nuttall James	100				
						Owin Benjamin		1			
						*Owin George		1			
						Owin George (P.C.)		1		1	
						Owin John (P.C.)	9 3/4	1			
						Owin John		1			
						*Owin William, Sr.		1			
2800	1	87	19	148	4	G-*Page Mann - Estate	1200				
						Page William		1	1	2	
						*Palister John		1		1	
		2	8			Parrott Ann					
						Parrot Augustine	2 3/4	1			
						Parrot George, Sr.		1	1	1	
25	1	1	2	6		*Parrott John, Senr.	33	1		1	
	1	1	2	2		Parrot John, Jr.		1			
						Parrot Michael		1	2	2	
						Parsons Absalom		1		1	
						Parsons Caty			2		
	1	6	1	5		*Parsons James					
60	1	4	1	6		*Parsons John - Estate	60				
						Parsons Mary			1		
						[Peed] Pead Andrew	16 2/3	1		1	
						Pead Dorothy	4				
						Pead George, jr.		1			
62						Peed Hunley	22 1/3	1			
						Junr. *Pead James	10				
	1		1	3		Peed John	50	1	1		
50						*Peed Lewis, Senr.					
						*Pead Lewis	16 2/3	1			
						Pead Robert	10				
						Pead Richard	16 2/3	1			
						Pead Sarah	8		2		
						*Pead William	10	1		1	
						/Peek Thomas					
						Peters Robert		1			
						*Pew Elias		1			
						Pew Josiah		1			
						*Pew William					
2000	2	128	28	120		*Peyton Sir John, Estate	1650		68	4	Chair
						/Peyton Thomas, Capt.					
	1		1			Philground George					
	1	1	2			Picket Galin - Estate	50		2	1	
						Pleacy Charles		1			
						Pleacy John		1			
						Plummer Armistead		1			
						*Plummer George W.		1			
200						*Plummer Judith					
						/Plummer William, Senr.					
						*Plummer William	3	1			
						/Poole Thomas					
50						*Powell Henry		1	1		
	1			11		G-*Powell John	104	1	2	1	
	1	5	2	6		Pritchet John					
						Purkins George		1			
50	1	2	1	3		Purkins Whitney	50	1	2		
						/Purnal John					

Gloucester Tax List - 1782 Kingston Parish						Names	Mathews Tax List - 1791				
Acrs.	Men	Neg.	Hors.	Catl.	Whl.		Acrs.	Men	Neg.	Hors.	Riding-Carriage
						G-/Ransone Augustine, jr.		1	1		
						Ransone Eliot		1		2	
						/Ransone James, Estate					
124½		12		1		Ransone Letitia	124½		6		
	1	1	1			Ransone Robert		1	4	1	
						Ransone Thomas	54	1	5	1	
						Ransone William		4		1	
						Read Francis		1	2		
	1	2		2		Read John		1			
400						Read John - Estate					
						Read Lucy			1		
						/Reaves Jane					
						[Respess] Respass Henry	204				
						Ditto	1	1			
			2	8		Respass John		1		2	
109	1	6	3	15		*Respass Richard, Senr.	239	1	6	4	
						Respess Richard, jr.			5	1	
50						Junr. Respass Thomas					
120	1	9	3	6		*Respess William	120	1	7	1	
						Ditto	100				
						Ditto	153				
						Reynolds Peter		1			
						*Reynolds William		1			
25	1	1		2		Ripley Andrew	100	1	1	1	
25						*Ripley John	50				
						Ripley John	40	1			
40	1			3		Ripley Richard	40	1			
						Ripley Thomas	50	1			
	1	2	2	2		*Roberts Thomas					
						/Robins Albin					
150		1	2	7		Robins Ann [Anna]	50				
						Robins Anna	52				
16						*Robins Edmund					
						Robins James	16	1			
						Robins Mildred	52				
77	1	2		2		*Robins Peter	77				
						Robins Thomas (Respass)	30				
						*Robins William		1			
311	1	10	3	22		*Robinson John					
						Sadler Michael		1			
						Sadler Robert		1			
	1	5	5	16		Sadler Robin		2	5	5	
						Sadler Richard		1			
						G-Sadler Thomas		1			
						Sadler William		1			
						G-Saddler William		1			
						Sale Edmund		1	7	7	
25½	1	2	2	13		*Sampson John	100	1	2	1	
						/Savage Nathaniel L.					
						Scrosby James	450	1	7	6	
						G/Seawell John					
						/Sellers Ann					
						/Shackelford Benjamin					
50						*Shipley John	37	1			
						/Shipley Joseph					
45						*Shipley Ralph	45	1		1	
						Simmons Anthony		1			
	1			5		Simmons William		2			
						Singleton Henry		1	1		
						*Singleton John	15	1			
						/Singleton Richard					
						Singleton William		1			
508	1	18	7	16		Smith Armistead	508	1	14	5	Chair
276	1	18	8	40		*Smith Isaac, Junr.	94	1	4	2	
	1		4	14		G-Smith James	40	1			
	1	1	4	8		Smith John	276	1	6	3	
			(For Vanbibber)			Smith John		1			
						Smith Perrin		1			

Gloucester Tax List - 1782 Kingston Parish Acrs.	Men	Neg.	Hors.	Catl.	Whl.		Names	Mathews Tax List - 1791 Acrs.	Men	Neg.	Hors.	Riding-Carriage
132	3	11	5	10			*Smith Peter	132	1	4	1	
							Smith Peter, Jr.		1	1	1	
							Smith Robert	141	1	8	3	
							Smith Sands	141	1	1	2	
630	2	48	12	42	4	Maj.	*Smith Thomas, Senr.	630	2	31	8	Phaeton
11	1		2	5			Smith Thomas, Junr.	43				
							/Smith William, Capt.					
							Smith William		1			
60	2		1	3			Smith William Hudgin					
	1		2	4			Soaper John	50	1	1	2	
6							Soaper William	40	2	1	1	
						[Summers]	*Sommers Richard		1			
							Southcomb John	4				
		2		11			Sparks Estate					
							/Sparks Alexander					
							Sparks James	380	1	10	4	
							/Spencer Robert					
							Sprat James		1		1	
	1			5			*Stedder James	27	1			
	1		2				*Stedder John		1			
20	1		2	2			Stedder Thomas	20	1			
							/Stevens William					
		Tho. Booth's Over'sr					Stewart James [Steward]		1			
							*Stewart John		1			
							*Stewart William	50	1			
							/Summers John					
							/Tabb Edward					
212	1	19	10	13			*Tabb John	202	1	11	6	Chair
700	2	37	17	92	4		G- Tabb Philip	150				
200							Ditto	120				
176							Ditto					
							/Tabb Susannah					
710	1	44	14	70	2		Tabb Thomas	710	2	22	10	Post Chaise
							Ditto	44				
							/Tabb Toye- Estate					
							Taber Joseph		1			
							/Teacle Michael					
35							Terrier Philip [Terry?]	35	1	2	3	
							Terrier Simon	18	1	1		
							/Thomas - Doctor					
100							G-Thomas George - Estate					
							Thomas Humphrey		1			
100	1	5	2	6			*Thomas James, Sr.	100	2	5	1	
							Ditto	43				
							Thomas James (Son Wm.)		1			
							Thomas James (Son Morgan)		1		2	
		5	1	5			Thomas Johanna					
							Thomas John		1	2	2	
							Thomas Joshua		1			
							*Thomas Mark - Estate	25				
							Thomas Matthew		1			
							*Thomas Morgan		1			
102	1	2	4	6			*Thomas William	102	3	1	3	
							G-Thompson John		1		1	
560	1	56	8	45			Throckmorton Mordecai					
217							Ditto					
462		6		11			G-*Tomkies Charles	968				
100		2		7			Tompkins Hannah					
100	1	2	4	3		(Tomkins)	Tompkins William	98	3	2	2	
							Treakle Dawson		1		1	
							Treakle John		1			
	1			1		(Treacle)	Treakle William		1			
	1	9	2	4			Trice James					
		1					Turner Esther					
50	1	2	3	2			Turner John		1		1	
550	1	4	17	35			Vanbibber Abraham	925		6	7	
500							Vanbibber Isaac					

Gloucester Tax List - 1782 Kingston Parish Acrs.	Men	Neg.	Hors.	Catl.	Whl.		Names	Mathews Tax List - 1791 Acrs.	Men	Neg.	Hors.	Riding-Carriage
							Waddle Mordecai	5	1	1	2	
							Waters Elizabeth			1		
							Watson John		1			
							*Westcomb Nicholas - Estate			2	1	
							Weston Degge		1			
	1	1		6			Weston George	50	1		1	
41							Weston Judith			1	1	
							/Weston Major					
							Weston Robert		1			
							Weston Thomas		1			
87½	1	1		12		[Whyte]	*White Edward	87½	1	1	1	
30							*White James,Sr.-Estate	32				
30							*White James, Estate	30				
79	1	4	1	8			White James, Sr.		1			
							*White James, Jr.	12½	1			
							White James (Son John)		1			
							White James (Son Wm.)		1			
							White Jesse		1			
	1			3		Jr.	*White John					
							*White John (Son James)		1			
							*White John (Son Wm.)		1	2	2	
28	1			2			*White Richard, Sr.	28	1			
125	1	6		8			*White William, Senr.	125	1	2		
34½	1			7			*White William, Jr.	33	1	1	1	
							Ditto	12½				
1966	1	53	15	42			G-Whiting John	245½				
50						(Wyatt)	G-Wiatt Richard G.	50	1	1	1	
							G-Wiatt William E., Doctor		2	8	4	Phaeton
							Williams ____ - Estate	150				
138	1	10	2	9			*Williams Daniel - Estate	93				
							Williams Francis (P.C.)		1	3		
							Williams Gregory	45	1	3		
60							Williams John	60	1	4	2	
							Williams Margaret, Mrs.	212		7	2	Chair
		1					Williams Rose					
580	2	24	10	48	2		Williams Samuel					
50							*Williams Thomas	320	1	6	5	
							Ditto	35				
							Williams Thomas		1	2	1	
							Williams Thomas - Estate	40				
							Williams William (E.R.)	105	1	2	2	
							Williams William		1	4	3	
							/Willis Ann					
							Willis George		1			
							/Willis Henry					
	1			3			*Willis James		1			
62						(Senr.)	*Willis John, jun.	24	1			
							/Willis Richard					
							G-/Willis Thomas					
							*Willis William	40	1		2	
50							G-Winder Ann					
40						(Window)	Winder Edmond (Edward)	40	1	1		
							Window Edmond, Jr.		1			
							Window James	50				
							*Window John	67	1			
88							*Window Thomas, Senr.	88	1	1		
							Window Thomas, Jun.	60	1			
							Wise Abel	35	1	1	2	
							Wood Nicholas				1	
30						(Wooden)	*Wooding George	30	1		1	
30							Wright William	130		1		
							Wylie John		1		1	
	1	12	1	6			Wyley William					
							Yeatman Muse	103	1	4	2	

In making up the following lists of Gloucester Burgesses, Council and Court members and county officers, the names have been obtained from original sources wherever possible. However, it has been necessary to use secondary sources to some extent.

The following sources have been used in making up the lists: Journals of the House of Burgesses and Minutes of the Council and Court as edited by McIlwaine; Land Office Patent Books; Records of other counties; private papers of Gloucester families; Colonial Virginia Register, Stanard; Virginia Historical Magazine and William and Mary College Quarterly references in the Virginia Historical Index, Swem; Calendar of State Papers.

As far as possible it is indicated whether the men in each list were residents of the section now Mathews County or Gloucester by "M" or "G", just as shown in the land grant records. Several Burgesses are shown as of York in the sources, while these men were of Gloucester when it was cut off from York and made a separate county. This is indicated in the lists.

...............ooXoo.............

MEMBERS OF THE HOUSE OF BURGESSES

County	Name	Served
M.	Armistead John, Col.	1680-1686
M.	Armistead Henry	1727-1734
G.	Baylor John	1692
G.	Beverley Peter	1700-1714
G.	Breman Thomas	1654-1655
G.	Buckner John, [Sr.]	1682-1693
G.	Buckner John [Jr.]	1715
G.	Buckner Thomas	1698-1718
M.	Buckner Samuel	1744
G.	*Burwell Nathaniel	1710
G.	Burwell Lewis	1742-1744
G.	Burwell Lewis	1769-1776
G.	Cant David	1659-1660
G.	Cooke Mordecai	1696-1714
G.	Cooke Giles	1722-1726
M.	Dudley Ambrose	1710-1712
M.	Elliott Anthony, Lt. Col.	1657-1658
M.	Gwynne Hugh (York)	1639-1652
G*M	Iversonn Abraham	1653-1676
G.	Jennings Peter, Capt.	1659-1666
M.	Kemp Matthew, Col.	1680-1686
G.	Knight Peter	1659-1660
G.	*Lee Richard (York)	1647
M.	Page John (North End)	1752-1768
G.	*Page John (Rosewell)	1771-1773
G.	Page Mann (College)	1761-1765
G.	Pate Richard	1653
G.	Pate Thomas	1684
G.	Ramsey Thomas, Capt.	1655-1658
M.	Ransone James, Capt.	1692-1706
G.	Smith John	1685-1692
G.	Smith Lawrence	1688-1734
G.	Walker John, Lt. Col.	1655-1656
G.	Walker Thomas	1660-1676
G.	?Warner Austin (York)	1652
G.	Warner Augustine	1658-1659
G.	Warner Augustine, Speaker	1675-1677
G.	Webb Wingfield	1654
G.	Whiting Henry, Major	1682-1684
G.	Whiting Beverley	1742-1754
G.	Whiting Thomas	1755-1776
G.	Willis Francis	1652-1660
G.	Willis Henry	1718-1734
G.	Willis Francis	1727-1749

....

* Note: Nathaniel Burwell given as of Jamestown. His family residence was in Glo'str.
" Iverson land was in both Gloucester and Mathews.
" Richard Lee is referred to in a York deed as living on the Gloucester side of York River before 1646.
" John Page of Rosewell also represented the College of William and Mary.

....

MEMBERS OF THE COUNCIL AND GENERAL COURT.

County	Name	First Served	Born-Died
M.	Armistead John	1688	1697
G.	Beverley Peter	1719	1668-1728
G.	Burwell Lewis	1702	1650-1710
G.	Burwell Lewis, Pres.	1744	1710-1756
M.	?Elliot Anthony	1658	
M.	Gwyn Hugh (Charles R.)	1639	
G.	Jennings Peter	1670	1671
M.	Kemp Matthew, Col.	1681	1683
G.	Lee Richard	1651	1664
G.	Lewis John I	1704	1669-1725
G.	Lewis John II	1748	1694
G.	Page Matthew	1699	1659-1703
G.	Page Mann	1714	1691-1730
M.	Page John (North End)	1768	1720-1774
G.	Page John (Rosewell)	1773	1744-1808
G.	Pate John	1670	1672
G.	Porteus Robert	1713	
G.	Read George	1657/8	1671
G.	Robins John	1648	
G.	Smith John	1704	1719/20
G.	?Walker John	1657/8	
G.	Warner Augustine I	1660	1610-1674
G.	Warner Augustine II	1677	1642-1681
G.	?Willis Francis (York)	1670	1691
G.	Whiting Henry	1690	1695

.......;..................

Edmund Berkeley, on Council 1713, owned Purtan and lived in Gloucester until circa 1712. He died 1718. Robert Beverley, John Cheesman, Humphrey Higgenson, George Menifie owned land.

The following lists have been made up from a search of all the sources given on the page of Burgesses and Council members, with the additional use of the Vestry Books for Kingston and Petsworth Parishes, as edited by C. G. Chamberlayne. Names for the later years have also been checked with the tax lists published herein. It is not claimed that these lists are complete.

CLERKS OF THE COURT OF GLOUCESTER

County	Names	Served
G.	Beverley Peter	from 1694/5 to 1719
G.	Buckner John	circa 1677 " 1693
M.	Clayton John	from 1720 " 1772
M.	Clayton Jasper [Deputy?]	
M-G	Morris Thomas	in 1657 and 1661
G.	Nelson Thomas	from 1774 circa 1790
G.	Nelson Thomas, Jr.	in 1797
G.	Pryor Christopher, Deputy	1783 - 1790
G.	White Richard	in 1671
G.	Whitehouse Richard [?]	in 1665

....

JUSTICES OF THE PEACE

County	Names	Served
G.	Alexander David	1714-1740
G.	Alexander John	1726
G-M	Anderson Matthew	1782
M.	Armistead John, Col.	1680
M.	Armistead Henry	1714-1726
M.	Armistead John	1727
M.	Armistead William	1765
M.	Bernard Robert	1737
G.	Booker Richard	1702-1705
G.	Booth Thomas	1726-1782
G.	Booth Mordecai	1743
G.	Booth George	1765
G.	Booth George, Jr.	1769-1775
G.	Buckner Thomas	1702-1705
M.	Buckner Samuel	1740
G.	Burwell Nathaniel, Maj.	1714-1719
G.	Burwell Lewis	1765-1775
G.	Cooke Mordecai	1702-1714
G.	Cooke Giles	1726
G.	Cooke Mordecai, Jr.	1737
G.	Cooke John, Jr.	1769
G-M	Curtis Thomas, Major	1662
M.	Debnam Charles	1737
G-M	Dixon John	1782
M.	Dudley Ambrose, Col.	1698-1702
M.	Dudley Ambrose	1737
G.	Fontaine James M.	1776
M.	Glasscock Thomas (York)	1652
M-G	Gregory Anthony	1702-1705
M.	Gwyn John	1702
G.	Hall William	1798
M.	Hayes Thomas	1726-1737
M.	Hayes William (Dece'd)	1769
G.	Huberd James	1737-1765
G.	Huberd James, Jr.	1765
M.	Hudgins Houlder	1790
G.?	Hughes John	1765
G-M	Iverson Abraham	1656
G.	Kemp Peter	1702-1714
G.	Kemp William	1714
G.	Knight Peter	1657
M.	Knowles Sands	1702
G.	Lewis John	1727
G.	Lewis Warner	1743
G.	Lewis Warner, Jr.	1769-1776
G.	Lightfoot Philip, Lt. Col.	1680
G.?	Nicholas George	1726
G.	Page Mann	1743
G.	Page Mann, Jr.	1769-1775

JUSTICES OF THE PEACE (Continued)

County	Names	Served
M-G	Page John	1765
M-G	Page John, Jr.	1765
G.	Pate John	1660
G.	Pate Thomas, Col.	1681
G.	Perrin Thomas	1727
G.	Perrin John	1782
M.	Peyton Sir John	1776
G.	Randolph Beverley	1743
M.	Ransone Peter (York)	1652
M.	Ransone James	1702-1705
G.	Reade Thomas, Jr.	1714-1726
G.	Savage Anthony	1660
M.	Savage Nathaniel	1782
M.	Seaton George	1670?
G.	Smith Augustine	1714
G.	Smith John	1702-1737
G.	Smith Philip	1714
G.	Smith William	1714
G.	Smith Lawrence	1737
M.	Smith Thomas	1765-1782
M-G	Tabb Phillip	1782
M.	Tabb Thomas	1787
G.	Throckmorton Gabriel	1702-1714
G.	Throckmorton Robert	1737-1765
M.	Throckmorton Mordecai	1782
G.	Throckmorton Warner	1782
G.	Thruston John	1740-1772
G.	Tomkies Charles	1714-1726
G.	Tomkies Charles	1765-1775
G.	Tomkies Francis	1765
G.	Tomkies Morgan	1789
G.	Todd Thomas	1698-1702
G.	Todd Christopher	1727
G.	Warner Augustine (York)	1652
G.	Watson Jonathan	1772
G.	Whiting Henry, Dr.	1680
G.	Whiting Henry	1714
G.	Whiting Thomas	1722-1765
G.	Whiting Beverley	1740
G.	Whiting Kemp	1765
G.	Whiting Peter Beverley	1765
G-M	Whiting John	1782
G.	Willis Francis	1726
G.	Willis Henry	1726
G.	Willis Francis, Jr.	1743-1769
G.	Wyatt Conquest	1702-1705

....

SHERIFFS OF GLOUCESTER

County	Names	Served
M.	Armistead John, Col	1675
M.	Armistead John	1729
M.	Ayres R., Sub-Sheriff	1790
G.	Baytop James	1790
G.	Booker John	1789
G.	Boswell Thomas	1753
G.	Burwell Lewis	1767
G.	Cluney Abra., Sub-Shrf.	1682
G.	Cooke Mordecai	1698
G-M	Dixon John	1782-1785-1788
M.	Dudley Richard	1657
M.	Elliott William, Sub-Sh.	1682
M.	Hayes [?] Jasper " "	1791

*SHERIFFS OF GLOUCESTER (Continued)

County	Names	Served
G.	Hopkins Charles	1792
G.	Hughes [?] Jasper, Sub-Shrf.	1792
G.	Kemp Peter	1702
G.	Lee Richard [York]	1646
G.	Lightfoot Phill., Col.	1688
G.	Neale Thomas	1700-1706
M.	Peyton Sir John	1783-1784
G.	Randolph Beverley	1756
G.	Savage Anthony	1660
G.	Smith John, Lt. Col.	1692
G.	Smith Philip	1706?
M.	Smith William	1770
G.	Stubbs Thomas	1731-1734
M-G	Tabb Philip	1790
G.	Thruston Robert	1790
G.	Todd Philip	1730
G.	Tomkies Charles	1756
G.	Tomkies Francis	1767
G.	Willcocks John	1715-1730
G.	Willis Francis	1727
G.	Willis Francis	1770's
G.	Willis Henry	1716
G.	Whiting Francis	1718
G.	Whiting Henry	1723
G.	Whiting Peter	1728
G.	Whiting Henry	1739
G.	Whiting Matthew	1741
G-M	Whiting John	1789
G.	Whiting Peter Beverley	1797
G.	Wyatt Conquest	1705-1707
G.	Wyatt Edward	1740
G.	Wyatt James	1741
G.	Yates Robert	1780's

* It is evident from the dates given that some of those listed as Sheriffs must have been Sub-Sheriffs or Deputies, though not identified as such in the sources.

*SURVEYORS OF GLOUCESTER

County	Names	Served
G.?	Beverley Robert	1670-1673
G.	Booker Lewis	1785
M.	Booker James	1780's or 90's
G.	Cook Thomas	1712-1723
G.	Duval William	1786-1804
G-M	French John	1740-1745
G.	Lewis John	1675-1676
G.	Mumford Thos.	1747-1753
G.	Perry Ro:	1733-1736
G.	Smith Lawrence	1683-1689
G.	Smith John	1709
G.	Throckmorton John	1751-1767
G.	Tomkies Francis	1768-1769

* Gloucester Surveyor's Book was also a source for some of those listed

....

GOVERNOR:

Lewis Burwell, as President of the Council served as Acting Governor, 1750-1751, until the arrival of Governor Dinwiddie.

SECRETARY OF STATE:

Richard Lee..................1649-1652

AUDITOR GENERAL:

Peter Beverley...............1716

TREASURER:

Henry Whiting................1692-1693
Peter Beverley...............1710-1723

ATTORNEY GENERAL:

Richard Lee..................1643
Peter Jennings...............1670-1671

....

MATHEWS COUNTY OFFICIALS 1791 - 1800

CLERKS OF THE COURT OF MATHEWS COUNTY

Name	Served
Cary John	1792-1794
Jones Richard C., Deputy	1793-1794
Patterson John	1795-1799

....

JUSTICES OF THE PEACE OF MATHEWS

Name	Served
Briggs Edmund, DR.	1800
Buckner William	1795
Cary Dudley	1795
Hudgins Houlder	1795
Jarvis John D.	1800
Smith Armistead	1795
Smith Thomas, Sr.	1793
Smith Thomas, Jr.	1795
Tabb Thomas	1800
Van Bibber Andrew	1800
Williams Thomas	1791

SHERIFFS OF MATHEWS

Name	Served
Ayres Richard, Deputy	1797
Billups Richard	1796
Glasscock Milton	1798
Gregory Richard	1797
Guthrie George, Deputy	1792
Hudgins William H.	1798
Humphries John	1794
Smith Thomas, Esq.	1792
Tabb Thomas	1791-1793

Between the years 1651, when Gloucester was first mentioned as a county, and the year 1654, November 20th, when the Virginia Assembly ordered that the County of New Kent be formed, all of that area west of the Poropotank Creek in what is now King and Queen County was, for those years, a part of Gloucester.

Lands granted in the present area of King and Queen between 1651 and 1654 are described in the patent books as lying in Gloucester County. For this reason many names have formerly been erroneously included in lists of landowners in the present area of Gloucester.

The following patents were issued for Gloucester lands which fell into the county of New Kent in 1654, and subsequently became a part of King and Queen when that county was formed in 1691.

GLOUCESTER PATENTS WHICH BECAME NEW KENT IN 1654
AND KING AND QUEEN IN 1691

NAMES	DESCRIPTION	COUNTY	BOOK	PAGE	DATE	ACRES
		Gloucester				
ABRAHALL Robert, Capt.-	SE side of Mattapany R.	"	3	30	April 27,1653	400
ABRALL " "	" " " Metopony	" "	3	337	Feb. 20, 1654	600
BALLARD Thomas, Mr.	SE " " Mettopony " now called New Kent.	"	3	350	July 16, 1655	1000
BARNEHOUSE Richard, Jr.	SE side of Mattapony R.	"				
	Renewed with same description,	Glo.	4	33	1655	
COALE William	S side of Matty	Gloucester	3	223	Nov. 23, 1653	100
DALE thomas	N side Mattapony [Note: Renewal of patent 1653]	"	5	435	May 24, 1664	350
DIGGS Edward	N side of Matapony R.	"	3	16	June 1, 1653	2350
DIGGS Edward, Gent.	N side of " "	"	3	32	April 18,1653	700
FORD Peter	NE side of " "	"	3	340	March 25,1655	500
GREEN Ralph	See Morgan					
HANCKS Thomas	SE side Mettopony "	"	3	369	Feb. 16, 1653	100
HANSFORD John	N " of Narrowes "	"	3	223	Dec. 16, 1653	950
LANGSTONE Anthony, Mr.	NW right against Rickocke, adjoining Mr. Hammond.	"	3	211	Sept. 6, 1653	1303
LEVISTONE John	W side of Poropotank	"	3	227	Dec. 16, 1653	400
LEWIS William, Major	NE side of Matty. R.	"	3	237	May 25, 1654	640
" " "	[Incomplete description]	"	3	237	" 25, 1654	1200
" " "	Above patent renewed as NE side of Matty. R.	"			1656	
" " "	NE " " " "	"	3	238	" 25, 1654	200
MADDISON John	N side of Metopony R.	"	3	217	Jan. 4, 1653	600
MOONE Abraham	SE side of Matty R.	"	3	326	Nov. 1, 1654	300
MORGAN Francis, Capt &)	SE side of Mattapony R.	"	3	166	Jan. 13, 1652	500
GREEN Ralph)	Renewal, Green survivor	"	4	577	Feb. 10, 1662	
PECK Thomas, Mr.	NE side of Mettopony R.	"	3	338	April 6, 1655	1000
PRICE Arthur	NE " " Mattapony "	"	3	27	April 3, 1654	300
RIVES Thomas	Assigned From A. Moone	"	5	335	1663	300
SYMPSON Edward	SE side of Mattapony R.	"	2	324	Dec. 2, 1651	100
SOANES Hen., Gentleman	NE " " " "	"	3	27	March 10,1653	200
" Henry, Mr.	E'most side " "	"	3	213	July 1653	700

NAMES	DESCRIPTION	COUNTY Gloucester	BOOK	PAGE	DATE	ACRES
TAYLOR William, Col.	N side of Mattapony R.	"	3	191	April 18,1653	1050
WALKER Thomas, Major	On N side of Matty R. called Mattapony Fort Above granted Edw.Diggs	"	5	616	Feb. 26, 1665 1653	2350
WEST John, Capt.	NE side of Mattapony R.	"	3	10	May 27, 1654	1000
WEST John, Capt.	Renewed above	"	4	150	1657	
WEST Toby		"	3	10	May 27, 1654	500
WILCHIN Richard	NE side of Poropotank	" [?]	3	289	Sept. 30,1654	300
WYAT William	On Matapony R.	"	3	4	April 27,1653	400
" "	Renewal	"	5	286	1663	
WYATT "	SE side of Matty.	"	3	233	Dec. 20, 1653	400

HR: - Head right. Only one family name spelling indexed. Tax List surnames only indexed.

HR: - Head Right. Only one family name spelling indexed. Tax List surnames only indexed.

HR: - Head Right. Only one family name spelling indexed. Tax List surnames only indexed.

HR: - Head Right. Only one family name spelling indexed. Tax List surnames only indexed.

HR: - Head Right. Only one spelling of family name indexed. Tax List Surnames only indexed.

HR: - Head Right. Only one spelling of family name indexed.. Tax List surnames only indexed.

HR: - Head Right. Only one spelling of family name indexed. Tax List surnames only indexed.

HR: - Head Right. Only one spelling of family name indexed. Tax List surnames only listed.

HR: Head Right. Only one spelling of family name indexed. Tax List surnames only indexed.

HR: - Head Right. Only one spelling of family name indexed. Tax List surnames only indexed.

HR: - Head Right. Only one spelling of family name indexed. Tax List surnames only indexed.

HR: - Head Right. Only one spelling of family name indexed. Tax List surnames only indexed.

HR: - Head Right. Only one spelling of family name indexed. Tax List surnames only indexed.

HR: - Head Right. Only one spelling of family name indexed. Tax List surnames only indexed.

HR: Head Right. Only one spelling of family name indexed. Tax List surnames only indexed.

HR: - Head Right. Only one spelling of family name indexed. Tax List surname only indexed.

HR: - Head Right. Only one spelling of family name indexed. Tax List surname only indexed.

HR: - Head Right. Only one spelling of family name indexed. Tax List surnames only indexed.

HR: - Head Right. Only one spelling of family name indexed. Tax List surnames only indexed.

HR: - Head Right. Only one spelling of family name indexed. Tax List surnames only indexed.

HR: - Head Right. Only one spelling of family name indexed. Tax List surnames only indexed.

www.ingramcontent.com/pod-product-compliance
Lightning Source LLC
Chambersburg PA
CBHW080250030426
42334CB00023BA/2760